KANT ON PLEASURE AND JUDGMENT

Were there interactions between the development of Kant's aesthetics and the development of his moral philosophy? How did Kant view pleasure and displeasure and what role did they play in the formation of his system of the faculties? In this book, Alexander Rueger situates Kant's account of pleasure and displeasure in its eighteenth-century context, with special attention to Leibniz, Wolff, Crusius, and Mendelssohn. He traces the development of Kant's views on pleasure from the 1770s to his *Critique of Aesthetic Judgment* in 1790 and shows that, throughout, Kant understood pleasure as the satisfaction of faculty interests. The significance of this theory for the completion of Kant's critical system in his third *Critique* is discussed in detail. Rueger's study illuminates both the role of pleasure and displeasure in Kant's thought and their important connections to the power of judgment.

ALEXANDER RUEGER is Professor Emeritus in the Department of Philosophy at the University of Alberta. He has published widely in the history and philosophy of science and on Kant's aesthetics.

KANT ON PLEASURE AND JUDGMENT

A Developmental and Interpretive Account

ALEXANDER RUEGER

University of Alberta

CAMBRIDGE
UNIVERSITY PRESS

Shaftesbury Road, Cambridge CB2 8EA, United Kingdom

One Liberty Plaza, 20th Floor, New York, NY 10006, USA

477 Williamstown Road, Port Melbourne, VIC 3207, Australia

314–321, 3rd Floor, Plot 3, Splendor Forum, Jasola District Centre, New Delhi – 110025, India

103 Penang Road, #05–06/07, Visioncrest Commercial, Singapore 238467

Cambridge University Press is part of Cambridge University Press & Assessment, a department of the University of Cambridge.

We share the University's mission to contribute to society through the pursuit of education, learning and research at the highest international levels of excellence.

www.cambridge.org
Information on this title: www.cambridge.org/9781009380379

DOI: 10.1017/9781009380362

© Alexander Rueger 2024

This publication is in copyright. Subject to statutory exception and to the provisions of relevant collective licensing agreements, no reproduction of any part may take place without the written permission of Cambridge University Press & Assessment.

First published 2024
First paperback edition 2025

A catalogue record for this publication is available from the British Library

ISBN 978-1-009-38034-8 Hardback
ISBN 978-1-009-38037-9 Paperback

Cambridge University Press & Assessment has no responsibility for the persistence or accuracy of URLs for external or third-party internet websites referred to in this publication and does not guarantee that any content on such websites is, or will remain, accurate or appropriate.

Contents

Acknowledgments		*page* vii
List of Abbreviations		viii
	Introduction	1
1	The Early Reception of the Third *Critique*	8
2	The Completion of the System of the Powers of the Mind, 1770–1790	16
	2.1 The Completion of a Long-Standing Project?	16
	2.2 What "Systematic Unity" Does Not Mean	17
	2.3 The Selection Criterion for Inclusion in the System	18
	2.4 The Table of Faculties	21
	2.5 The Proof of Completeness	22
	2.6 Architectonic Problems	25
	2.7 The Development of the System in the 1770s	26
3	Kant's Theory of the Feeling of Pleasure and Displeasure (I)	33
	3.1 Background and Development: Wolff, Mendelssohn, and Kant	33
	3.2 The Transcendental Definition of Pleasure and the Satisfaction of Faculty Interests	47
4	Kant's Theory of the Feeling of Pleasure and Displeasure (II)	62
	4.1 What Pleasure Is Not	62
	4.2 An Alternative Theory of Pleasure	73
5	Consequences of the Theory	85
	5.1 'Judging Precedes Pleasure' and the Determining Ground of Judgments of Taste	85
	5.2 From the Pleasure of Taste to a New Faculty	95
6	The Principle(s) of the Power of Judgment	106
	6.1 Two Versions of One Principle?	107
	6.2 The Principle of Systematicity: Its Introduction and Function	110
	6.3 The Power of Judgment and Rules of Apprehension	120

7	The Interest of the Reflecting Power of Judgment and the Deduction of Judgments of Taste	125
	7.1 What Is the Interest of the Faculty of Reflecting Judgment?	125
	7.2 "Cognition in General"	131
	7.3 The Comparison Model	135
	7.4 The Deduction of Judgments of Taste	138
	7.5 Problems with an 'Intuitive Principle': Mistaken Judgments of Taste	148
	7.6 "Taste as a Kind of *sensus communis*"	152
	7.7 Conclusion	157
8	The Imagination in Its Freedom	159
	8.1 Problems with the 'Free Play' of the Faculties	159
	8.2 The Freedom of the Imagination, Genius, and Taste	162
	8.3 The Antinomy of Taste	176
	8.4 Symbolizations of the Ideas of a Supersensible Ground	181
	8.5 Concluding Remark	185
9	The Transition from Nature to Freedom	187
	9.1 Teleology: The Logical Transition	189
	9.2 The New 'Gulf'	198
	9.3 The Aesthetic Transition	203
	Conclusion: The Autonomy of Taste	208
	Bibliography	213
	Index	223

Acknowledgments

I thank the Social Sciences and Humanities Research Council of Canada for supporting my research from 2009 to 2013 and the students who worked with me during those years and beyond, most notably Emine Hande Tuna. For encouragement and discussions, I am grateful to Şahan Evren, Paul Guyer, Susan Hahn, Charles Roger, and Catherine Wilson. Thanks are also due to two anonymous reviewers for Cambridge University Press who provided helpful criticisms and suggestions. Finally, I am much indebted to W. during the time I wrote the book.

In Chapters 4 and 9, I used, with permission, material from my previously published article, "Kant on Feelings and Sensations and the Gap between Rationality and Morality," *Kantian Review* 25 (2020), 125–48. Parts of Chapters 3 and 5 include altered versions of material found in my articles, "Pleasure and Taste in Kant's Theory of Taste," *Kant-Studien* 109 (2018), 101–23 and "Kant on Beauty and Morality, c. 1784." In: *Proceedings of the XII. International Kant Congress* (ed. V. Waibel et al.) vol. 4, Berlin: deGruyter, 3063–70.

Abbreviations

References to Kant's works are indicated by the following abbreviations with volume and page number of the *Akademie* edition, for example (5: 190), except in the case of the KrV, where I refer to the first or second edition, for example (A 99) or (B 101).

Anthropologie	*Anthropology from a Pragmatic Point of View*
Fortschritte	*What Real Progress Has Metaphysics Made in Germany since the Time of Leibniz and Wolff?*
GMS	*Groundwork of the Metaphysics of Moral*
KpV	*Critique of Practical Reason*
KrV	*Critique of Pure Reason*
KU	*Critique of the Power of Judgment*
MS	*Metaphysics of Morals*
R	*Reflexion* (Notes and Fragments)
Religion	*Religion within the Boundaries of Mere Reason*

Translations Used

I usually follow the translations of Kant's works in the Cambridge edition. Where I have modified a translation, I indicate this with an asterisk, for example (5: 170*).

All other translations are mine unless indicated otherwise.

Introduction

In the *Critique of Judgment* of 1790, Kant listed three separate higher faculties of the mind – the understanding, the (reflecting) power of judgment, and (practical) reason – and claimed that this list was now complete. The introduction of the newest member, the power of judgment, into the system is the topic of my study. Although the faculty has other important employments – in concept formation and teleology – it is supposedly in judgments of taste about beautiful objects that its operation finds its purest expression, "unmixed with any other faculty of cognition." Such judgments document a special kind of feeling, the pleasure of taste, and Kant indeed insisted that it is only in this kind of pleasure that the power of judgment 'reveals' itself:

> It is ... properly only in taste, and especially with regard to objects in nature, in which alone the power of judgment reveals itself as a faculty that has its own special principle and thereby makes a well-founded claim to a place in the general critique of the higher faculties of cognition, which one would perhaps not have entrusted to it. (20: 243f.; cf. 5: 246)

Were it not for the connection with this pleasure, he wrote, the discussion of the faculty's teleological employment could have been included in the critique of theoretical reason (as indeed they were in the *Critique of Pure Reason* of 1781). At one point in the unpublished draft of the Introduction, Kant even refers to the KU as a "critique of the feeling of pleasure and displeasure" (20: 207).

These remarks motivate the approach I take in this study: I start with a reconstruction of Kant's theory of pleasure and its development from the 1770s to the KU. The perhaps surprising result of this investigation is that Kant – along with many other eighteenth-century German philosophers – thought of pleasure as the satisfaction of interests or the attainment of aims. Although he mentions such a view briefly in the Introduction of KU (5: 187), it has seemed to many commentators that it cannot possibly be his 'general theory of pleasure', as Paul Guyer suggested in 1978; an aim-satisfaction theory seemed too clearly in conflict with the famous 'disinterestedness' of judgments of taste. Kant, however, held this view from the 1770s on and furthermore connected different kinds of pleasure with the satisfaction of the interests of specific faculties of the mind. Insofar as these faculties belong to the higher kind, their interests count as a priori, and the associated pleasures, therefore, can in principle make a claim to universal validity.

The following study is divided into three main parts, addressing: (1) the theory of pleasure (Chapters 3–5), (2) the interest of the faculty of judgment and the deduction of its a priori principle (Chapters 6–7), and (3) the role that the free operation of the imagination plays in the employment of reflecting judgment in taste (Chapters 8–9).

The new faculty, the power of reflecting judgment, is first presented in the Introduction to KU as distinguished from determining judgment, which is the capacity to subsume particulars (intuitions, concepts, laws) under given universals (more general concepts and laws). Reflecting judgment, however, is charged, to put it paradoxically, with subsuming given particulars under a universal that is not yet known. With its own a priori principle, it is supposed to assist us in finding empirical concepts for given intuitions or for searching for more general laws that unify known particular laws. Its principle is the "presupposition" that the multitude of nature's particular laws can be arranged in a system, or, in an alternative formulation, that "for all things in nature empirically determined concepts can be found" (20: 211). Even though Kant gives a transcendental deduction of this principle from the requirement that our experience of the empirical world has to be unified, the principle itself does not qualify as a law of nature in the sense in which the principles of the understanding function as most fundamental laws. The latter laws are, in Kant's terms, "constitutive" for the experience of objects (any object of possible experience is guaranteed to satisfy these laws), while the principle of reflecting judgment is merely "regulative" for cognition by guiding the attempts at expanding our knowledge of nature. It advises us to search for concepts and laws so as to fit them into a systematic arrangement, but it does not legislate that there are such concepts and laws.

It is notoriously obscure what this principle of judgment may have to do with taste, even though Kant assures the reader of the Introduction that judgments of taste have a "relation" to that a priori principle, a relation that supposedly accounts for the claim to universal validity that we make in such judgments and that distinguishes them from judgments in which we merely state that some object is agreeable to us.[1] Having an a priori principle of its own, however, is only a necessary condition for a faculty's inclusion in the system of powers of the mind that Kant presents in the Introduction; it is not sufficient, as the omission of *theoretical* or speculative reason from the system shows (5: 198; 20: 245f.). This faculty, which received its transcendental investigation at great length in the first *Critique*, clearly has a priori principles of its own but they are assigned, like the principle of the power of judgment, a merely regulative role for cognition; they are not, like the principles of the understanding, constitutive for knowledge of nature. And they differ from the moral law, which is constitutive for the faculty of desire. If the role of reflecting judgment with respect to cognition is merely regulative, then, in order to be included among the cognitive faculties, the power of judgment has to also play a constitutive role. And Kant indeed assigns such a role to it: it is constitutive for the feeling of pleasure and displeasure. Because of this constitutive role, the pleasure of taste takes on fundamental significance: it is only in this pleasure that the "power of judgment reveals itself as a faculty that has its own special principle" (20: 244). A transcendental investigation into this feeling, then, is supposed to show us something important about the system of our cognitive faculties, namely, that it has to contain, beside the understanding and (practical) reason, a further member, the power of reflecting judgment, and that only with this addition can the system be shown to be complete. As I shall argue, it is only the combination of the a priori principle from the Introduction and the 'fact' of the pleasure of taste that accomplishes the task of establishing the power of judgment as a faculty of its own.

In the first part of my study, accordingly, I attempt to reconstruct Kant's "general theory of pleasure," starting from notes and lectures of the 1770s and following the development to 1790. The core of this theory, I suggest, is the link between purposiveness and pleasure. Representations that give us pleasure are (subjectively) purposive for us: being conscious of the purposiveness of X means that we are conscious that X satisfies an *interest* of ours, an interest of our faculties.[2] In fact, in several places, Kant

---

[1] Judgments of taste can make a claim to universality "through the relation of the subjective purposiveness of the given representation for the power of judgment [manifested in the pleasure of taste] to that a priori principle of the power of judgment, of the purposiveness of nature in its empirical lawfulness in general" and, therefore, this power "can be justified in finding a place in the critique of the higher pure faculties of cognition" (20: 243).

[2] Paul Guyer suggested in 1978 (1997: ch. 3) that this is Kant's "general theory of pleasure" but he thought it doubtful that it fits into the transcendental framework of the KU. Guyer's precedent has,

seems to understand the link as an identity: the consciousness of subjective purposiveness *is* nothing but the feeling of pleasure. An immediate consequence of this is that pleasure is not a sensation separate from that consciousness and that there is, in particular, no causal relation between judging a representation to be subjectively purposive and the feeling. That the pleasure of taste indicates a "purposiveness without purpose" and is "disinterested" then means that in this case the interest of the faculty of desire is not involved, nor that of the faculty of understanding.

Although Kant explicitly introduced the concept of such faculty interests only in the *Critique of Practical Reason* (1788), the idea can be traced back to Kant's notes and lectures of the 1770s. The analysis of judgments of taste Kant presents in the four "moments" of the Analytic of the Beautiful – in particular, the result that such judgments are not based on concepts of objects and that they make a claim to universal validity – can be understood as showing that the pleasure of taste consists in the satisfaction of a *unique* interest, namely, that of the reflecting power of judgment. Kant extracts from our practice of making such judgments characteristics of the pleasure of taste that could not be connected with the satisfaction of the interests of the other two higher faculties. A further immediate consequence of the theory is that in the case of the faculties of judgment and of practical reason, judgment indeed precedes (in a logical sense) the feeling of pleasure – a result that Kant famously calls "the key to the critique of taste" (5: 216).

What is the unique interest of the power of judgment? Both determining and reflecting judgment aim at bringing the imagination, which delivers manifolds of intuition, and the understanding, the faculty of concepts, into agreement or harmony. I show that it follows from the general theory of pleasure that in the case of *reflecting* judgment, the aim must be to seek a *free* harmony of those faculties, in which the imagination is not apprehending intuitions according to an available concept (which is the task of determining judgment). It is a free agreement because it does not depend on previously formed concepts and it is required in the process

---

to my knowledge, not met with much sympathy in the subsequent literature. The basic idea, however, is old. Thus, Wilhelm Windelband, the later editor of the KU in the Academy edition, wrote in 1880: "the critique of reflecting judgment [is] an investigation into the a priori forms of our *Gefühlsleben*. Every feeling contains either pleasure or displeasure. This ... can only be based on the fact that the object ... corresponds to some desire or other, or does not so correspond. In the most general sense, we call these desires purposes, and it follows that everything purposive is combined with a feeling of pleasure . . . . In every feeling we thus see a subordination of a represented object under a purpose." If it can be shown that there are "necessary and universal" ways of reflecting on objects, then these will be "connected with equally necessary and universal feelings" (1880: 149)

of concept formation, in which the principle of judgment is supposed to assist the understanding and the imagination in finding new concepts. Success in this process – that is, the satisfaction of judgment's interest – Kant explains, is accompanied by a "noticeable pleasure." Once a concept has been found, of course, the harmony turns into an "unfree" agreement. The pleasure connected with successful concept formation (or the systematization of particular laws) is therefore transitory; it tends to be forgotten (5: 187): we do not feel it in the application of a concept to intuitions in 'ordinary' cognition; that is, unfree harmony is not pleasurable.

This "original pleasure of predication,"[3] however, cannot simply be identified with the pleasure of taste, even though several commentators have tried to do so.[4] The conditions under which we experience beauty are quite different from the conditions of concept formation, not least because we find objects beautiful even though we already have concepts for them, as we do in Kant's examples of a tulip, a rose, crystals, sea shells, and so on. Regarding such objects, Kant says that nature is beautiful insofar as it looks like art (5: 306). This is an expression of the "idealism of purposiveness," namely, that nature, unintentionally and accidentally, on occasion generates objects whose forms evoke the pleasure of taste in us, just *as if* an artist had designed those products of nature for us. The claim, however, can be given a more substantial interpretation.[5] When we find the form of a natural object beautiful, we compare this given form with a hypothetical work of art, a work that we (or an artist) could have produced, and we find agreement. This may seem as too literal a reading of the nature-as-art formula, but I suggest that this is what Kant actually meant. When he reflects – in an underappreciated passage – on the fact that the imagination in the apprehension of a *given* form has no opportunity to play freely – and this is, of course, the paradigm case in which we make judgments of taste – he proposes that "the object can provide it [the imagination] with a form that contains precisely such a composition of the manifold as the imagination would design in harmony with the lawfulness of the understanding in general if it [the imagination] were left free by itself," that is, if the imagination were indeed "productive and self-active (as the authoress of

---

[3] Hogrebe (1992 [1981]: 73).
[4] Most recently Geiger, who notes, however, that these interpretations create a "tension" in Kant's view because Kant insists that in experiencing beauty we have no intention of acquiring or forming a concept (2022: 197). See Chapters 6 and 7 for further discussion.
[5] Cf. Hermann Cohen's gloss on these passages: Unless we are conscious of art, nature exists for us "only as mechanism, perhaps as organism" but not as "self-sufficient" beauty. "Only art reveals to us the beauty of nature, as natural science discovers [nature's] necessity" (1889: 200).

voluntary forms of possible intuitions)" (5: 240f.). We thus compare a given form (the product of "purposeless mechanism") with a form our imagination could have produced freely, without constraints from the understanding. The accidental agreement of such a free creation of the imagination with a form that we cognize under a concept ensures that the freedom of the imagination is in harmony with the requirements of the understanding. The free form, however, is a product of art.

In this reconstruction of Kant's view, the aim of the reflecting power of judgment, free harmony, can be attained in two ways, in each of which we compare forms of objects: (i) forms given in empirical intuition, which can lead to concepts of the objects and the transitory "pleasure of predication" and (ii) we compare a given form of a conceptualized object with a free form, which can result in the pleasure of taste. The view of the "free play" of the faculties I am suggesting is quite different from other extant interpretations that often understand the free harmony, induced by an object, as the feeling that the given form of the object is especially suitable for conceptualization.[6] On my view, these interpretations have it backwards: the already conceptualized form rather 'feels' like one that could have been imagined freely, without guidance from a concept. It is not that the manifold of intuition we perceive is such that it induces us to search for a concept – we already have plenty of concepts to subsume it under – and that this search, even though it does not ultimately succeed, is somehow pleasurable, merely because we 'feel' that the manifold "contains the promise of a specific concept that the understanding might supply."[7] Instead, I suggest that the manifold *is* conceptually determined and that the supposed conceptual inexhaustibility actually pertains to the free form or its mode of generation, from which the given conceptualized manifold inherits it in virtue of its agreement with the free form.

The revised understanding of the free harmony as a comparison of a conceptualized and a free form will be the basis of my interpretation of the deduction of judgments of taste and of the role that the a priori principle of judgment – that we can find concepts for all things in nature – plays in taste. What Kant tells us about the operations of the 'imagination in its freedom,' however, is only to be found in the sections on art in KU, that is,

---

[6] Cf. a recent representative formulation of this view by Horstmann: "an object is judged to be beautiful just in case the judging subject, without having a concept under which to subsume the intuition of that object, can feel in the act of trying to find a concept that fits this intuition (in the act of reflecting about it) a certain 'reciprocal harmony'... between the activities of ... the understanding and the imagination" (2018: 59f.).

[7] Horstmann (2018: 75).

in the sections in which he is concerned not only with taste but with the productive activity in the artist that results in objects that taste can then judge. The imagination is free here in a different sense than in concept formation: in the latter case, it is bound to apprehend a given manifold and operates according to the law of association; in the former case, the imagination is under no such constraints, it is "self-active" and guided by (indeterminate) rules that "lie higher in reason" (5: 314). This ultimately inscrutable activity is the production of "aesthetic ideas." I thus agree here with commentators who have suggested that we take seriously Kant's remark that *all* beauty, even beauty in nature, is the "expression of aesthetic ideas" (5: 320).[8]

Overall, then, this study takes us from the theory of pleasure, which Kant adapted from empirical psychology into the transcendental framework of faculty interests, to the deduction of judgments of taste and thereby to the completion of the task of introducing the power of judgment into the system of the higher cognitive faculties.

---

[8] I argue that the beauty of works of art, too, can be understood along these lines in Chapter 8.

I

The Early Reception of the Third Critique

Although a developmental approach that studies the emergence of Kant's views on pleasure and taste out of the traditional empirical psychology is neither new nor, in principle, in need of a special motivation, in this chapter, I draw attention to a perhaps not well-known fact about the reception of the KU in the first few years after its publication. This, I suggest, indicates an additional reason for pursuing the details of how Kant's views developed out of the Wolff–Baumgarten tradition. It is the fact that Kant's opponents – philosophers who had responded very critically to the first two *Critiques* – received the KU with approval.

This benevolent reception, at first glance, is surprising because Kant saw his own accomplishment as nothing less than revolutionary. Only the replacement of traditional analyses of taste – roughly, in either an empiricist or a rationalist version – by a 'transcendental' investigation, he claimed, could rescue the pleasure of taste from collapsing into the delight in the agreeable or the good. "And so," he concluded dramatically, "all beauty in the world would be denied" (5: 346f.). Similarly dramatic claims are familiar from the other two *Critiques*.[1] In these cases, however, 'the tradition' had responded, in the form of reviews and other publications, swiftly and very critically. Not so in 1790. The KU was not regarded by the early readers as the radical break with traditional views that Kant and later commentators saw in it – nothing like the "aesthetic revolution" the young Friedrich Schlegel, for instance, in his pre-Romantic phase, expected the KU to inaugurate.[2] In the reviews that appeared during the first five years after the *Critique*'s publication,[3] Kant's notion of beauty was

---

[1] In 1781, for instance, he announced that the critical philosophy might attain, "even before the end of the present [century] what many centuries could not accomplish ... namely, to bring human reason to full satisfaction in that which has always, but until now vainly, occupied its lust for knowledge" (A 856).
[2] Schlegel (1797: 187). This essay was written in 1795 but published only in 1797.
[3] They are listed in Klemme's edition of the KU: Klemme (2006: 564f.).

often understood as virtually equivalent with the traditional notion of 'unity in variety'; his insistence that judgments of taste cannot be derived from rules, though apparently directed against a dominant view at the time, was not perceived as such; and the connection between taste and morality Kant proposed seemed in line with widespread opinion. The tone of these reviews was usually reverential; the reviewers celebrated an admirable achievement of the by now sixty-six-year-old philosopher who had written an "outstanding, deeply thought out, and masterful work."[4]

We can get a first impression of the difference in attitude towards the KU from some remarks Johann August Eberhard made in 1791 – not in a review of Kant's just published work but in a response to criticisms of his own, long-standing efforts in aesthetics. In 1788, Eberhard had started his famous attempt to rehabilitate the Leibniz–Wolff tradition against Kant's criticism in the KrV, which provoked a lengthy reply from Kant that he published in 1790 together with the KU; the reply, in turn, stimulated further responses from Eberhard and his allies in the following years.[5] On both sides, it was a heated exchange. The same year, 1790, also saw the third, "improved" edition of Eberhard's handbook of aesthetics (*Theorie der schönen Künste und Wissenschaften*), a compendium of the Wolff–Baumgarten tradition in this field that aimed at deriving (or at least make plausible) principles of art from basic philosophical claims and, in particular, the claim that we ascribe beauty to an object when we confusedly perceive the object's perfection. The reviewer of the Kant-friendly *Allgemeine Litteratur Zeitung* sharply reproached Eberhard for having neglected the opportunity in the new edition to correct the old doctrines in light of Kant's criticisms of the Wolff–Baumgarten views, especially with respect to the "indeterminate and ambiguous" concept of perfection.[6] The interesting point here is that – even though Eberhard was obviously hurt by the review – he refused to engage in an attack on the KU and instead granted Kant's "subjective" point of view as a legitimate option that he did not criticize ("*ich tadle nicht*") and instead just emphasized his right to prefer the "objective" approach of Baumgarten's school in which the effect of beauty is correlated with features of the object as its causes. The reason he gave is pragmatic: only the objective approach can be made useful for critics and artists. In this respect, he pointed out, the traditional doctrine had proven overwhelmingly successful in giving "the German art critics the advantage over the critics of all other educated nations . . . . This

---

[4] Schulze (1793: 398).   [5] Cf. Beiser (1987: 217–25) for a brief overview.
[6] Anonymous (1790: 778): Eberhard just plays "the old game" with this concept.

certainly speaks in favor of the correctness and fruitfulness of these [Baumgartian] concepts."⁷

What looked like an offer of peaceful coexistence from Eberhard was reflected in the early reviews of the KU. The most substantial of the early reviews were authored by Kant's old enemy, the Lockean Johann Georg Feder, co-author of the famous Garve–Feder review of the KrV, and by the Humean Gottlob Ernst Schulze.⁸ They made it clear that much of what Kant said sounded familiar to them. Thus, Feder noted that Kant's view on beauty and sublimity "finds my complete approval" and he suggested that it was not in these (apparently familiar) results but rather "in the derivation, elaboration and application" of them "where ... [Kant's] original genius shows itself."⁹ Schulze recommended that somebody should carefully compare the KU with "Baumgarten's, Sulzer's, and Mendelssohn's analyses of the beautiful" because "the agreements of the latter with the former ... are not as small as some may believe."¹⁰ A contemporaneous essay by an anonymous author indeed performed such a comparison and concluded that Kant's theory could be, more or less, translated into Baumgarten's.¹¹ Even a decade after the publication of KU, August Wilhelm Schlegel in his lectures on *Schöne Literatur und Kunst* presented a (quite critical) summary of Kant's "analysis of the form of so-called judgments of taste" and found that the "positive message" turned "out to be nothing other than: beauty is the form of objects that agrees with the needs of the understanding; which [message] has, properly speaking, not more content than the [traditional] definition: beauty is unity in the manifold."¹² Finally, the results Kant arrived at with respect to the relation of taste to morality also would have seemed familiar to readers in 1790 – the results, though not the reasoning that led to them. These results seemed to be commonplaces. Compare, for instance, the conclusion of § 59 of the KU that "taste as it were makes possible the transition from sensible charm to the habitual moral interest without too violent a leap" and that it teaches us "to find a free satisfaction in the objects of the senses even without any sensible charm" (5: 354), with Johann Georg Sulzer's entry in his encyclopedic *Allgemeine Theorie der schönen Künste und Wissenschaften* (1771–74): "How can we begin to apply the human being's inborn inclination to sensibility in order to ennoble his way of sensing [*Sinnesart*] and to use it, in particular cases, as a means to stimulate him

---

⁷ Eberhard (1791: 150f.). ⁸ See Beiser (1987: chs. 6 and 9) for these classifications.
⁹ Feder (1791: 189, 1790: 1140). ¹⁰ Schulze (1793: 424). ¹¹ Anonymous (1792).
¹² Schlegel (1989: 231).

irresistibly to his [moral] duty?"[13] Taken by itself, what I call (in Chapter 9) the aesthetic transition from taste to morality is not further remarkable in the eighteenth-century discussion.[14]

Even though much of what Kant said sounded familiar to the early reviewers of the KU, there were complaints, similar to Eberhard's point, that the theory did not seem to be useful for art critics or artists (which Kant had emphasized himself, e.g., 5: 170) or that Kant's claims about a priori principles of our higher faculties were doubtful on the basis of previously rehearsed objections.[15] To later readers, however, Kant's view that there cannot be principles of taste – that is, basic propositions under "which one could subsume the concept of an object and then by means of an inference conclude that it is beautiful" (5: 285) – has often seemed one of the most obvious ways in which he parted with eighteenth-century traditions. Indeed, the German rationalists had the ambition to 'explain' the pleasure of taste by deriving it from principles of what was called 'empirical psychology.' In 1771, Moses Mendelssohn, for instance, found it regrettable that a "great observer of nature" like Burke, in his *Philosophical Enquiry* (1757), was not able to explain his acute observations about beauty and sublimity "from the nature of the soul," because he was unaware of the German philosophers' theories about the human mind.[16] In his aesthetics textbook mentioned earlier, Eberhard, for instance, claimed that all such rules had to be derived from the "final and highest aim" of artworks, which is to give us pleasure. Since pleasure is always the sensible perception of perfection – a principle from the empirical psychology part of rationalist metaphysics – the rules must be instructions of how to represent such perfection in a sensible way. Therefore: "Beautiful works are here regarded as means and hence as effective causes of pleasure."[17] When Eberhard and others labelled Kant's approach as 'subjective', it seems therefore that they did not mean to criticize his focus on the effect of beauty but his claim that we can investigate the causes of the effect only empirically and not derive them from a priori principles.[18]

---

[13] Sulzer (1774: 622f.; s.v. "Künste; schöne Künste").
[14] For further similarities between Sulzer's views and Kant's, see Rueger (2008a).
[15] Cf. Schulze (1793: 426): "has the critical system, by deriving certain properties of our cognition from the essential arrangement of our mind, really proceeded to the utmost limits of all philosophy?"
[16] Mendelssohn (1771: 400). For the program of explaining the pleasure of taste in Baumgarten and his followers, see Beiser (2009: 133–38).
[17] Eberhard (1786: 7f. and 16).
[18] Beiser (2009: 138) has suggested that what the Baumgarten school meant by 'a priori rules' were rules derived "from higher psychological principles, which determine the place of aesthetic experience within our mental economy." Kant's insistence that there cannot be rules of taste that are derived "from some source entirely outside experience" would then be directed at a straw man

In any case, the contrast between Kant and the eighteenth-century efforts concerning rules of taste did not appear to contemporary readers as stark as it seems in hindsight. First of all, whatever difficulties contemporary readers may have had with grasping the 'transcendental point of view,' it could occur to them that Kant was not competing with efforts to find rules of taste, properly understood, that is, rules that can be found inductively from examples of great art. Art critics, he wrote, through the application of such empirical rules, criticize "the products of fine art just as the former [the transcendental critique] criticizes the faculty of judging them itself" (5: 286). Thus, the KU, officially at least, left the eighteenth-century practice of judging works of art untouched.[19] Second, although the necessity of rules of taste for judging and for producing art was generally accepted, it was also evident to many theorists that these rules could not function as 'principles of taste' in Kant's sense because their correct application to particular cases depended on – taste. Thus, the Swiss *Kunstrichter* Johann Jacob Breitinger admitted in his seminal treatise on poetics (1740):

> It is ... impossible to teach and present good taste through rules that constitute a complete system of fine art because its judgments refer to particular occasions [*Stellen*], which have to be judged according to the [poet's] particular intentions and according to the qualities [*Beschaffenheit*] of particular things.[20]

The poet C. F. Gellert echoed this sentiment, adding that not even the possession of genius can compensate for the shortcoming of the rules:

> The usefulness of the rules is very limited, even when we have genius. They are general and imperfect. They instruct us what we have to do in general but not how much and how little in each case. The application [of the rules] is determined by our insight, by our taste.[21]

---

rather than at philosophers such as Baumgarten, Mendelssohn, or Eberhard. Although I am not sure the proposed interpretation adequately captures what Baumgarten meant by 'a priori,' it would contribute to explain the relatively tolerant reception of the KU.

[19] I say 'officially' because privately Kant did express the hope that the transcendental critique of taste could lead to practical consequences in art criticism. Cf. the letter to the musician Johann Friedrich Reichardt (15 October 1790) in which he related that "it would please me if a connoisseur truly conversant with the products of the faculty of taste could give a more concrete and explicit account of the characteristics of that faculty, so difficult to fathom, that I have tried to outline" (11: 228). For a systematic and pioneering exploration of the possibility of art criticism within Kant's framework, see Tuna (2016).

[20] Breitinger (1740: 430).

[21] Gellert (1774: 171). Cf. also Sulzer: Works of the fine arts are those whose "mere presentation requires genius and taste, because it cannot be accomplished according to determinate rules" (1774: 626; s.v. "Kunst; künstlich"; cf. 1771: 462; s.v. "Geschmack").

At some level, these were Kant's points: what he called 'mechanical' rules were required in art (cf. 5: 304; 310) – for judging and producing it – but they could not account for a more basic capacity, namely, taste. This more basic ability to discern beauty, in a way that can make a justified claim to universal agreement, he tried to subject to a transcendental (as opposed to an empirical) investigation, that is, he aimed at deriving "the possibility of such a judging [in taste] from the nature of this faculty as a faculty of cognition in general" (5: 286). This sort of investigation, in analogy with the first *Critique*, was supposed to answer the question: *Assuming* that judgments of taste, with their pretension to universal validity, are actual, how are they possible? If we can understand their possibility, through connecting them with our cognitive faculties, then the assumption can be lifted and we can *assert* that we indeed have the capacity to make such judgments and their claims are, in principle, justified.

In light of the comparatively tolerant reception of the KU by the reviewers, it is somewhat ironic that early followers of Kant, such as Schiller and Friedrich Schlegel, also saw a problem with this 'subjectivity' of Kant's theory but took it – against Kant's own pronouncements – as an unnecessary limitation, a blind spot in Kant's view that could be overcome through the efforts of a younger generation of philosophers. Kant's "revolution in the philosophical world," wrote Schiller in early 1793, "has toppled the current system of aesthetics (if it indeed deserves this name)." But although Kant did not see this, his philosophy actually provides the "firm fundament [*Grundsteine*] for erecting a [new] system of aesthetics."[22] In this envisaged system, Schiller planned to give the connection of beauty and morality its proper due, which Kant could not do because he understood the experience of beauty as "a mere subjective play of the imagination that can have no other than empirical rules."[23] Instead, Schiller wanted to show that "the original laws of reason also have to be the laws of taste."[24] The rationalists' ambition – as characterized or mischaracterized by Kant – would thus be realized on a supposedly Kantian basis in a system of "objective" rules.[25]

My diagnosis of the reasons for the early benevolent reception of the KU has left out some circumstances that presumably also played a role, in particular, the fact that Kant's reputation and stature in German philosophy in 1790 may have motivated a certain reverence on the reviewers' part or

---

[22] Letter to the Duke of Augustenburg, 9 February 1793 (Schiller 1992: 184).
[23] Letter to the Duke of Augustenburg, 9 February 1793 (Schiller 1992: 186).
[24] Letter to the Duke of Augustenburg, 9 February 1793 (Schiller 1992: 185).
[25] See the analysis of this project, started but not completed in Schiller's *Kallias Briefe*, in Beiser (2005: ch. 2).

that the KU was just too difficult to understand, as Karl Leonhard Reinhold, one of Kant's most prominent followers, admitted privately so as to excuse the three-year delay of his review; he just could not grasp what Kant was trying to say in the Introduction and the aesthetic part of the work.[26] But if my diagnosis is roughly correct, it would, of course, still not be justified to infer from the early reviews that the KU indeed did not contain much that was new. What is in need of explanation, however, is the striking fact that the reviewers found, despite Kant's protestations, so much agreement with views in the rationalist tradition. The search for such an explanation motivates a developmental approach, that is, an investigation into the transformation of tenets familiar in 'empirical psychology' into a framework that denied the empirical aspects, an inquiry Kant labelled 'transcendental.' This transformation was the culmination of Kant's old plan to write a 'critique of taste,' for which he had copious materials in his notes and lectures from the 1770s, and historians have long noticed that much of these materials were absorbed, more or less unchanged, into the new KU. My focus in the following chapters, as I explained in my Introduction, will be on the notion of pleasure and its varieties, a topic standardly discussed under the heading of empirical psychology.

During the eighteenth century, there were numerous attempts at defining or explaining pleasure in German philosophy and although the Leibniz–Wolff school's connection of pleasure with the perception of perfection was clearly dominant, after the middle of the century modifications of this view were explored and anti-Wolffian proposals – which insisted that pleasure had nothing to do with perfection but consisted in the satisfaction of desires – were explored. I discuss these positions in some detail because they appear, at least at first glance, similar to Kant's later efforts. In particular, what Kant presented as a "transcendental definition" of pleasure in the KU, and which he motivated with the conjecture that pleasure has "an affinity with the pure faculty of cognition a priori" (5: 177n; 20: 230n), was a widely accepted definition – though, of course, without the label 'transcendental.' In Chapter 2, I start the investigation into the development of Kant's theory of pleasure by exploring what he meant when he claimed that the introduction of the power of judgment in the system of faculties of the mind 'completes' this system. Similarities of his list of faculties with the Wolff–Baumgarten views will be shown, as well as the differences, which became important to the final version of the system in the KU.

A developmental approach of the kind I am pursuing is, in large parts, unavoidably speculative and conjectural. In the case of the KU, this

---

[26] See Fabbianelli (2004: lxxxiii).

uncertainty includes the chronology of the work's preparation. Although we can reconstruct the transformation of concepts and doctrines in the notes and lectures from the 1770s onwards, it is not possible, on the basis of these materials, to determine precisely what precipitated Kant's change of mind about the a priori grounds of the pleasure of taste between 1781, when he denied such grounds in KrV, and 1787, when he announced the discovery of such grounds in a famous letter to Reinhold.[27] Nor do we know exactly why Kant assigned much more significance to feeling in the moral-philosophical works from the KpV onwards – a significance that is reflected in the role of the pleasure of taste in the aesthetic transition from nature to freedom in the KU. For both developments, I offer conjectural grounds that differ considerably from other proposals in the literature.[28] These grounds, I suggest, are to be found in contemporaneous changes in Kant's moral philosophy. First, throughout the 1770s and up to 1781 Kant seemed reluctant to seriously consider the pleasure of taste to be universally valid. The main obstacle here, I suggest in Chapter 5, was that he perceived a universally valid feeling as a threat to his project of a "pure" moral philosophy, which was to be based on reason but not on any kind of feeling. The obstacle was removed in 1784 when he discovered that the moral law, without being based on moral feeling, provides its own incentive in the form of the "self-wrought" feeling of respect for the law. Thus, once morality became fully autonomous in this sense, a 'critique of taste' as a critique of a faculty with its own a priori principle became possible. Second, to understand and appreciate the role that the pleasure of taste is assigned in the transition project, I argue in Chapter 9, one has to take into account a development in Kant's moral philosophy after 1785. In 1786/7 he realized that the deduction of the categorical imperative in the *Groundwork* (1785) was unsuccessful; the effects of this insight were visible in the second *Critique* (1788)[29] as well as in later works, in which the receptivity to moral feeling took on a systematically more important role. The 'affinity' of such feeling with the pleasure of taste, which Kant emphasizes in the KU, explains the role of aesthetic feeling in the 'transition' from nature to freedom.

---

[27] See (A 21fn.) and the letter to Reinhold (10: 513–15).
[28] For alternative reconstructions, see Zammito (1992); Guyer (2005: ch. 7); and Frierson (2018). The most recent study of the development of Kant's views on taste (Clewis (2023)) contains rich material about his "early aesthetics" (from the 1760s through the 1770s) but does not focus on the transition to the KU.
[29] This view of the relation of the GMS and the KpV, though widely shared, is, of course, controversial. See Chapter 9.

2

The Completion of the System of the Powers of the Mind, 1770–1790

With the KU, Kant announced in the Preface, "I bring my entire critical enterprise to an end" (5: 170). What had to follow now, he hoped, was the "doctrinal part," that is, the metaphysics of nature and the metaphysics of morals. The critical investigation of the higher cognitive powers – understanding, power of judgment, and reason – was in 1790 considered complete and Kant presented at the end of both (unpublished and published) introductions to KU a table, variously labelled "a complete system of all the powers of the mind" (20: 244) or an "overview of all the higher faculties in accordance with their systematic unity" (5: 197). The term 'system' or 'systematic' indicates that the table is not to be understood as a mere enumeration of elements but that these elements are organized according to some principle or idea and that in virtue of this organization the list of entries can be seen to be complete: nothing has been left out and nothing can be added. A footnote in the published introduction (5: 197n.), in very condensed form, is supposed to justify the claim of completeness.

Before we look more closely at the note, it is worthwhile to reflect on what the 'completion' of the critical enterprise might mean.

2.1   The Completion of a Long-Standing Project?

This statement from the KU preface marks the endpoint of a development that started nine years earlier with the KrV and, at that time, the prospect, or the necessity, of further critiques was, for all we know, not envisaged by Kant. Most obviously, in the KrV the power of judgment was not regarded as a separate faculty and its employment in subsuming particular cases under general rules, with the rules given by the understanding, did not require a principle of its own. Moreover, Kant argued that there could not be such a principle, on pain of circularity: if the power of judgment is the capacity to apply general rules to particular cases, then a special principle of this capacity would itself have to be applied to cases of subsumption, which would require a further principle for these applications, and so on (A 133). Only in the KU did Kant discover that there is an employment of the power of judgment that does necessitate a principle of its own and hence requires a separate critique.

The case is in some respect similar to that of the second *Critique*. It is very likely that Kant did not envisage the need for a critique of practical reason at the time of the KrV.[1] Whatever the insights may have been that led him to work on a further critique, he was not aware of them in 1781 because in the Appendix to the Transcendental Dialectic he announced that the deduction of the ideas of pure reason "is the completion of the critical enterprise of pure reason." (A 670)[2]

Thus, in 1781, the task of subjecting to a critique whatever faculties were in need of such treatment was apparently already accomplished. But the critical enterprise generated further tasks in the years between 1781 and 1790. It is not the case that at the beginning the scope of the enterprise was clear and that Kant then gradually manufactured critiques until he had exhausted what lies within this scope.

2.2 What "Systematic Unity" Does Not Mean

A misleading way of understanding the completion of the critical project in KU could be motivated by the remark in the introduction, quoted above, that in 1790 the higher faculties are presented "in accordance with their systematic unity." One might associate this with other pronouncements by Kant, made in various places, about a possible (and desirable) unity of theoretical and practical reason. In 1788, for instance, he remarked on "the expectation of bringing some day into one view the unity of the entire pure rational faculty (both theoretical and practical) and of being able to derive everything from one principle." Although he obviously did not think that this unification had been accomplished yet, it "is an unavoidable need of human reason, as it finds complete satisfaction only in a perfectly systematic unity of its cognitions" (5: 91). And already in the Canon of the KrV, Kant had announced that the "systematic unity of ends" in the moral (or intelligible) world "leads inexorably to the purposive unity of all things" in

---

[1] For a discussion of the genesis of KpV, see Klemme (2010).
[2] I have replaced Guyer/Wood's "critical business" with "critical enterprise" to emphasize the same wording as in the KU preface (see above).

nature and thereby "unifies practical with speculative reason" (A 815).³ Doesn't the KU introduction, with the alleged display of the "systematic unity" of the faculties, make good on this expectation?

Not in any straightforward sense. There is no "one principle" in KU that would serve as the premise from which to derive a new way of seeing theoretical and practical reason as different employments of ultimately one faculty, let alone some kind of unification. What the KU offers is, first, the insistence on "the great chasm" that separates the domain where the understanding prescribes laws to nature and the domain of practical reason that legislates freedom; a "bridge from one domain to the other" is *not* possible (5: 195); and, second, the power of judgment is shown to provide "a mediating concept ... which makes possible the transition from the purely theoretical to the purely practical" (5: 196; 5: 175f.). Whatever this might mean, a 'transition' does not seem equivalent with a derivation "from one principle." In the KU at least – ignoring later attempts by Kant in the *Opus postumum* – there is no unification in this sense and the announced "systematic unity" has to be understood differently.⁴ I'll discuss this further below in Section 2.4.

2.3 The Selection Criterion for Inclusion in the System

Another observation about the table of all higher faculties in KU concerns the absence of theoretical reason and what this tells us about the criterion that decides which faculties belong into the system. In the triad of faculties – understanding, power of judgment, reason – Kant makes it clear that he understands reason here only as practical reason. This is, at first glance, perplexing because the ultimate aim of the KrV was to determine the limits of the legitimate use of precisely the faculty of theoretical reason or, what amounts to the same, to find out to what extent the claims of traditional metaphysics to knowledge can be justified. One symptom of this omission of theoretical reason is Kant's effort in KU to portray the KrV as a critique of the faculty of *understanding* alone: "the critique of pure reason," he now says, "consists of three parts: the critique of the pure understanding, of the pure power of judgment, and of pure reason" (5: 179). The title of a critique of pure reason here seems to have taken on a different meaning than the one it had in the actual first critique;

---

³ Cf. also (A 840): philosophy "contains the natural law as well as the moral law, initially in two separate systems but ultimately in a single philosophical system."
⁴ Cf., for instance, Kleingeld (1998) and Förster (2000: ch. 5).

2.3 The Selection Criterion for Inclusion in the System

the faculty that this book subjected to a critique is no longer regarded as a topic for the critique of pure reason. Pure reason, thus, is restricted to practical reason.[5] The motive for this modification is clearly announced by Kant: the critique of pure reason, in the revised sense, is only concerned with faculties that not only operate according to a priori principles but in which these principles furthermore function as "constitutive principles of cognition a priori" (5: 167). This selection criterion for inclusion in the table is satisfied by the understanding but – as a result of the KrV's Transcendental Dialectic – not by theoretical reason. The "transcendental ideas" of reason, whose deduction Kant believed in 1781, completed the critical enterprise, or the corresponding "maxims of reason" (A 666) were shown to have only a "regulative" role to play in cognition. Constitutive principles of a faculty of cognition are laws that anything that is to be a cognizable object for us has to satisfy. This is most easily illustrated by the concepts and principles of the understanding. In order for a given manifold of intuitions to be experienced by us as an object, the manifold has to be such that it satisfies the Axioms of Intuition, the Anticipations of Perception, and the Analogies of Experience. Nothing can be an object (of nature) for us that, for instance, does not fall under the law of causation. "The conditions of the possibility of experience in general are at the same time conditions of the possibility of the objects of experience" (A 158). In this sense, as Kant explains in KU, the concepts of the understanding have a "domain," a set of objects for which the concepts are "legislative"; whatever is in the domain necessarily falls under the concepts and the domain assigned to the understanding is nature. The case of such a priori concepts is contrasted with *empirical* concepts for objects where it is "contingent" whether an object falls under them or not (5: 174).

There is only one other domain, besides nature, for which a faculty is legislative, that is, for which it has constitutive a priori principles. That is the domain where "legislation through the concept of freedom takes place through reason" (5: 174) in the sense that reason "contains constitutive principles a priori nowhere except strictly with regard to the faculty of desire" (5: 168). Briefly, this means that the (higher) faculty of desire is determined a priori by laws of practical reason, which determination is manifested in the feeling of respect for the moral law. This, again, is contrasted with empirical incentives influencing the will.

---

[5] Cf. the discussion in Brandt (2007: 497–501).

The power of judgment, finally, in order to be included in the table – and thereby complete it – would have to have its own a priori principle, which is indicated as "purposiveness," but this principle could not merely have a regulative role to play in cognition; it would also have to be constitutive for – what? A 'principle of purposiveness,' Kant makes clear in the introductions to KU, does not legislate to nature and hence does not compete with the laws of the understanding. The power of judgment, therefore, has no domain in Kant's sense. If 'purposiveness' means that we are somehow entitled to regard nature as purposive for our cognitive capacities – for instance, if the principle is expressed as "for all things in nature empirically determinate concepts can be found" (20: 211) – it is clear that the power of judgment is supposed to "orient" us "in the face of this excessive multiplicity in nature" that the constitutive laws of the understanding left undetermined (5: 193). But since such purposiveness is not constitutive of (objects of) nature, and hence functions in a similar way as the "maxims of reason" in KrV, namely regulatively, it cannot establish the power of judgment as a separate faculty in the table of higher faculties, even though the principle is a priori. And Kant is explicit about this: the regulative employment of the principle of purposiveness in the sense just sketched "could always have been appended to the theoretical part of philosophy" (5: 170) – just like its precursor (the maxims of reason) had been included in the KrV.

It is therefore only the relation of the power of judgment to the feeling of pleasure and displeasure that can secure the faculty's inclusion in the table. Kant again emphasizes this in several places:[6] judgment's a priori principle has to be constitutive for feeling. But how could it play this legislative role? This is "puzzling," says Kant, because he had always insisted that from concepts – and hence from any principle expressed in conceptual form – "an immediate inference to the feeling of pleasure and displeasure can never be drawn" (5: 169f.). Further questions arise about the puzzle: Is, for instance, the moral law (again, a conceptually formulated law) not also constitutive for the feeling of respect? More generally, it is indeed not straightforward to grasp what it might mean for any principle to be constitutive for a feeling. As we'll see later, Kant indeed has to fight off such doubts in order to defend the status of the power of judgment. For now I only want to point out that a priori principles that play *both* constitutive and regulative roles are also found in KrV and that such a double function is therefore not peculiar to judgment's principle. The

---

[6] Cf. (20: 244); (5: 246).

Analogies of Experience are regulative with respect to intuitions (for which the Axioms of Intuition and the Anticipations of Perception are constitutive) but constitutive for experience (A 664).

2.4 The Table of Faculties

The "complete" table of powers of the mind in the published introduction is this (5: 198):

All the faculties of the mind [Gemüt]
 Faculty of cognition
 Feeling of pleasure and displeasure
 Faculty of desire

Alongside these are listed the members of the

[Higher] faculty of cognition
 Understanding
 Power of judgment
 Reason

with their

A priori principles
 Lawfulness
 Purposiveness
 Final end

and these principles'

Application to
 Nature
 Art
 Freedom

The table is to be read in the following way:[7] The operation of the faculties of cognition, feeling of pleasure and displeasure, and of desire are regulated either by empirical factors or by a priori principles. Insofar as they are determined a priori, such determination comes from the associated "higher cognitive faculties" (20: 245f.): the a priori aspect of cognition depends on the principles of the understanding (the fundamental laws of nature); the extent to which the faculty of desire can be determined a priori depends on

---

[7] I am combining here elucidations from both introductions.

the moral law, given by practical reason; and insofar as there are feelings that can be determined a priori, they would depend on the principle of the power of judgment. The first two critiques had established these connections for the faculty of cognition and that of desire by justifying the corresponding a priori principles. It is a main task of the KU to accomplish such a justification for the principle that determines the feeling of pleasure and displeasure. Since this justification is not fully presented in the introductions, Kant reminds the reader that the table of the faculties "should properly have its place only at the conclusion of the treatise" (20: 245).

The a priori principles of the understanding are summarily characterized in the table as "lawfulness" and its domain of application (or, in the unpublished introduction: its "product") is nature – nature as "the existence of things, so far as it is determined according to universal laws" (4: 294). Why Kant specifies the a priori principle of practical reason not as 'the moral law' but as the "final end" (or, in the earlier version, as "purposiveness that is at the same time law") will be explained in Section 2.5. The principle of the power of judgment is "applied" to (or has as its "product") art. This initially puzzling claim is elucidated in the unpublished introduction. Even though the principle can be "applied" to nature (in the way mentioned), it does not legislate; nature is certainly not its "product." But insofar as we regard nature as suitable for our cognitive aims – that is, suitable "for finding in the immeasurable multiplicity of things in accordance with possible empirical laws sufficient kinship among them to be brought under empirical concepts" – we regard nature "as art," as organized with the aim of such suitability, hence, as (analogous to) an artifact.[8] In contrast to the understanding, which "can make its principle valid as a law," the power of judgment's principle (with respect to nature) is "only a necessary presupposition" (20: 215). How it can be a necessary presupposition even though it is only regulative for the cognition of nature I'll discuss in Chapter 6.

2.5 The Proof of Completeness

The footnote attached to the table indicates the reason for why there has to be a tripartite division ("trichotomy"); in other words, why the list of

---

[8] Cf. also (5: 246): According to the principle of the purposiveness of nature "with respect to the use of the power of judgment in regard to appearances," the latter "must be judged as belonging not merely to nature in its purposeless mechanism but rather also to the analogy with art."

2.5 The Proof of Completeness

higher faculties and their principles would not be complete without the power of judgment in addition to understanding and practical reason.

> It has been thought suspicious that my divisions in pure philosophy almost always turn out to be threefold. But that is in the nature of the matter. If a division is to be made a priori, then it will either be *analytic*, in accordance with the principle of contradiction, and then it is always twofold.... Or it is *synthetic*; and if in this case it is to be derived from *concepts* a priori (not, as in mathematics, from the a priori intuition corresponding to the concept), then, in accordance with what is requisite for synthetic unity in general, namely (1) a condition, (2) something conditioned, (3) the concept that arises from the unification of the conditioned with its condition, the division must necessarily be a trichotomy. (5: 197)[9]

Suppose we start out with the concept of 'a priori principles' and 'analytically' divide it into those principles that refer to purposes and those that do not. The latter have the characteristic (fall under the concept) of lawfulness and correspond to the principles of the understanding. The principles about purposes can be further divided into those that determine purposes that are not governed by laws (the principle of purposiveness of nature) and those that specify purposes that have the property of lawfulness (the final end, that unique purpose the realization of which the moral law prescribes as a duty). In this way, a complete division of the concept of a priori principles has been achieved: principles that concern lawfulness without involving purposes, those that pertain to purposes without lawfulness, and those that concern purposes that are governed by laws. It is obvious that this list satisfies Kant's remark about what is "requisite for synthetic unity": the concept of principles that do not involve purposes has the characteristic of lawfulness; it is the "condition" that conditions that the other elements of the division must fall under 'principles involving purposes'; the third one of these indeed represents the "unification of the conditioned with its condition" because this kind of principle combines the character of the condition, lawfulness, with the character of the conditioned that involves purposes.

One can also see that the division would not be complete had we stopped with lawful principles not involving purposes and those lawful ones that do concern purposes. Similarly, the list of "products" or 'applications' of this triad of principles would be incomplete had we omitted

---

[9] A detailed interpretation of this text has been given by M. Wolff (1995: 164–70), which I follow here. Wolff, however, does not apply his analysis to the KU table. See also Pollok (2017: 71f.).

"art" (that is, nature regarded as if it were art) and only retained "nature" and "morals." Furthermore, we can now understand why Kant does not characterize the a priori principle of (practical) reason as the moral law in the table but rather as the "final end" or as "purposiveness that is at the same time law": only in this formulation does the synthetic character of the principle (with respect to the division) become clear.

Since my suggestion about why theoretical reason does not appear among the powers of the mind in KU stands in contrast to another popular explanation, I should point out why I prefer my account. It seems, at first glance, plausible to say that there is no need for listing theoretical reason because the power of reflecting judgment has now taken over central tasks that were assigned to reason in the KrV. If it is true that "the principle of reflective judgment actually generates ... merely the heuristic or methodological principles presented in the first *Critique* as products of the regulative use of reason," one could plausibly assume that it is simply more economical to suppress the faculty of theoretical reason in the new system.[10] This, however, is too simple — at least if 'no need to list' is meant to imply that Kant could have included theoretical reason, were it not for considerations of economy. But Kant thought that he could prove that the list of faculties in KU is complete, and the argument for completeness, as we have seen, relies crucially on the principle of the purposiveness of nature as the a priori principle of the power of judgment. This is not the same as the principle or maxim of systematicity assigned to theoretical reason in the KrV.[11] In the Appendix to the Transcendental Dialectic, purposiveness — understood as arrangement according to a purpose — is the highest form of systematicity (cf. A 686), while in the KU systematicity (of the particular laws of nature) is merely one version of the principle of purposiveness, the other being the so-called principle of taste (see Chapter 7). Without this 'architectonic' change, the proof of completeness of the system of faculties would not go through. What is essential for the argument is the shift from systematicity to the more general notion of purposiveness (for our faculties); and it is the latter concept, as we shall see in subsequent chapters, that allows the power of judgment to play a constitutive role for the feeling of pleasure and displeasure.

---

[10] Friedman (1992a: 251f.); cf. also Guyer (2005a: 11). Förster (2000: 7) disagrees with this view, although not for quite the same reasons I do.
[11] As Allison pointed out (2004: 513 n. 33). See below, Chapter 6.

Reflecting on the table of faculties and the demonstration of its completeness gives us the 'architectonic' meaning of the transitional or mediating function that Kant assigns to the power of judgment. With respect to the higher faculties, the power of judgment mediates between the understanding and practical reason: it makes the concept of purpose or purposiveness, which originates in reason, applicable to nature. With respect to the other powers of the mind, the power of judgment, because it is constitutive for a special kind of feeling, the pleasure of taste, mediates between the kind of pleasure that depends on sensibility (the agreeable) and the feeling for what is morally good. (In Chapter 9, these mediations are discussed as the 'logical' and as the 'aesthetic transition', respectively.)

2.6 Architectonic Problems

Some questions about the architecture of the system of the powers of the mind will have to be taken up again in later chapters. I already mentioned the difficulty that arises from the dual characteristic of the power of judgment: its a priori principle, which is identified as the 'presupposition' of the subjective purposiveness of nature in the organization in its particular laws, is supposed to function regulatively for cognition but in a constitutive role with respect to the faculty of feeling and thereby as the principle of taste. Though one can understand, as I explained above, why Kant had to impose these requirements in order to complete the system of the mind, it is clearly a further problem to understand how he may have imagined the principle to discharge its dual role.

A second issue concerns the place of the teleological use of the power of judgment in the system. Teleological principles are not mentioned in the table. But one might suggest that the entry 'purposiveness' in the table could, on the face of it, be understood as referring to both subjective *and* objective purposiveness, which we ascribe to organisms in teleological judging. Similarly, the entry 'art' could conceivably cover both kinds of purposiveness: if we judge nature as (subjectively) purposive for our faculties, we consider it in "analogy with art" (5: 246); similarly, Kant considers the capacity of nature to produce "organized products" as "an analogue of art" but ultimately rejects the comparison because "strictly speaking, the organization of nature is ... not analogous with any causality that we know" (5: 374f.). It is thus not clear whether teleological judgment is indeed included in the system. We should also remember that, according to Kant's Preface and the

First Introduction, teleology has no a priori principle of its own (5: 169f.; 20: 243f.) and has therefore no relation to the faculty of feeling.[12] Kant insists on the 'primacy of taste' because only in this respect does the power of judgment establish itself as a faculty while its teleological use could have been dealt with in a treatise like the KrV. The question, of course, arises whether he is entitled to attribute both employments of judgment to the same faculty.[13]

The discussion so far has made it clear that the primacy of taste – the experience of the pleasure of taste in natural beauty – is motivated by the requirement that a faculty, in order to be included in the system of the higher faculties, has to have not only an a priori principle of its own but also has to have a constitutive role with respect to another power of the mind. It is therefore appropriate that Kant calls the third *Critique* a "critique of the feeling of pleasure and displeasure" (20: 207). The "puzzling" relation of the power of judgment to the feeling should accordingly take center stage in understanding the KU. Since relations between faculties and pleasure and displeasure have played a role in Kant's thinking long before the KU, it will be helpful to look at his earlier views.

2.7 The Development of the System in the 1770s

We can compare the KU table of faculties with earlier lists Kant presented in his metaphysics lectures of the 1770s. Though there are obvious differences, the important point that emerges is that in these pre-critical lectures on 'empirical psychology' Kant associates with each faculty a specific kind of feeling of pleasure and displeasure.

The powers of the mind are listed, as in KU, as cognition (or "capacity of representations"), desire, and pleasure and displeasure. Each of these powers has a lower and a higher part, depending on whether their operation is receptive (passive) – that is, dependent on affection by objects – or spontaneous. The collection of the lower powers is labelled "sensitivity," that of the higher powers "intellectuality" (28: 228f.).[14]

---

[12] See Pollok (2017: 305), who considers this as a flaw in the system of the powers of the mind.
[13] The most ambitious recent attempt to answer the question positively is Zuckert (2007). I will not pursue this issue.
[14] Sensibility is further divided into the "capacity of the senses themselves" and the "*bildende Kraft*" (28: 230), a precursor of the KrV's power of imagination. See, e.g., Dyck (2016). For the system of the faculties, see also Wuerth (2014: ch. 6).

2.7 The Development of the System in the 1770s

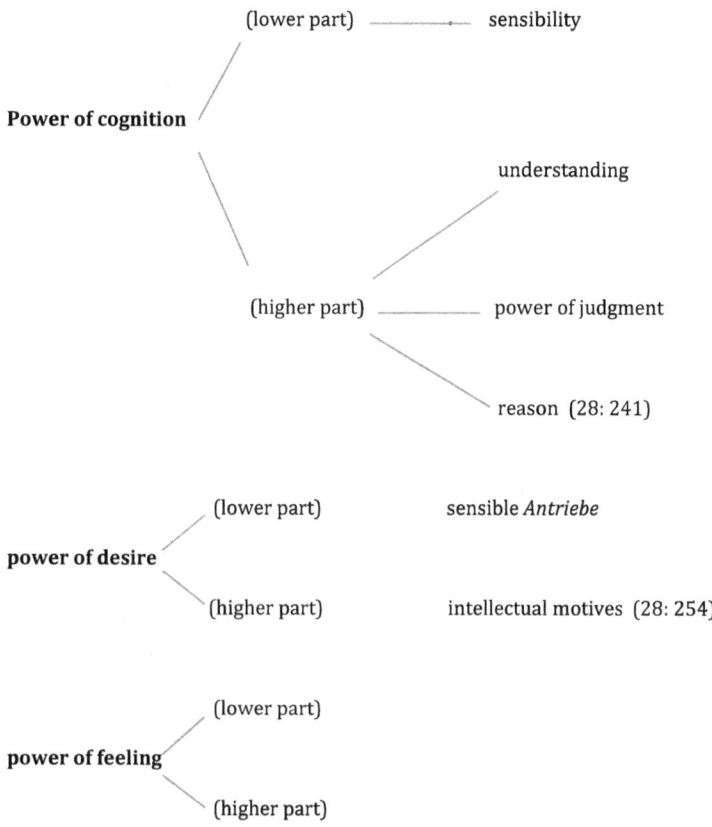

The division of the higher capacity of cognition (or "the understanding in general") looks, at first glance, exactly as in KU: understanding, power of judgment, and reason (28: 241). The operation of these faculties is briefly illustrated (similar to KrV) as follows: the understanding forms judgments (or "rules"), the power of judgment subsumes cases under such judgments (or rules), and reason is the capacity to form inferences (28: 241f.). There is, however, some confusion in the way the lectures specify the role of the power of judgment. At times this role is described, just like in KrV, as subsumption of the particular under a general rule, that is, as what Kant in KU calls "determining judgment." Sometimes, however, the role is reversed and the power of judgment is taken to be the capacity "to cognize the general from the particular" or to "make a general rule out of the given particular" (28: 242), which is the way "reflecting judgment" is characterized in the KU.[15]

More generally, Kant says, the power of judgment is "a capacity for making distinctions [*Unterscheidungsvermögen*]" (28: 243), namely, for whether a particular case falls under a rule or not. Considering judgment as a capacity for discernment is supposed to establish a "transition from the higher faculties of cognition to the capacity for distinguishing objects according to the feeling of pleasure and displeasure." Here Kant discusses our ability to compare representations with respect to their agreement or differences under the traditional titles of *Witz* and *Scharfsinn* (28: 244).[16] To what extent he intends to distinguish these capacities from the power of judgment does not become clear and he asks himself, at the end of the discussion, whether *Witz* and *Scharfsinn* are to be placed among the higher or the lower cognitive faculties. He tends to the former view because "in general" the capacities for comparison "are the higher cognitive faculty, applied to the lower" (28: 245).

Thus, the status of the power of judgment, though explicitly ranking among the higher cognitive faculties, is not entirely clear. Insofar as the faculty is a higher one, it has spontaneity, which presumably means it operates according to 'intellectual' principles – though Kant does not specify what these might be. But there also is the *sinnliche* power of judgment (28: 248), which judges a given particular with the aim of finding a general rule or concept. Since Kant closes the discussion of the power of judgment as a discerning capacity by announcing a "transition" to the other discriminating power, the feeling of pleasure and displeasure (28: 244), it is tempting to assume that the sensible power of judgment, or some aspect of its employment, is closely related to the discrimination through feeling. And indeed, the special sort of pleasure we take in beauty is "the feeling according to a general [or common] sense [*allgemeiner Sinn*], by means of the sensible power of judgment" (28: 248).[17] "Taste is therefore the power of judgment of the senses" (28: 251).

---

[15] See also R 842 (from the late 1770s): "the *sinnliche* power of judgment goes from the particular to the all of comprehension, from the manifold to the unity either of composition or of the idea and intention" (15: 375). The *sinnliche* power of judgment figures also in the lectures (e.g., 28:248).

[16] Wolff, for instance, had discussed *Witz* as the ability to detect similarities (or agreement) among representations of objects (1751: § 858); for *Scharfsinn*, see (1751: § 850). Similarly Baumgarten (1783: §§ 426–28). In Kant's *Anthropologie*, *Witz* is characterized as the capacity "to think [*auszudenken*] the general to the particular" (7: 201).

[17] At (28: 249) Kant also uses the expression "common and generally valid sense" [*gemeinschaftlicher und allgemein gültiger Sinn*].

2.7 The Development of the System in the 1770s

This connection is well-known in the tradition:[18] Baumgarten distinguished between a *Beurtheilungsvermögen* that judges the perfection of things distinctly – hence an intellectual or higher faculty – and sensible judgment, a lower faculty; the latter is "taste in the wider meaning." The sensible judging of perfection, however, is the feeling of pleasure.[19] Although Kant rejects – in the lectures (28: 246) and elsewhere – this close association of perfection and pleasure and replaces it with a different view about pleasure,[20] he obviously retains the connection of a sensible power of judgment, taste, and pleasure.

The capacity for feeling pleasure and displeasure is, like the power of judgment, a capacity to discriminate whether "a representation agrees [*zusammenstimmt*] with the entire power of the mind, with the principle of life" (28: 247). If such an agreement occurs, we feel pleasure; if a representation conflicts with the entire power of the mind, displeasure results. This is obviously meant to be a general claim: pleasure results from, or indicates that, a representation of any kind (sensations, intuitions, concepts, ideas) satisfies the requirements of the entire power of the mind. Although one might at first suspect that the reference to the "entire power" implies that a pleasing representation has to agree with the requirements of *all* the powers together, it soon becomes clear that this is not what Kant intends. The "principle of life" – whatever it may be – turns out to fall under three headings, animal, human, and spiritual (or intellectual) life, and hence he concludes that there are three different kinds of pleasure.[21] Each type of life is correlated with the operation of one of the powers of cognition: sensibility, power of judgment, and understanding/reason. "Animal pleasure consists in the feeling of the private senses. Human pleasure is the feeling according to the general [or common] sense, by means of the sensible power of judgment; it is an intermediate thing [*Mittelding*].... Intellectual pleasure is ideal [*idealisch*] and is recognized from pure concepts of the understanding" (28: 248).

---

[18] Against Frierson (2018).
[19] Baumgarten (1783: §§ 452 and 482). Wolff (1751: § 152) understands perfection as the agreement of the manifold in a thing with the purpose for which the manifold has been arranged. He distinguishes two 'directions' of such judging: from knowledge of the manifold, we can infer the purpose; and from knowledge of the purpose, we can check the manifold for agreement (1751: § 157). See also Buchenau (2013: 63).
[20] See Chapters 3 and 4.
[21] In what sense the feelings are distinguished from each other is problematic. In R 6871 (from 1776–78), for instance, Kant seems to suggest that even though the objects that cause our feelings are different, the feeling of pleasure (and displeasure) is nevertheless *qualitatively* the same. This he takes to be required, at this time, for making *quantitative* comparisons between pleasures and, e.g., preferring something agreeable to what is morally good (19: 187). See Chapter 3.

The standard Kantian terms for the kinds of pleasure are introduced: Objects that are "agreeable" are those that agree with "the particular subject", that is, with its particular sensibility; "beautiful" objects are those that agree with the "universal sensibility [*allgemeine Sinnlichkeit*]"; and satisfaction in what is "good" indicates "agreement with the universal power of cognition [*allgemeine Erkenntniskraft*]" (28: 248f.). In the case of beauty, we judge through the sensible power of judgment that a given representation harmonizes or agrees with principles characteristic of the faculty of sensibility, among which Kant at this time still counts laws comprising "order, proportion, symmetry, harmony in music" (28: 251f.). In the case of moral satisfaction, the relevant harmony or agreement – according to Kant's view at the time of the lectures, which we can reconstruct from other notes[22] – consists in the agreement of a representation or action with the idea of order and regularity of our conduct.

Each type of pleasure thus corresponds to an agreement of representations with a particular cognitive power, where the agreement is recognized by the power of judgment. Accordingly, the feelings are divided into "subjective" and "objective" ones, depending on whether or not they are based on judgments that are "universally valid and hold for everybody." The pleasure of the agreeable, therefore, is merely subjective since it depends on the "private senses" and not on a higher faculty. The feeling we associate with what we judge to be good, by contrast, is an objective satisfaction since it is based on the understanding and reason. And the 'intermediary' pleasure of taste likewise counts as objective because it indicates agreement with the "*allgemeinen Sinne*" (28: 248). What Kant later in KU calls the 'aesthetic quantity' of such judgments – the sphere of subjects for which they claim to be valid – depends, according to the lectures, on the cognitive powers that are involved: the subjectivity and objectivity of feelings is inherited from those powers.

It is tempting to understand Kant's classification of the pleasure of taste as objective, and hence valid for everybody, as an anticipation of his later claim that this pleasure is universally and necessarily valid and that it therefore must be based on some a priori principle.[23] There are indeed places in the lectures where Kant is reported to have said that we judge about beauty a priori; but these are usually combined with – what at least sounds like – a denial of such claims. For instance:

---

[22] E.g., R 6867 (from 1776–78; 19: 186) and many other *Reflexionen* from this time.
[23] Guyer (2005: 166) argues along these lines. He is rightly opposed by Frierson (2018).

2.7 The Development of the System in the 1770s

> One could say: that some rules of taste are a priori; but not immediately a priori rather than comparatively, so that these a priori rules themselves are based on general rules of experience. For example, order, proportion, symmetry, harmony in music are rules that I cognize a priori and understand that they please everyone; but these [rules], in turn, are grounded in general rules a posteriori. (28: 251f.)

> What is good has to please everybody necessarily. The beautiful, however, does not please everybody necessarily; the agreement of the judgment [about beauty] is accidental. (28: 249)

In a note from the time of the lectures, Kant states that "taste is what is similar to reason [*das Vernunftähnliche*] in the sensible power of judgment." One judges "as it were [*gleichsam*] a priori" about what will please others (R 818; 15: 365; late 1770s). This is an allusion to Baumgarten's *analogon rationis*, the capacity of some of the lower faculties (in Baumgarten's classification) to judge things indistinctly that the higher faculties judge distinctly; among those lower faculties that are able to, as it were, imitate reason is the "*sinnliche Beurtheilungsvermögen*."[24] There is, however, no suggestion that because of this similarity taste must be literally based on a priori principles.

Kant's power of judgment in the 1770s detects the agreement or disagreement of representations with the principles of other faculties (and thus is connected with the capacity for feeling) but it is, to say the least, not clear that he thinks judgment has a principle of its own, let alone an a priori principle. And, as we have seen, in the letter to Reinhold from 1787 Kant reports that he has found such a principle only recently (10: 514f.).

Overall we gain from the lectures a picture in which, as Kant says at one point, "pleasure consists in desiring,"[25] that is, we desire to have representations that "promote life" in the sense of agreeing, rather than conflicting, with the "entire power of the mind, the principle of life." The role of the power of judgment in this picture is, in this respect, similar to the role it plays in Wolff and Baumgarten:

Cognition → judgment → pleasure or displeasure
　　　　　　of perfection (Baumgarten, Wolff)
　　　　　　of agreement with faculty (Kant)

---

[24] Baumgarten (1783: § 468).
[25] (28: 247); also (29: 890, 894). Zuckert (2007: 255 n.41) has noted these pronouncements and concluded that in these lectures (from the 1770s and early 1780s) the distinction of the faculties of desire and of feeling is "unstable" in Kant's mind. In Chapter 3, I'll suggest that the connection of pleasure with desire (in a sense to be specified) is actually central even to Kant's mature views in the KU.

I'll reconstruct the development of Kant's theory of the feeling of pleasure and displeasure in more detail in Chapters 3 and 4. This will point to a possible (but conjectural) way in which he could have come to postulate the power of judgment as a genuine member of the system of higher faculties with its own a priori principle, a principle that is constitutive for the capacity of feeling.

3

Kant's Theory of the Feeling of Pleasure and Displeasure (I)

Since the power of judgment is established as a separate faculty and as a member in the three-part system of the higher cognitive powers only through its constitutive role with respect to feeling, Kant characterizes the third *Critique* as a "critique of this feeling of pleasure and displeasure" (20: 207). Although this remark occurs only in the unpublished Introduction to KU, I take it as my starting point, in this and Chapter 4, for a reconstruction of Kant's views on the nature of feeling. The feeling of pleasure, I try to show, registers an achievement, the satisfaction of an interest or purpose. To make my claim plausible, I sketch the eighteenth-century background of theories of pleasure and follow the emergence of Kant's own views from this background during the 1770s. This will prepare the reconstruction of the theory found in the KU. Since the notion of purpose or interest is so closely connected with the faculty of desire, its employment in the aesthetic context – where the pleasure of taste is famously characterized as "disinterested" – requires a generalization that loosens the notion's affinity with desire. This is provided in § 10 of the KU if we supplement the "transcendental definition" of pleasure given there with the concept of interests that are specific to the higher faculties, a concept made explicit only in the KpV but implicit in many of Kant's notes and lectures from the 1770s.

3.1 Background and Development: Wolff, Mendelssohn, and Kant

In agreement with other eighteenth-century philosophers, Kant readily admits that he cannot provide a definition or explanation of what feelings are. The KU summarizes his earlier declarations on this issue: "pleasure or displeasure, since they are not kinds of cognition, cannot be explained by themselves at all, and are felt [require to be felt], not understood; hence they can be only inadequately explained through the influence that a representation has on the activity of the powers of the mind by means of this feeling" (20: 232).[1] Whatever the merits of this claim may be, it echoes earlier views, as expressed, for instance, in Walch's *Philosophisches Lexicon* of 1726: "pleasure [*Lust*] belongs among those things that can be clearly sensed but cannot be intelligibly explained, precisely because it is an agreeable sensation."[2] Leibniz himself had expressed such doubts already in the late 1670s, based on his more general view that nominal definitions of sensory qualities like colors are impossible.[3]

Such humility notwithstanding, there were of course numerous philosophical views on the nature and origin of pleasure and displeasure that Kant presumably was familiar with and that I shall briefly sketch as the background to a reconstruction of his own views. The development of eighteenth-century philosophers' views about the nature pleasure can be traced back, with only slight exaggeration, to two short passages in Descartes: a letter to Princess Elizabeth from 1645, in which he linked pleasure to perfection, and a few paragraphs in the *Passions of the Soul* (1649), in which he remarked that it is "the movement of the spirits which excites the passion of joy."[4] The first of these was the inspiration of Leibniz, Wolff, and their followers. The second seems to have entered the German discussion through widely read French authors, Jean-Baptiste Dubos and Lévesque de Pouilly, whose views were combined with the Leibniz-Wolffian doctrine by philosophers like Sulzer and Mendelssohn.

3.1.1 *Wolff and His Critics: Perfection and the "Desires of the Soul"*

Within the rationalist tradition – from which Kant drew the textbooks he used for his lectures – the feeling of pleasure and displeasure was discussed under the heading of 'empirical psychology' and the basic claim was that pleasure was connected with the perception (or cognition) of perfection. At the beginning of the tradition, Wolff attributed the insight into this connection to a sentence in one of Descartes' letters to Princess Elizabeth, which Wolff paraphrased in 1721 as: "Pleasure consists in an intuitive cognition of perfection."[5] Though Descartes seems to have intended to explain pleasure as a response to noticing a perfection in one's *own* mind – that we are conscious of possessing a good – Wolff elaborated the idea into

---

[1] Earlier statements are found in the metaphysics lectures of the 1770s, e.g., (28, 246).
[2] Walch (1726: 1686).   [3] See Schwaiger (1995: 122). Cf. also Leibniz, *New Essays* II.21. § 42.
[4] Descartes (1985: § 91, 1991: 263).
[5] Wolff (1751: § 404). Wolff used a Latin translation of the letters. The original is translated as: "all our contentment consists simply in our inner awareness of possessing some perfection." Descartes to Princess Elizabeth, 1 September 1645 (1991: 263).

3.1 Background and Development 35

a more complex doctrine: pleasure is the perception of perfection in *both*, the object of perception and, correspondingly, in the perceiver's mind. In much of the later historiography, the second aspect of Wolff's theory (which is the one that probably corresponds to Descartes' proposal) has mostly been ignored in favor of the first.[6] Even his immediate followers seem to have focused exclusively on the first view that locates the source of pleasure in the perfection of the object.

Wolff followed Leibniz (without acknowledging it)[7] in emphasizing that pleasure arises from the *confused* – that is, clear but not distinct – cognition of perfection; hence the label "intuitive cognition." At the same time, however, he insisted that our pleasure increases the more our cognition of the object gains in distinctness and illustrated this claim with many examples. One of these is an architect's pleasure in the sight of a building that is arranged according to the rules of *Baukunst*, so that the "general rules of perfection have been meticulously observed"; others, however, "who do not understand the art, pass it [the building] by and look at it without any sensation."[8] It's the expert's superior knowledge – a more distinct cognition of the object – that enables her to experience more pleasure. And with respect to grasping "deep truths" or mathematical proofs, Wolff claims that the more effort we invest in understanding such truths, the greater our pleasure will be when we succeed.[9]

Wolff's followers found this "strictly Rationalist position"[10] difficult to confirm empirically – an increase in distinctness of cognition seemed to actually decrease pleasure – and therefore often focused on the link between pleasure and clear but indistinct perception of perfection.[11] It seemed empirically implausible to them that the effort invested in achieving distinct perception could be correlated with an increase in the pleasure derived from a beautiful object.

Wolff, however, was quite aware that the claim that more distinct knowledge leads to more pleasure seemed to contradict the basic definition

---

[6] For more on this, cf. Buchenau (2013: 61f.). The double aspect view had already been emphasized by Leibniz as a modification of Descartes' definition; see Schwaiger (1995: 124f.).
[7] Leibniz had suggested to Wolff (in a letter from April 1705) that pleasure (voluptas) is "sensus perfectionis." See Leibniz (1860: 18).
[8] Wolff (1751: § 411). [9] Wolff (1751: § 412).
[10] Buchenau (2013: 63): "the greater one's cognitive effort and the more distinct one's knowledge, the greater the pleasure."
[11] Cf., e.g., Meier (1744: § 38) and the famous illustration he used to support the claim that more distinct cognition detracts from the pleasure of beauty: human skin, indistinctly perceived, looks beautiful while studied more distinctly under a microscope appears ugly (1754: I, § 23). Cf. also Mendelssohn (1755: 59).

of pleasure as indistinct cognition of perfection and made an effort to resolve the problem. He held onto the claim that more and more distinct perception of an object is a necessary condition for correctly cognizing its perfection. But, he continued, "even if we cognize distinctly what is required for judging perfection, the representation of perfection itself is only clear and without distinctness." Thus, distinguishing the cognition of the object from forming a representation of its perfection is the key to resolve the apparent difficulty. The architect, from the earlier illustration, has distinct cognition of the building but he represents its "agreement with the rules" of architecture, in which its perfection consists, only indistinctly. This is inevitable, said Wolff, because the time it takes the architect to look at the building and form a distinct perception is not long enough for him to explicitly think of all the rules and infer from them that the building agrees with them. Thus, even when there is distinct cognition of the object, the judgment about its perfection is 'intuitive,' not based on conscious inferences from rules.[12] The same holds with respect to the pleasure one derives from cognizing the perfection of one's mind (or understanding) when making an effort to grasp a mathematical proof or some other "deep truth"; here we too have "an intuitive cognition of the perfection of our understanding at the same time as of the object, which we cognize distinctly."[13]

What is perfection in Wolff's sense? His notion of perfection as the agreement of a manifold to a unity – or in Baumgarten's formulation: "When many things together contain the sufficient ground of One, they agree (*consentiunt*) in this One. The agreement itself is the perfection (*perfectio*), and the One in which they agree is the determining ground of the perfection"[14] – has often been understood as a purely ontological characterization, as a sort of orderliness in a manifold of things or parts. This is aspect of order is certainly part of the meaning of the term but one needs to add that the 'agreement in (or: to) One' has to be explained as "agreement of the manifold to an intention or purpose."[15] Wolff's examples of perfection clearly illustrate this goal-directed aspect of perfection: the parts of a clock or of a painting are arranged 'to perfection' to the degree to which they operate together to achieve the purpose of the

---

[12] Wolff (1751: § 415). In this moment, the rules of architecture (which the architect once learned) are only presented to him by his "imagination" (according to the law of association) and hence the judgment or representation of perfection is intuitive rather than distinct.
[13] Wolff (1751: § 412).   [14] Wolff (1751: § 152); Baumgarten (1783: § 73).
[15] E.g., Meier (1752: § 22). Beiser (2009: ch. 2) emphasizes this point and so does Buchenau (2013: 53).

respective object: indicating time correctly or resembling the object that is represented in the painting.

On this view, one takes pleasure in contemplating such objects only under the condition that one is aware what the intended purpose of the object is. In the case of natural things or the world as a whole, this would require insight into the divine intentions; in the case of artifacts, one needs to know what the artisan or artist's aim was. If all the parts of the clock work together ('agree') so as to correctly indicate time, then one perceives perfection, the adequacy of the thing for its purpose, the agreement of its manifold parts with what it is supposed to be or do.

Critics of Wolff early on pointed out that the claim that pleasure arises from perceiving the agreement of an object with the artist or creator's aim led to empirically implausible consequences. Rüdiger and his followers – among them Crusius – took pleasure to be the response to a *subject's* purposes being satisfied – but these purposes were, in general, not the artist or creator's purposes.[16] While the Wolffians held that experience makes it plain to everybody that we enjoy perceiving perfection (in Wolff's sense), the critics claimed that in many cases even having the perfection of a building explained to her, a person may still not experience pleasure in its contemplation. What is required for a pleasure-response is that the building in some way corresponds to a purpose the person herself has. Walch's *Lexicon* summarized Rüdiger's objection: Since people often do not agree in which objects they find pleasing, "one must not search for the ground of pleasure in the perfection of the thing itself and its cognition." If we perceive perfection and feel no pleasure, this shows that "such a perfect thing has no connection with our desires." And, of course, there are the cases where we do not know the purpose of a thing at all and still find it beautiful (see Section 3.1.3). The proposed alternative theory of pleasure is therefore: "Pleasure arises when the desires [*Begierden*] of the soul are being satisfied."[17]

Since Wolff himself had explained perfection as grounded on purposes, what is the difference? In Wolff's case, the purpose or aim was determined by the process of production of the object (the creator or artist's plan) while for the critics the relevant aim was one that the audience or the users of an object held. Pleasure for Wolff depended on insight into the producer's plan; if the object agreed with the plan, it manifested a perfection and gave rise to pleasure. On the opposed view, pleasure arises from perceiving that the object satisfies an interest of the spectator. Only on the Wolffian

---

[16] Rüdiger (1721: §§ 5–7); Crusius (1767: § 24).   [17] Walch (1726: 1687f.)

view did perfection of the object play a recognizable role because the unique aim of the producer allowed one to assign a unique perfection to the object, one that other subjects would have to make an effort to cognize. For the critics, it would seem, aims could in principle be indefinitely varied in different subjects and their pleasure depended merely on whether an object happened to satisfy those aims.[18]

3.1.2 Mendelssohn: Engaging the Soul's Powers of Knowing and Desiring

Later admirers of Wolff, like Baumgarten and Mendelssohn, still had to face some of these issues, among them the question of whether distinct cognition contributes to the experience of pleasure or actually distracts from it and the problem of explaining our pleasure in the beauty of objects whose purpose we are not aware of. In 1753, Kant raised the latter issue in a *Reflexion* where he argued that the Leibniz–Wolffian school makes it impossible to infer, in physico-theological fashion, from the beauty of nature to the existence of an intelligent designer – who has purposively arranged things in nature – because, on the school's theory of pleasure, we would first have to know the divinely decreed purposes of the objects before we can find them beautiful.[19]

Baumgarten's response to such problems was to assign different notions of perfection to the lower and the higher faculties.[20] In this framework, beautiful objects, to use Kant's later terminology, are 'purposive' with respect to the specific aim of the lower faculty and this had to be characterized differently from the aim of the higher faculty in order to hold on to the perfection–pleasure connection. Mendelssohn's adaptation of this in his *Briefe über die Empfindungen* (1755) took the form of a distinction between beauty, in which we take a "terrestrial" pleasure, and perfection, the perception of which gives us "heavenly" pleasure. While the latter requires insight into the purpose (or even "final purpose") of things, the former requires only attention to the arrangement of the parts of an object.[21] Similarly Sulzer: "The perfection of a thing cannot be either distinctly or indistinctly felt, unless one knows, or at least feels with some clarity, what the thing is supposed to be." Since there are many things about which we neither know nor feel what they are meant to be, one

---

[18] Only 'in principle' since Crusius, e.g., provides a list of human basic drives [*Grundtriebe*], among them the "drive for our own perfection" (1767, §§ 111ff.).
[19] See R 3705 (17: 238) and Buchenau's discussion (2013: 215f.).
[20] First in his *Reflections on Poetry* (1735). [21] Mendelssohn (1755: 60f.).

should say that "the beautiful is the perfection of [a thing's] external form or shape [*Gestalt*]."²² (Kant's later 'purposiveness without a purpose' is related – at least in hindsight – to these developments within the Wolffian tradition.)

Wolff had proposed that pleasure arises from perceiving perfection in the object *and* from noticing the perfection of the mind that, as it were, is ennobled by perceiving the perfect object. As Mendelssohn pointed out, these two aspects of pleasure require, strictly speaking, two different notions of perfection.²³ The *consensus-in-varietate* concept applies to objects that are composed of parts but is not suited for simple substances like the mind that have no parts that could agree to One. If the mind enjoys perceiving its own perfection, an alternative concept has to be employed. Leibniz himself had suggested such an alternative concept to Wolff: Perfection "is the degree of positive reality, or what comes to the same thing, the degree of affirmative intelligibility, so that something is more perfect in which more things worthy of observation are found."²⁴

This increased-reality notion of perfection obviously applies to simple substances, and one could conclude that *any* stimulation of the mind represents a reality and hence increases perfection. Mendelssohn pursued this line of thought in the *Rhapsodie* of 1761, which enabled him to connect the developments that originated from Descartes' remark about perfection and pleasure in his 1645 letter to Princess Elizabeth with the tradition that elaborated on his other proposal (from the *Passions of the Soul*), viz., that it is the "movement of the spirits," which excites the feeling of pleasure, regardless of what sort of passion – even sadness or hatred – stimulates such activity.²⁵

This latter approach was made widely popular by Dubos (1719) and de Pouilly (1747). Dubos elaborated the Cartesian model and motivated it with the horror that the soul senses when inactive – the horror of boredom. Aesthetic experience, understood as a stimulation of the powers of the mind, meant an escape from such boredom and was therefore pleasurable: "Man has ... a greater dread of the heaviness ["ennui",

---

²² Sulzer (1774: 1038; s.v. "schön")   ²³ Mendelssohn (1755: 98–100; 118f.).
²⁴ In a letter from Winter 1714/15: see Leibniz (1989: 230). In answer to questions by Wolff, Leibniz argued in subsequent letters that this notion implies the 'agreement in variety' concept (1989: 233). See also *Monadology* (1989: 218), which was not published until 1720, and the *Theodicy* (1966, § 33).
²⁵ Descartes (1991: 263), quoted above, and *Passions*, § 94: "we naturally take pleasure in feeling ourselves aroused to all sorts of passions – even to sadness and hatred – when these passions are caused merely by the strange happenings we see presented on the stage" (1985: 362).

boredom] which succeeds inaction, and finds in ... the tumult of his passions, a motion that amuses him."[26] Activity, stimulation, is a basic need of the mind and any relief from inactivity (or boredom) is experienced as pleasure, the indication that the basic need has been satisfied. This theory could explain people's enjoyment of gladiator games and tragedies, insofar as they 'set the mind in motion,' even though the perceived objects are plainly lacking any perfection and which therefore presented a long-standing problem for advocates of the pleasure–perfection link.

Furthermore, the theory easily accounted for the observation that pleasure could result from objects – visual or poetic – that showed a certain irregularity, a "beau désordre," as Boileau famously labelled it in the discussion of odes in his *L'art poetique* (1674).[27] This was meant to contrast with the classicist rules for beauty, which emphasized regularity, symmetry, and proportion; in many cases – for example, in Boileau himself and much later in Mendelssohn – the contrast led to theories of the pleasurable effects of the *un*beautiful, most notably, the sublime.[28]

In the *Briefe*, Mendelssohn gave a characterization of the two opposed doctrines: on the one side there were "those who claim our soul as the only seat of pleasure have said that sensual pleasure arises from the obscure representation of a perfection." The opposed view claimed "that the ground of all pleasure lies in ... a certain movement and irritation of the nerves that occupies their activity without tiring them."[29] Mendelssohn's aim was to develop a theory that preserved the pleasure–perfection link while adapting the observations of Dubos and his followers, that is, phenomena that had been used as counterexamples to the perfectionist view. When we feel, for instance, pity for a tragic hero, we are displeased or pained because we perceive a manifest imperfection while we still, in some sense, enjoy the tragedy – a "mixed sentiment" in Mendelssohn's terminology. (Similarly with the experience of the sublime or with depictions of natural catastrophes.) But – this was Mendelssohn's proposal in a simplified form – our exercising the capacity for disliking imperfections, just like

---

[26] Dubos (1748: I, 8).
[27] "Chez elle [i.e., l'ode] un beau desordre est un effet de l'art": Boileau (1970: 67). Following Boileau, Dubos points out: "'Tis impossible for either a poem, or picture, to produce this effect, unless they have some other merit besides that of regularity and elegance of execution. The best drawn picture imaginable, or a poem disposed in the most regular manner, and written with the greatest accuracy of style, may prove frigid and tiresom [*sic*]." (1748: II, 2)
[28] See Zelle's (1995) detailed study of this "double aesthetics." See also Rueger (2009).
[29] Mendelssohn (1755: 81f.).

the capacity for liking perfections, is itself a manifestation of the perfection of our mind, an increase in its reality, to which we respond with pleasure:

> On the side of the object and in relation to it, we feel, to be sure, displeasure and disfavor in the intuitive cognition of its deficiencies. But on the side of the mind's projection, the soul's powers of knowing and desiring are engaged, that is, its reality is enhanced and this must necessarily cause pleasure and satisfaction.[30]

Thus, even the mixed sentiments that had seemed problematic for the perfectionist could in the end be analyzed as instances of the pleasure–perfection link if one employed the double notion of perfection. The *realitas*-concept of perfection allowed to interpret even our, as it were, first-level displeasure (about tragedies etc.) as an increase in the mind's positive characteristics and thus, at a second level, explain the origin of a further pleasure.[31]

Shortly before Mendelssohn published the *Briefe*, Sulzer (1753) had already tried to accommodate the premises of Dubos and some of his followers within a perfectionist framework. The desire of our soul to be in constant activity – which Sulzer interpreted as a desire to produce representations ("ideas") – could be taken to be an effort to increase its perfection (in the *realitas* sense) and, Sulzer inferred, whatever facilitates – that is, makes easier – this activity is therefore pleasant. What stimulates the soul's "original power of representations to lively activity" gives us pleasure; whatever hinders its operation causes displeasure.[32] If the representation of an object promises to the mind to be a "rich font" of ideas that it can "work on with ease and rapidly," that is, without tiring, it feels pleasure.[33] Sulzer's introduction of the qualification that the activity of the mind should proceed 'easily and rapidly' is owed to his reception of Dubos and, especially, de Pouilly's *Théorie des sentimens agréables* (1747), which was translated into German twice in 1751. It was de Pouilly who derived the traditional aesthetic qualities of symmetry, harmony, proportion, and contrast straightforwardly from the soul's desire for easy and non-tiring occupation; objects with those qualities, he suggested, were especially suited to facilitate the mind's grasp of the manifold of the parts of such objects.[34] Indeed, it is the agreement of the parts to a purpose – just as in

---

[30] Mendelssohn (1771a: 389).
[31] On Mendelssohn's theory see, e.g., Guyer (2020: ch. 6); Beiser (2009: ch. 7); and Pollok (2018).
[32] Sulzer (1773: 11f.; 18).   [33] Sulzer (1773: 13; 20f.).
[34] De Pouilly (1751, § 31).
  Altmann (1969: 99) has shown Sulzer's dependence on Dubos and de Pouilly.

Wolff's view – that is important for the easy occupation of the mind and proves its perfection.³⁵ The combination of the 'effortless occupation' doctrine as the ground of pleasure with the ingredients from the perfectionist views must have been striking for German readers and probably explains de Pouilly's wide reception.³⁶

3.1.3 Kant's Views in the 1770s

Kant followed the views about pleasure quite closely in his logic lectures from the early 1770s (*Logik Blomberg* and *Logik Philippi*).³⁷ "What promotes our life, that is, which as it were sets our activity in play, pleases us. Something becomes easy for us if it is in order. Order is, therefore, a means to the agreement of our cognition with the object with which it is concerned" (24: 45). And he even labels the claim that "our sensibility is in constant activity and also always wants this [activity]" as a, or perhaps 'the,' "fundamental law of sensibility" from which we can derive "the rule of taste: if an object of sensibility should please us, it must have a manifold in it, so that it [sensibility] is provided with material with which it can occupy itself" (24: 353). The features that facilitate this activity – and hence are pleasing – are "variety [manifoldness], symmetry, harmony and clarity ... so that sensibility can grasp the object without effort, [and] can easily distinguish the impressions of the object and feel them" (24: 353). And in the anthropology transcripts from the same time, one of the "laws of sensibility" is explicitly formulated: "Whatever facilitates [*erleichtert*] and expands sensory intuition, pleases us according to objective laws that hold for everybody" (25: 378 [*Anthropologie Parow*]; also 25: 118f. [*Anthropologie Collins*]).³⁸

These are examples of Kant's use of a *facilitation model* of the origin of pleasure in beauty,³⁹ according to which the perception of the beautiful object is especially conducive to assist the mind in its original task – that is,

---

[35] De Pouilly (1751: § 41).
[36] Cf. Zelle (1987: 337) on the "exchangeability" of perfectionist and physiological terms in the German reception of de Pouilly. – The 'easy occupation' idea is also present, e.g., in Gerard's *Essay on Taste*: "moderate difficulty, such as exercises the mind, without fatiguing it, is pleasant." Again, it is objects with properties like uniformity, variety, and proportion that "enter easily into the mind" and produce "a grateful exertion of its energy" (1759: 3; 30–32).
[37] Also, e.g., R 625 (15: 271; from 1769/70) and R 1793 (16: 117; from 1769/70).
[38] Such forms, appealing to our sensibility, would also enable us to grasp abstract concepts easier – in the sense of giving illustrations, vivid examples, etc. for such concepts. Cf., e.g., (24: 43). See also Dumouchel (1997).
[39] Guyer (1997: 17ff.).

3.1 Background and Development

having representations that agree with their objects – by making this task easier. The facilitation, and thus the pleasure, is oriented towards the goal of cognition. This model, as we have seen, derived from Descartes via the modifications introduced by de Pouilly and Sulzer.

We can detect in Kant's notes from the 1770s, however, remarks that are not obviously in line with the facilitation model. These notes are, one could say, expressing a *stimulation view* of pleasure, without a clear orientation towards cognition. In reflections from the mid-1770s, Kant characterizes "spirit" [*Geist*] as "the inner ... principle of the stimulation [*Belebung*] of the powers of the mind .... Spirit is the original stimulation which arises from us and is not derived [from elsewhere]" (R 934; 15: 415). The way spirit stimulates the powers of the mind is through the production of ideas. And Kant emphasizes here that, in general, "the stimulation of sensibility through [an] idea is spirit," which term, he adds, can be used interchangeably with genius (R 933; 15: 414). These notes thus agree quite closely with the characterization of spirit that Kant gives much later in the third *Critique*:

> Spirit, in an aesthetic significance, means the animating principle in the mind. That, however, by which this principle animates the soul, the material which it uses for this purpose, is that which purposively sets the mental powers into motion, i.e., into a play that is self-maintaining and even strengthens the powers to that end. (5: 313)

In contrast to the early reflections, however, the free play of the faculties is first introduced in the KU without any reference to spirit, which makes its official appearance only in the sections on artistic beauty. In the 1770s, spirit is not only the "stimulating principle" of the powers of the mind, it more specifically induces these powers to "a free play" (R 817; 15: 364). Or, as Kant puts it in a "*summa* of sensibility" from the mid-1770s: "The harmonious [*einstimige*] animation of the understanding and of sensibility is spirit" (R 1486; 15: 708). The original conception of the free play thus included the stimulation of the mind by ideas, produced by spirit. The free play is in these notes brought about by spirit; at the same time, the ideas involved in this stimulation perform the task of giving unity to the playing powers. In R 811 (from 1776–78), for example, Kant employs a contrast between work (*Geschäft*) and play:

> [Work] constrains our powers to some extent by directing them onto a certain purpose; [play, by contrast] ... sets them into free motion which occupies them proportionally and enlivens them .... Without a purpose, the powers do not become unified enough; without play, they do not get

exercised enough. Thus, even when we play we need to have an idea or a theme, which is a single representation that permeates the whole activity, so that the stimulation [of the powers] is more complete through [their] unification. (15: 360f.)[40]

In summary, then, the free play of the faculties originally involved an idea, a "theme"; without such a theme, the play would not have the unity required to stimulate and exercise our faculties.

Traces of the stimulation model are also found in the KU, for instance, when Kant denies that regular, highly symmetric figures are aesthetically significant and declares them to be even displeasing because they don't "stimulate" or "animate" the powers of the mind (5: 241f.). Such figures do not provide the escape from boredom required for the pleasure of taste. What is needed for the experience of beauty is spirit as it expresses itself, for example, in the "beau désordre" of English gardens.

The two models of the origin of pleasure are obviously at a tension with each other and this apparent conflict was Mendelssohn's starting point when he presented the facilitation and stimulations views as opposed in the *Briefe* (see Section 3.1.2). His attempt to bring them together in the theory of mixed sentiments, by employing the realitas notion of perfection, was impressive. Although it does not seem that Kant ever commented on this theory, he was aware of the basic tension between the two views. From early on – as the reflections from the 1770s quoted above concerning the "laws of sensibility" indicate – he thought that the facilitation view, with its orientation towards cognition, would secure whatever degree of general validity judgments of taste could claim to have. In a note from 1772/73, Kant distinguishes explicitly the two models in terms of "the movement (and occupation) of the mind" through sensations and through concepts (the latter is called "spirit"), on the one side, and "the arrangement [*Anordnung*]" of the manifold of an object through sensations and through concepts, on the other. "The movement of the mind," he writes,

> is based on the specific [*eigenthümliche*] constitution of the mind because what matters here is life and the proportion of the forces. Arrangement, by contrast, aims at what is cognition for everyone ... hence at what is universally valid. (R 779; 15: 341*)

At least in this note, then, Kant voiced doubts about whether the stimulation model is suitable to account for universally valid judgments of taste

---

[40] Cf. also (R 807; 15: 358) and (R 817; 15: 364), from 1776–78; furthermore, cf. (7: 177). Tonelli (1966) discusses many of these notes.

because it refers to specific, non-universal features of the mind; if such judgments are the target of analysis, the facilitation model has to be used.

Kant himself had by this time apparently become deeply suspicious about the pleasure–perfection link. In 1771/72, he wrote: "It has to be noted that pleasure and displeasure are not representations of perfection but rather the latter presupposes the former; hence, because we find pleasure in an agreement, it is for us a perfection; but not every pleasure signifies a perfection, only the pleasure through the understanding." (R 746; 15: 328; from 1771/72 or 1775) This sounds very similar to a position one of the friends in Mendelssohn's *Briefe* ("Euphranor") holds at one point, before he gets corrected by his wise counterpart ("Palemon"). Euphranor argues that pleasure and perfection must be independent because there are many cases – for instance, the pleasure of wine or erotic attraction – in which a perfection in the sense of a unified manifold of concepts stirred up in the mind by the pleasing object cannot be postulated. Perfection is not the ground of pleasure – rather the other way around: "the pleasure we receive from certain objects is the ground why we call them perfect."[41] In the metaphysics lectures from the 1770s, Kant likewise argued that

> perfection is not the feeling of beauty and the agreeable but perfection is the completeness [*Vollständigkeit*] of an object. It is true that all perfection pleases us ... but to cognize the completeness, that is, the perfection of the object is not a cognition of pleasure; it is rather a further question whether it [the cognition of perfection] is connected in certain cases with pleasure or displeasure. If we assume that the thing is an object of pleasure, then its perfection pleases us and then its completeness is not always required for pleasure .... Pleasure and displeasure are capacities for discerning objects, not with respect to what we find in them themselves but with respect to how their representation affects our subject and how our feeling is stirred. (28: 246*)[42]

It is remarkable that Kant focuses on a notion of perfection as completeness and seems to ignore Wolff's definition in terms of purposes. In the logic lectures *Philippi*, he used Meier's *Auszug aus der Vernunftlehre* (1752) as a textbook and followed Meier in distinguishing logical and aesthetic perfection but replaced the textbook's definition of

---

[41] Mendelssohn (1755: 73).
[42] Already in the 1760s, Kant had made a dismissive comment on Sulzer's attempt to explain pleasure by adding to the perfection–pleasure link the further requirement that the pleasing object should promote the "natural activity of the soul" in an "easy way." Kant replies to this: "This only shows that it [the object] promotes the natural strife for pleasure" (20: 137).

perfectio cognitionis – "when the manifold contained in a cognition agrees to an end [*Absicht*] or contains the sufficient reason for the end"[43] – with the characterization of logical perfection as "agreement of a cognition with the laws of the understanding," while aesthetic perfection refers to such "agreement with the laws of sensibility" (24: 360).[44] As we saw in Chapter 2, in the empirical psychology part of the metaphysics lectures this agreement with the laws of a faculty was Kant's explanation for various kinds of pleasure. Taking these claims together, it is obvious that Kant still subscribed to the pleasure–perfection link – but with a modification of the notion of perfection: the 'agreement of a manifold to an end' is understood by Kant to refer to the end or interest of different faculties.[45] Thus, when he rejects (perception of) perfection as the ground of pleasure in the 1770s, he is rejecting an unsuitable notion of perfection; if the latter is taken as agreement with the end of a faculty, however, Kant still holds on to the link. "What agrees with the laws of a power of representation pleases" (R 1895; 16: 151; late 1770s).

One can only speculate about the reasons for this re-orientation. If our experiencing pleasure in a beautiful object depends on our having insight into the *Absicht* or purpose of the object, as Meier seemed to suggest, then lack of such insight would interfere with the pleasurable experience. Kant made this point, as I mentioned, already in 1753,[46] when he complained that this view would make a physico-theological argument from natural beauty to the existence of a wise designer impossible because the basis of the argument (beauty) would already presuppose what was supposed to be the conclusion (knowledge of the designer's purpose). In 1769, he noted:

> The inner perfection of an object has a natural relation to beauty. This is because the subordination of the manifold under a purpose requires a coordination of the manifold according to [*gemeinschaftlichen*] laws. That's why the same property that renders a building beautiful is also conducive to its usefulness [*Bonität*].

This brief argument connects the traditional notion of perfection with the idea that the beauty of an object is grounded in its sensible manifold being

---

[43] Meier (1752: § 22).
[44] In the slightly earlier *Blomberg* lectures, however, he recites Meier: "With all perfection we always need to have an end [*Absicht*], an examplar, *ein Vor- und Urbild* before our eyes," which provides the standard against which to judge perfection (24: 50).
[45] In an early note, Kant makes this (almost) explicit: he quotes Meier's definition of perfection and then continues, as if he was merely explicating: "If everything agrees according to the rules of the lower cognitive faculties, then it is aesthetically perfect" (R 1748; 16: 100; from mid-1750s).
[46] See (R 3705; 17:238).

3.2 The Transcendental Definition of Pleasure

'coordinated', that is, arranged according to 'laws of sensibility'.[47] But Kant continued that

> in many objects in nature we recognize beauty but no purposes; it is plausible that the pleasure we receive from their appearances is not their purpose [*Absicht*] but rather a consequence of their [unkown] purpose. (R 628; 15: 273f.*)

This seems to say that even though perfection requires agreement with laws, the pleasure we derive from experiencing such agreement is not dependent on awareness of the perfection, defined as agreement to a purpose. It follows that the explanation of pleasure should just be 'agreement according to laws' but not perfection as subordination under a purpose. This kind of agreement, however, is nothing other than the aim or interest of the lower cognitive faculty. It is the frequent lack of insight into an object's purpose that may have motivated Kant's later claim, quoted above, that "because we find pleasure in an agreement, it is for us a perfection" and that attributions of perfection to an object presuppose the feeling of pleasure (R 746, quoted above).

3.2 The Transcendental Definition of Pleasure and the Satisfaction of Faculty Interests

3.2.1 *A Nominal Definition of Pleasure, 1750–1780*

In 1705, Leibniz had written to Wolff that although we do not have a "nominal definition" of pleasure, he can give a "real definition" in terms of what occasions pleasure, namely, the perception of perfection.[48] Fifty years later, Mendelssohn attributed this "*Sacherklärung*" to Descartes, as Wolff had done, and supplied a "*Worterklärung*" as well, which he had found in Maupertuis' *Essai de philosophie morale* (1749).[49] This nominal definition became important in Kant's own approach to pleasure and led to the famous definition he gave in the KU (20: 230 and 5: 220).

In the German translation of Maupertuis' essay, which Kant owned, the definition reads: "Gratification or pleasure, in my view, is called nothing other than that sensation of which the soul prefers to feel it rather than not feel it."[50] Two issues are to be noted about this *Worterklärung*:

---

[47] 'Coordination' is the term Kant uses in the *Dissertation* (1770) to characterize the operation of sensibility and differentiate it from that of the understanding (subordination).
[48] Leibniz to Wolff, 4 April 1705, in Leibniz (1860: 18).   [49] Mendelssohn (1755: 112).
[50] Maupertuis (1750: 7).

Maupertuis, first, takes pleasure to be itself a sensation, separate from whatever representation might give rise to it; and, second, he explains it in terms of preference, an act of the mind that is usually connected with (the faculty of) desire. In Mendelssohn's rendering of the nominal definition, the first aspect is subtly changed: that an object gives us pleasure means that we prefer to have the representation of the object in our mind rather than not have it;[51] there is no claim that it is a separate pleasure sensation that we prefer to have. Mendelssohn, however, follows Maupertuis in arguing that pleasure and desire (or willing) are distinguished only in their "degree" (willing being "stronger", *heftiger*), not in their basic structure.

In both desire and pleasure, he explains, we begin with the contemplation of an object, or the representation of it, and form a judgment that "this object is good," where 'good' indicates the various manifestations of perfection: utility, beauty, or moral goodness. This judgment is followed either by desire for the object, or for producing it, or "by the second judgment: I want to have this representation more than not have it."[52] The latter judgment, which occurs in the case of pleasure, is obviously the nominal definition: an object gives us pleasure if we prefer having the representation R of the object over not having R. As Mendelssohn explains elsewhere, the judgment that "this object is good" is the answer to the question: Does this object "agree with your inclination [*Neigung*] to perfection? Do[es it] agree with the true need of a rational being?"[53] Agreement of a representation with this need or inclination of our mind is the explanation for our preference for having the representation over not having it. Pleasure therefore is "an inner consciousness that the representation ... improves our state .... [It] is, as it were, an approving [*günstiges*] judgment of the soul about its actual state."[54]

In the second edition of his *Philosophische Schriften* (1771), Mendelssohn modified the nominal definition so that the judgment of goodness of the object now leads to either the "desire to make the object of such a representation actual" or to "*the striving of the mind to preserve the representation.*"[55] This modified formulation now looks like the disjunctive definition of pleasure Kant gave in the First Introduction to the KU:

> Pleasure is the state of the mind in which a representation is in agreement with itself, as a ground, either merely for preserving [or: maintaining] this state itself ... or for producing its object. (20: 230)

---

[51] Mendelssohn (1755: 66; 112). [52] Mendelssohn (1755: 66). [53] Mendelssohn (1771: 257).
[54] Mendelssohn (1770?: 225). [55] Mendelssohn (1771: 258; my emphasis).

3.2 The Transcendental Definition of Pleasure

I shall call this the *maintenance definition* of pleasure. Note that in Mendelssohn's modified version, what was originally described as the act of preferring to have a representation has become a "striving of the mind," which suggests a causal activity of the mind.

In Kant's metaphysics lectures from the mid-1770 (L_1) we find a similar definition in terms of maintaining a representation in the mind, which he then connects with the needs or aims of our faculties.

> Feeling is the relation of objects not to the representation [which would be cognition], but rather to the entire power of the mind, for either most inwardly receiving them or excluding them [*innigst zu recipiren oder auszuschliessen*]. The receiving is the feeling of pleasure, and the excluding of displeasure. (28: 247)

After having identified the "entire power of the mind" with "the principle of life," he explains that when we 'most inwardly receive' a representation, "a representation harmonizes ... with the principle of life"; and the harmony or agreement "is *pleasure*" (28: 247). As we saw in Section 2.7, there are three kinds of pleasure, each defined as the agreement of representations with the appropriate principle of life: animal, human, and spiritual (28: 248f.). Objects that give us the pleasure of the agreeable are those that agree with "the particular subject," that is, with its particular sensibility; beautiful objects or representations harmonize with the "universal sensibility [*allgemeine Sinnlichkeit*]"; and what we experience as good agrees "with the universal power of cognition [*allgemeine Erkenntniskraft*]" (28: 248f.). Kant's account of pleasure in the 1782/83 *Mrongovius* lectures similarly moves from the maintenance definition to the satisfaction of the interest of a faculty. The definition here reads: "The feeling of pleasure is the ability of my power of representation to become determined by a given representation to its maintenance or promotion " (29: 890). From this Kant proceeds to the claim that "pleasure is thus the consciousness of the agreement of an object with the productive power of imagination of our soul" (29: 891).

None of this is (yet) original with Kant. Apart from Mendelssohn's precedent, we find, a few years later, in Sulzer's *Allgemeiner Theorie der schönen Künste*, the claim that the sensation of warmth is agreeable (pleasurable) when we "desire to remain in this state or to enjoy the sensation more intensely. If the state displeases us, the force that we regard as our own essence manifests a strife for a different state." And in Johann Nicolas Tetens' *Philosophische Versuche über die menschliche Natur* of 1777 – a work well known to Kant – the same view can be found. Tetens characterizes the "most perfect satisfaction" in having a representation of an object (i.e., pleasure) as "a tendency to maintain [or preserve] oneself in such a state." In such cases, he said, the representations of objects "agree with [*gemäss sind*] the faculties and powers that are concerned with them."[56]

Within the framework of empirical psychology, it is not further remarkable that Kant adopted seminal views on pleasure although the fact that he dissociated these views from the notion of perfection is a distinguishing feature. The two claims he adopted are (i) the *maintenance definition*, or nominal definition, of pleasure, and (ii) the principle that we already saw in operation in Section 2.7, the *achievement principle*: that pleasure indicates the achievement of an aim that is specific to a faculty (or the satisfaction of the faculty's interest, or the agreement with the faculty's basic principle). Later, in KU, this principle is formulated as follows: "The attainment of every aim is combined with the feeling of pleasure" (5: 187). The definition (i) together with the principle (ii) indeed form, as Guyer has argued, Kant's "general theory of the production of pleasure."[57] Together they correspond to Mendelssohn's combination of a nominal and a real definition (or explanation), although his reference to perfection (or the "inclination to perfection") is replaced by the aims of faculties of the mind.

What is original with Kant is the fact that in KU the definition of pleasure from empirical psychology is turned into a "transcendental definition" (20: 230n; 5: 177n.), apparently without much change. Leaving the status of the achievement principle aside for now, one has to ask why Kant thought it legitimate to import these empirical ingredients and argument structures into an "investigation of the faculty of taste ... from a transcendental point of view" (5: 170). The problem is this: If one has come to believe that a judgment of taste "gives itself out to be universally valid and therefore asserts a claim to necessity" – and Kant had come to believe this sometime before KU (see Section 5.2) – then "it would be absurd ... to justify [the judgment] psychologically," that is, with the means of empirical psychology. In fact, if such an empirical explanation were to succeed, "it would prove that the judgment could make absolutely no claim to necessity, precisely because its empirical origin can be demonstrated" (20: 239; cf. 5: 277f.).

The other question is: How can we understand the "usefulness" that Kant in KU attributed to such definitions "of concepts that are used as

[56] Sulzer (1774: 1084; s.v. "sinnlich"); Tetens (1777: 183; 181). [57] Guyer (1997: 70).

3.2.2 The Transcendental Definition of Pleasure

Since the notion of a transcendental definition is not common in Kant's works,[58] we have to try to extract its characteristics and its role from the hints he provides in the KU. A first clue is given in the First Introduction. If one wants to have an "explanation" of the feeling of pleasure, Kant writes, "considered in general, without regard to the distinction whether it accompanies sensation, reflection or the determination of the will," then such an explanation – or definition (20: 230n) – "must be transcendental" (20: 230). In more detail, to ensure the generality of the definition, it should only refer to "the influence that a representation has on the activity of the powers of the mind by means of this feeling" (20: 232). The influence itself is characterized in terms of the relation between the state of mind when it receives a representation and a consecutive state: a representation is accompanied by pleasure if it functions "as a ground, either merely for preserving this state itself ... or for producing its object" (20: 230f.). One can call this a functional definition[59] because it characterizes pleasure in terms of its functional role in connecting the initial state of mind – the ground, containing the representation – and a later state – the consequence – that either still contains the representation or leads to some action for producing the object. The relation of ground and consequence is obviously a causal relation, as Kant also emphasizes in § 10 of the KU, where the definition reads: a representation is pleasurable if we are conscious of its "causality ... with respect to the state of the subject for maintaining it in that state" (5: 220).

The transcendental definition, as a functional definition that refers to a cause-effect (or ground-consequence) relation, is supposed to satisfy the general requirement for such a definition that Kant states in the Introduction: it is "a definition ... through pure categories, insofar as these alone already yield the distinction between the concept in question

---

[58] To my knowledge, the term appears for the first time in the marginalia to Kant's copy of the first edition of the KrV (23: 41). The definitions sketched there resemble the ones given in the KpV (5: 9n; see Section 3.2.4).
[59] See Morrisson (2008: 76).

[i.e., pleasure] and others" (5: 177n).⁶⁰ In the KpV, he applies the same strategy to arrive at a transcendental definition of the faculty of desire as "the faculty ... of causing, through its representations, the reality of the objects of these representations." And he points out again that the *definiens* here "consists only of terms belonging to the pure understanding, i.e., categories, which contain nothing empirical." (5: 9n). That the *definiens* is free of anything empirical, however, does not mean that the concepts so defined themselves are not empirical concepts. It is, Kant insists, an empirical fact that we are in possession of a faculty of feeling and a faculty of desire: "the concept of a faculty of desire as a will must still be given empirically (it does not belong among the transcendental predicates)" (5: 182). Similarly, the 1787 edition of the KrV states that "the concepts of pleasure and displeasure, of desires and inclinations etc. ... are all of empirical origin" (B 29).⁶¹ In all of these cases, transcendental characterizations of the respective concepts can be given but it is an empirical question whether there is anything that falls under them, that is, whether we have feelings, desires, etc. Transcendental definitions, therefore, are intended to be given for concepts that do not properly belong in transcendental philosophy⁶², even though the definitions themselves contain only 'transcendental predicates.'

What is the use of transcendental definitions? It has become clear that they are supposed to provide a transition from empirical psychology to a transcendental investigation by making empirical concepts like feeling or desire amenable to such an investigation. As Kant puts it in KU: "It is useful to attempt a transcendental definition for concepts that are used as empirical principles" in those cases where "one has cause to conjecture that they [the concepts or principles] have an affinity [*Verwandtschaft*] with the pure faculty of cognition a priori" (5: 177n). It now remains to be seen how the definition of pleasure in terms of the category of causality alone can assist in revealing that "affinity."

---

⁶⁰ It is not clear to me how seriously one should take Kant's emphasis on "pure categories" here. If we take it seriously, we would have to exclude schematized categories from the definition, that is, we should not think of the relation between the 'ground state' and the 'consequence state' in temporal terms. But this view would complicate the understanding of many passages in which Kant writes about maintenance. It would also be in conflict with interpretations like Zuckert's that characterize the relevant state of mind as "future directed" (2007: 234). In the following, I will use the schematized category of causality.

⁶¹ Cf. also the *Metaphysical Foundations of Natural Science*, where Kant takes as his starting point the empirical concept of matter.

⁶² In the KrV, Kant therefore explicitly excludes "the supreme principles of morality" from transcendental philosophy, even though they are clearly a priori principles (A 14f. and, modified, B 29).

3.2 The Transcendental Definition of Pleasure

I'll suggest in the following that the task requires, first, connecting the maintenance definition of pleasure with the achievement principle in a way that shows that the latter is not merely a principle of empirical psychology but can be employed in a transcendental investigation. Second, it has to be argued that the achievement of a faculty interest, which manifests itself in the pleasure of taste, involves an a priori principle of a faculty that is distinct from the principles of the other higher faculties of cognition but, in virtue of its a priori status, shows the faculty's "affinity" with these other faculties. The first task is discussed in the remainder of this chapter; the second is the topic of Chapters 6 and 7.

3.2.3 The Series of Transcendental Definitions in § 10

I reconstructed the way from the widely shared nominal definition of pleasure to Kant's transcendental definition as a translation of the first into causal language. It seemed fairly straightforward to understand my preference for having a representation R over not having it as my being conscious that R has a tendency to remain in my mind rather than being excluded from it. The tendency of R, in turn, can be analyzed as a tendency to cause its own preservation in the mind: the initial reception of R tends to cause R to remain in the mind at a later time.[63]

In § 10 of the KU, where the definition of pleasure is officially introduced, Kant, however, adopts a different strategy. He lays out a series of definitions, starting with the concept of a 'purpose' (or end), proceeding to 'purposiveness', 'pleasure', and finally to the 'faculty of desire'. Although he does not explicitly label them as transcendental definitions, they are recognizable as such because each of them is phrased in terms of causality. The series is constructed so that, for instance, the definition of 'purpose' does not refer to feeling or desire, nor does the definition of 'pleasure' rely on the other concepts in the series. This is how it should be, given the nature of transcendental definitions: since feeling and desire are empirical concepts, they cannot figure in the *definiens* of 'purpose,' which must

---

[63] I use 'tendency' here in order to indicate the *ceteris paribus* nature of the definition. We may be conscious of some R's causal tendency to maintain itself but, in fact and due to other factors, R does not get preserved. And we may be conscious of some other R*'s tendency to be deleted from our mind (a painful memory, e.g.) while in fact this R* is maintained. With respect to the first case, compare Kant's response to the objection that to define desire as the faculty that enables us to be through our representations the cause of the objects of those representations is to ignore mere wishes or "fantastic desires," desires that do not result in the realization of the objects. Kant points out that despite our impotence to cause the objects of such representations, "the representation of their [the representations'] causality is contained in every wish" (5: 178n).

contain only the category of causality (similarly for the other concepts). At the same time, this procedure allows Kant to use the concepts of purpose and pleasure independently from the concept of desire. And, famously, he can claim at the end of the section that "purposiveness can thus exist without an end" (5: 220).

The way in which the main concepts of § 10 are *empirically* connected, I think, is the principle, formulated succinctly in MS, that "every determination of choice proceeds from the representation of a possible action through the feeling of pleasure or displeasure, whereby we take an interest in the action or its effect, to the action" (6: 399; cf. 6: 211–13).[64] That is, if the representation of an object is accompanied by pleasure, the faculty of desire is determined to attempt the production of the object. In this paradigm case of human action, the faculties of cognition, of feeling, and of desire are involved. The cognitive faculty forms the concept of an object; if this concept is accompanied by an (anticipatory) feeling of pleasure in the existence or in further effects of the object, the faculty of desire is stimulated to an action, appropriate for the production of the object. In order to define 'purpose,' Kant abstracts from feeling and desire and is left with an underlying causal structure: the concept of the object functions as the cause of the object's existence. This causal structure now serves as the transcendental definition: a purpose is "the object of a concept insofar as the latter is regarded as the cause of the former" (5: 220). 'Purposiveness' in turn is defined as "the causality of a concept with regard to its object." The notion of causality is here to be distinguished from the notion of cause; the causality of a concept is what makes it into a cause, as Kant explains in the *Metaphysik Mrongovius*: "Causality ... is the determination of a cause by which it becomes a cause .... Thus the cause is always to be distinguished from the causality" (29: 893). Again, there is no reference to feeling or desire in the definition. But if we fill in what has been abstracted from – and thus return to the case of action – what turns a concept of an object into a cause of its production is the feeling of pleasure associated with the concept: "The relation of the representation to the subject as determination of its [the representation's] causality is the feeling of pleasure" (R 1050; 15: 469; from 1785–88?) The feeling of pleasure can also be described only in terms of the characteristic causal structure: "The consciousness of the causality of a representation with respect to the state of the subject, for maintaining it in that state, can here designate in general what is called pleasure" (5: 220). Finally, the faculty of desire, insofar as it

---

[64] For a detailed discussion of this scheme in Kant, see Frierson (2014: 56ff.).

3.2 The Transcendental Definition of Pleasure

qualifies as a will, concludes the series of definitions: "The faculty of desire, insofar as it is determinable only through concepts, i.e., to act in accordance with the representation of a purpose, would be the will" (5: 220).

The transcendental definitions in § 10 enable Kant to consider feelings of pleasure that are not necessarily connected with the faculty of desire. Such 'contemplative' pleasures are exemplified in the pleasure of taste, where the representation of an object is the cause of its own maintenance in the subject, without involvement of the will. The representation thus is purposive (in the sense defined) and an example of a purposiveness that "can exist without an end" (5: 220). We can summarize:

> **(P)** If the mental state of having a representation R is pleasurable, then the subject is conscious of this state's tendency to cause its own preservation in the subject (i.e., to continue having R).

3.2.4 Distinctions in the Notion of Purpose

The notion of purpose as defined in § 10 is peculiar.[65] We do not usually regard an *object* that is caused by a concept, that is, an object with a special kind of causal history, as a purpose; the more common understanding of 'purpose' rather is in terms of an interest or aim. The difference between the two senses is clear from the fact that a purpose, understood as an interest, can be achieved by objects that are not conceptually caused objects – as Kant himself notes when he considers "certain tools, e.g., a lever or an inclined plane, which have their effect in an end without a concept having to be their ground" (20: 219). To mark the different notions of purpose, I'll call the causal-history version *etiological*, while the common-sense notion is labelled as *teleological*.[66] As we shall see, the disambiguation of 'purpose' complicates the task of finding a connection between the maintenance definition (P) and the achievement principle.

(P) can be read as a generalization of what I called the paradigm of action from which Kant extracted the definitions in § 10. In the case of production of an object, a representation, the concept of the object, causes the existence of the object. According to (P), we can say that a (pleasurable) representation R itself takes on the role of a purpose because the presence of R in the mind at a time t_2 is caused by R's presence at an

---

[65] As many commentators have pointed out; see, e.g., Guyer (1997: 189f.); Wachter (2006: 15ff.); Zuckert (2007: 80ff.); Teufel (2011); Höwing (2013: 76ff. and ch. 3).

[66] I adopt these labels from Teufel (2011). For a different way of drawing the distinction, see Wachter (2006: 48ff.).

earlier t1. This is what maintenance of R means and the state of having R at t2 is analogous to a purpose as Kant defined it. Understanding (P) in this way, of course, requires widening the original definition of purpose: R does not have to be the *concept* of an object but should be allowed to range over *all* kinds of representations. In § 3 and § 5, Kant had distinguished the pleasure in the good (in both, what is intrinsically good and what is instrumentally good, i.e., useful), in the agreeable, and in the beautiful in terms of the different representations that are involved in the feeling, that is, concepts ("principles of reason"), sensations ("impressions of the senses"), or "merely reflected forms of intuition" (5: 206; cf. 209f.).[67] All of these kinds of representation – concepts, sensations, 'forms' – can serve as causes of their own maintenance in the mind and, therefore, (P) can apply to the three kinds of pleasure Kant distinguishes. This general nature of (P) is perhaps not immediately obvious because the definition seems to exclude the practical case and apply only to contemplative pleasure. In the version of the definition in the First Introduction, the two cases were distinguished as maintenance of a state of mind and production of objects. In the KU, this distinction is given up or suppressed and one has to wonder whether (P) is intended to apply to pleasure in general or only to the contemplative case. I shall adopt the former view, which is also supported, for example, by Kant's treatment of the pleasure of the agreeable according to (P) in the *Anthropologie* (7: 230f.).[68]

The differentiation between an etiological and a teleological notion of purpose presents a considerable obstacle to establishing a connection of (P) with the achievement principle that "the attainment of every aim is combined with the feeling of pleasure" (5: 187). Such a connection, I claimed, is desirable in order to understand why this principle is not merely an import from empirical psychology but, like (P) itself, a legitimate part of a transcendental investigation. If we were to read the achievement principle in terms of the etiological sense of purpose or aim, it would, of course, immediately follow from (P): if having a representation R is pleasurable, then R is maintained, that is, R at t1 causes the presence of R at t2 in the subject, which, according to the etiological reading, counts as

---

[67] The pleasure of taste is "connected with the mere apprehension ... of the form of an object of intuition without a relation of this to a concept for a determinate cognition" (5: 189).

[68] The generalist interpretation has been advocated, for instance, by Engstrom (2007); Zuckert (2007: 233ff.); and Höwing (2013: 111ff.). Longuenesse (2005: 269f.) takes the maintenance definition to apply only to contemplative pleasure.

3.2 The Transcendental Definition of Pleasure

the achievement of a purpose.[69] But this reading is of no help, since it is clear that the achievement principle has to be understood as employing the teleological notion of purpose or aim. Kant himself clearly understood it in this way in the KpV when he characterized the (anticipatory) pleasure that accompanies the representation of an object and influences the faculty of desire to attempt the production of the object. Such pleasure, he says, "is the representation of the agreement of an object or an action with the subjective conditions" of the faculty of desire (5: 9n.), where the "subjective conditions" refer to interests of the faculty, that is, to purposes in the teleological sense. If this is correct, then the transition from (P) to the achievement principle does not seem possible without ignoring the different senses of 'purpose.'

In fact, Kant has been accused of such an illegitimate transition in the sections following § 10. In § 11, Kant discusses whether the achievement of some purpose – in the teleological sense – could account for the pleasure of taste and seems to reject this possibility. The unannounced switch from the etiological notion in § 10 to the other sense in the immediately succeeding section has seemed unjustified and confusing to commentators.[70] In § 12, Kant characterizes the pleasure of taste as the "consciousness of the merely formal purposiveness in the play of the cognitive powers"; this consciousness, he continues, contains "a determining ground of the activity of the subject with regard to the animation of its cognitive powers, thus an internal causality (which is purposive) with regard to cognition in general." It is hard to see how this could be understood in any other way than as a claim about a process that is purposive for "cognition in general," that is, as a process that satisfies, or agrees with, the interest of the cognitive faculty.[71] Later on the same page, however, Kant claims that the pleasure of taste has "a causality in itself, namely that of maintaining the state of the representation of the mind" (5: 222). This statement is plausibly read in the etiological sense of purpose, according to (P).[72]

Thus, in order to connect the transcendental definition (P) with the achievement principle, we need a way of moving from (P) to the

---

[69] That is, achievement of an aim is *necessary* for pleasure. Kant's formulation of the principle at (5: 187) is ambivalent, as Allison pointed out (2001: 56f.); it could be read as stating that aim achievement is merely *sufficient* for pleasure. He rejects the reading in terms of a necessary condition.
[70] E.g., Guyer (1997: 191).   [71] On "cognition in general" see Section 7.2.
[72] Guyer therefore concluded that § 12 is operating with two different kinds of causality (and purposiveness) that must not be identified (1997: 194).

teleological understanding of the principle. Without such an argument – and if we agree, with Guyer, to regard the principle as the basis of Kant's theory of pleasure – we would have to judge the etiological definition of purpose and purposiveness in § 10 as well as the transcendental definition of pleasure as idle wheels, at least in the aesthetic part of the KU. The real work would be done by an empirical principle, imported from empirical psychology.[73]

3.2.5 The Achievement Principle, Faculty Interests, and the Transcendental Definition of Pleasure

Apart from the question of whether the achievement principle is merely an empirical principle, there are other well-known concerns that have been raised against assigning the principle a central role in Kant's theory. Even if the principle is supposed to specify the conditions under which pleasure, as characterized in (P), occurs, as Guyer suggested,[74] one could worry that such a role inevitably contradicts the Second Moment (5: 204f.), according to which the pleasure of taste is disinterested. "Every end," Kant insists, "if it is regarded as the determining ground of satisfaction, always brings an interest with it, as the determining ground of the judgment about the object of the pleasure" (5: 221). Achieving an aim therefore could at best be a sufficient condition for pleasure but not a necessary one, that is, a condition that is involved in all pleasures, including those that are disinterested. Put differently, if the achievement of an aim were a necessary condition for pleasure, then the pleasure of taste would be indistinguishable from pleasure in the good.

In reply to such objections one has to distinguish between a *narrow* and a *wide* notion of aim or interest. When Kant characterizes the pleasure of taste as disinterested, the relevant notion of interest, he points out, "always has ... a relation to the faculty of desire" (5: 204). This is 'interest,' understood in the narrow sense, as associated with the faculty of desire. Since the achievement principle, however, is intended to apply not only to the faculty of desire but to all faculties, the notion of aim or interest has to be taken in a wide sense. That Kant meant to apply it more generally is clear from passages like this:

> Now this transcendental concept of a purposiveness of nature ... represents the unique way in which we must proceed in reflection on the objects of

---

[73] This seems to be Guyer's view: see Guyer (1993: 417 n. 39, 2008).   [74] Guyer (1997: 70ff.).

3.2 The Transcendental Definition of Pleasure

nature with the aim of a thoroughly interconnected experience, consequently it is a subjective principle (maxim) of the power of judgment; hence we are also delighted (strictly speaking, relieved of a need) when we encounter such a systematic unity among merely empirical laws, just as if it were a happy accident which happened to favor our *aim*. (5: 184; my emphasis)

Kant is here using a notion of 'aim' that is wider than the notion associated with the faculty of desire. Since it is the latter notion that is employed in characterizing the pleasure of taste as disinterested, the wider notion does not automatically conflict with such disinterestedness. An explicit characterization of the more general sense of aim is to be found in the KpV: "To every faculty of the mind an interest can be ascribed, i.e., a principle which contains the condition under which alone its exercise is advanced" (5: 119). That is, each faculty has an interest, in the wide sense, in having representations that agree with "the conditions under which alone its exercise is advanced"; and if a given representation satisfies these conditions – satisfies the interest in question – the agreement is registered with pleasure.

The achievement principle can be stated in this way:

> **(S)** All pleasure involves the satisfaction of the conditions of the operation of a faculty of the mind by a given representation, that is, pleasure involves that a representation agrees (contingently[75]) with these conditions, which means that the interest or need of that faculty is met by the representation.[76]

According to this principle, achievement of an aim then is a necessary condition for pleasure to occur. But how can (S) be connected with (P) so that the quasi-transcendental status of the latter can be assigned to the former as well? For such a transition we have to assume, besides (P), the framework of faculty interests, which uses the teleological notion of purpose. Within this framework, (S) should then follow from (P): from the fact that a representation R is maintained in the mind (and therefore experienced with pleasure) it should follow that R satisfies the interest of a faculty F, which is the aim of having representations that promote the operation of this faculty, thereby securing or maintaining the "condition

---

[75] This qualification is introduced by Kant in order to restrict the pleasure resulting from achievement of the aims of the understanding to cases where success (agreement) is not automatic. In such cases of automatic satisfaction, it is actually not appropriate to speak of an interest, aim, or purpose since Kant reserves these notions to cases of (for us) contingent agreements of representations with the requirements of our faculties. Cf. (5: 187) and (5: 190). For more on this, see Section 4.2.2.
[76] For the application of (S) to specific faculties, see Chapter 4.

under which alone its exercise is advanced." Now if R is such that it has a tendency to cause its own maintenance in the mind, then R must agree with the operating conditions of some F. For if R did violate those conditions (hence, hinder the operation of F), R could not have the tendency to maintain itself in the mind. In this case, R would contain, as Kant says in § 10, the ground for "hindering" its maintenance or for "getting rid of" it (5: 220). If R, however, agrees with the operating conditions, then R satisfies the interest of F. Consciousness of the purposiveness (in the etiological sense) of R is pleasure according to (P); this etiological purposiveness of R, under the assumption of faculty interests, involves agreement with such an interest and R is, therefore, purposive in the teleological sense.[77] Therefore, the pleasure of taste, as Kant states in the Introduction, "expresses nothing but [a representation's] suitability to the cognitive faculties that are in play in the reflecting power of judgment" (5: 190).

This result justifies the initially worrying identification of the two kinds of causality in § 12.[78] There the pleasure of taste was first characterized as a consciousness that involves an "internal causality (which is purposive) with regard to cognition in general," which implied the teleological sense of purposiveness. Shortly afterwards, the pleasure was said to have "a causality in itself, namely that of maintaining" the state of mind (5: 222), that is, a causality in the etiological sense. But if the argument above is correct, the two senses, in this case, are extensionally equivalent. It does not follow, however, that they are always equivalent. It is, of course, possible that a conceptually caused object is pleasurable for you because it agrees with a subjective interest of yours, while it has no such interest for me. And an object that has not been caused by a concept can still be pleasurable because it satisfies an interest. But in the case that occupied us here, where a representation in the mind at t1 causes its own maintenance at t2, the two notions coincide.

The exportation of (P) from empirical psychology into a transcendental framework, together with the connection of (P) and (S), allows us to regard (S) as a principle that has equal status with (P).[79] And we can give an interpretation of Kant's claim that the definition of pleasure "through pure

---

[77] Kant explicitly excludes the possibility of "indifferent" representations, that is, representations that are not associated with some degree of either pleasure or displeasure (see 5: 277; 20: 226).
[78] See the quotations above in Section 3.2.4.
[79] When Fichte wrote his fragmentary and unpublished commentary on the KU in 1790/91, he emphasized the importance of this principle in a way that agrees with my interpretation: "It is important for what follows that we accept the claim 'the discovery of the contingent laws of nature as agreeing with our desire for cognition [*Erkenntnis-Bedürfnis*] is a source of pleasure' as not only confirmed a posteriori but as clearly a priori" (1962: 338).

categories" should be attempted if one suspects that the defined concept – at least in some cases – has "an affinity with the pure faculty of cognition" (5: 177n.). This "affinity" is a special case of the general connection that pleasure, understood in terms of the causality of a mental state, has with the faculties of the mind in terms of the achievement of their interests. In Section 5.2, we'll see how (S) can be employed to construct (or reconstruct) a conjectural path from the 'fact' of the pleasure of taste to the existence of a 'new' faculty in the group of faculties of cognition, the power of reflecting judgment.

4

Kant's Theory of the Feeling of Pleasure and Displeasure (II)

The transcendental definition of pleasure and the achievement principle are the central ingredients in Kant's theory of pleasure. Both originated in the empirical psychology of 'the school' and were imported into the framework of the KU in a way that allowed Kant to integrate them into a transcendental investigation of taste. It remains to draw out some further consequences from these basic ingredients, in particular with respect to the question of what the feeling of pleasure and displeasure actually is for Kant, and how it is to be classified (if at all) among the kinds of representation he recognizes. Is pleasure itself a sensation about which we can say that we prefer to have this sensation over not having it? Although the title of the section does not indicate it, Kant devotes a good part of § 3 of the KU to a discussion of this question and concludes that pleasure is *not* a sensation. In this chapter, I try to understand the argument in § 3 and then suggest a reconstruction of Kant's view as an 'attitudinal' theory of pleasure.

4.1 What Pleasure Is Not

One might wonder why this should be an important issue after the definition (P) and principle (S) have been secured. But Kant makes it plain that the status of pleasure is, for him, at first glance, of implausibly urgent significance. The argument he develops claims that if pleasure were a sensation, then morality would be reduced to hedonism. Such an argument is bound to look erratic since we know that Kant, from early on, insisted that the basic principle of morality could not be based on feelings.[1]

---

[1] The argument of § 3 has therefore received very little attention in the literature, with the notable exception of Zuckert (2007: 245–48) who comes to similar conclusions as I do, although through a different route.

4.1 What Pleasure Is Not

I first clarify which view on pleasure Kant is rejecting in KU. It has often seemed to commentators that this supposedly rejected view is one that Kant himself held only two years earlier in KpV. I argue against this reading and suggest a conjecture about the immediate occasion that may have induced Kant to emphasize in KU that pleasure is not a sensation. I then reconstruct Kant's argument for rejecting the erroneous view on pleasure.

4.1.1 The View Kant Is Rejecting

In § 3 of KU, Kant argues that if feelings were sensations, then the subjects in this counterfactual scenario would assess their engagement with what we in fact distinguish as the agreeable, the beautiful, and the morally good according to one standard and with only one goal: the amount of "gratification" they expect, that is, the amount of pleasure in the agreeable. These subjects would lack what Kant calls taste and, in particular, they would be unreceptive to the concept of duty. If we restrict the notion of happiness to gratification, we can say that the subjects deliberate exclusively according to the 'principle of happiness' (PoH); they would be a species of hedonists. The argument to this conclusion proceeds in two steps: (i) from the assumption that all pleasure is a sensation it follows that there can be only the pleasure of the agreeable (ii) from this intermediary result, Kant infers further that the subjects would follow the PoH in all their affairs. This is taken to be a *reductio* of the assumption about the nature of pleasure.

Here is the first step:

> The agreeable is that which pleases the senses in sensation. Now here there is an immediate opportunity to reprove and draw attention to a quite common confusion of the double meaning that the word 'sensation' can have. All satisfaction [*Wohlgefallen*] (it is said or thought) is itself sensation (of a pleasure [*Lust*]). Hence everything that pleases [*gefällt*], just because it pleases, is agreeable. (5: 205f.)

How is the "common confusion" about pleasure to be understood? If feelings of pleasure were sensations, wouldn't it still hold that, for example, pleasure taken in the representation of a morally good deed is pleasure taken in a *conceptual* representation and therefore does not fall under the rubric of the agreeable? Kant seems to be claiming that if pleasure is a sensation, then the three types of pleasure he generally distinguishes according to their source – sensations, concepts, and "merely reflected forms of intuition" (5: 206) – cannot be differentiated anymore; they all turn out to be "what pleases the senses in sensation."

Kant's result follows in this way: Pleasurable representations, R – of any of the three kinds distinguished – are representations that we prefer to have rather than not have. Under the assumption that pleasure is a representation *distinct or separate* from whatever R occasions it, we would prefer to have *this* distinct representation and we would take pleasure in R only indirectly or mediately: as a means to achieve the separate pleasure representation. This means–end structure follows from the assumption of separateness; it leaves it open what sort of representation pleasure is. If we further assume that the pleasure representation itself is a sensation, then all pleasure falls under the notion of the agreeable as that which "pleases the senses in sensation."

The target of Kant's criticism therefore is the conjunction of the separateness and the sensation assumption:

> **(A)** Pleasure is a sensation, a representation that is separate from the representation that occasions it.

If we read 'occasions' as 'causes,' (A) expresses a view that has often been ascribed to Kant and in § 3 of KU, at least on the face of it, Kant is explicitly rejecting this view. The result of the first step of the argument – all pleasure reduces to the agreeable – sounds very much like Beck's presentation of Kant's supposed view: "Whether the origin of the pleasure lies in some physical stimulation, the physical fulfillment of a desire, or some idea held in contemplation, the feeling is always an effect upon our sensibility . . . there is no place for qualitative differences." Similarly, Guyer suggested that for Kant "all feelings of pleasure are a qualitatively uniform kind of sensation" and that therefore pleasures are "internally opaque with regard to their diverse . . . relations to their objects."[2]

But it seems clear that Kant is arguing against such a view, summarized in (A). In fact, (A) does have a tradition in eighteenth-century philosophy that extends well into the twentieth century.[3] One can point to Locke's influential characterization of pleasure as a "simple idea," distinct from other ideas that it may accompany, and to Hutcheson who – for the case of the pleasure of taste – postulated a special sense that enables us to perceive the "idea of beauty," which is identified with the sensation of pleasure, while the other (external) senses receive other sensations of objects.[4] And

---

[2] Beck (1960: 93f.); Guyer (1997: 104f.).
[3] Such theories are often called 'felt-quality theories.' They are distinguished from 'hedonic tone' views, which do not postulate a separate pleasure sensation but claim that what, e.g., pleasurable sensations have in common is a characteristic way they feel (namely, 'good'). See Section 4.2.
[4] Cf., e.g., Guyer (2014: 101–3) or Guyer (2018: 150–52).

closer to Kant's time, Tetens, in 1777, asked: "Is the sensation of being affected [agreeably or disagreeably] a separate [*besondere*] sensation that follows on the sensation of the object?" and spent some time on refuting philosophers who gave a positive answer to the question.[5]

Beck and Guyer support their interpretation of Kant by drawing on passages in the KpV. If Kant indeed held the pleasure-as-sensation view two years before the KU, there seems to be a choice for commentators: either the argument of § 3, far from correcting a "common confusion," is itself confused and should be ignored because it is in conflict with Kant's real view (as expressed in KpV)[6] or § 3 is to be taken seriously and Kant changed his mind in the short time between the second and third *Critique*.[7] A closer look at the KpV shows, I want to argue, that Kant did not reveal his real view there and that he did not undergo a change of mind between 1788 and 1790.

4.1.2 Did Kant Hold the Pleasure-as-Sensation View before the KU?

Although the textual evidence for the Beck–Guyer interpretation – that Kant affirmed the pleasure-as-sensation view in KpV – seems impressive, a preliminary hint that we should be cautious in reading Kant in this way is provided by the widely and highly regarded review of the KpV by August Wilhelm Rehberg, published in 1788.[8] One of Rehberg's main objections was that Kant did *not* explicitly come out in favor of the pleasure-as-sensation view and that he regarded moral pleasure (the pleasurable aspect of respect) as a feeling instead of as a sensation. For Rehberg, only as a sensation could respect for the moral law have any influence on the faculty of desire. At least this reviewer thus read the KpV differently than the later commentators. (I'll return to Rehberg below.)

The relevant passages in the KpV are found in the first "Remark" of § 3 of the Analytic. Kant argues that those philosophers who accept the PoH as the only practical principle cannot legitimately introduce a distinction of

---

[5] Tetens (1777: 204f.)
[6] This is Guyer's position. The argument in § 3 is dubious, he says, but since it doesn't serve any purpose, it is also harmless: "in fact [Kant] has no need to disprove the view that delight always consist of the same sensation of pleasure – the view, of course, that he himself generally maintains" (1997: 153). Guyer has recently revised his view on what Kant's theory of pleasure was; the quotations here should therefore not be taken to reflect his current interpretation. See Guyer (2018) and my discussion in Section 4.2.
[7] This is Zuckert's view (2007: 238). Kant's reference to a "common confusion" would then involve self-criticism.
[8] Rehberg (1975).

a lower and a higher faculty of desire "by noting whether the representations which are associated with the feeling of pleasure have their origin in the senses or in the understanding" (5: 22f.). The premises of the argument are (1) the doctrine that all desire is determined by the feeling of pleasure and displeasure (the PoH) and (2) no prior distinction within the faculty of desire is assumed. The attempt to introduce a differentiation within the faculty of desire fails, says Kant, because "the pleasure which is given to us by these intellectual ideas and which is the only means by which they can determine the will is of exactly the same kind as that coming from the senses .... The principle of one's own happiness ... contains no other determining grounds for the will than those which belong to the lower faculty of desire" (5: 24).[9]

Taken out of their context, these quotations do seem to show that Kant held that all feelings of pleasure are of "exactly the same kind" as the agreeable. But the context in which he makes these pronouncements is decisive. All of the claims concerning the sameness of feelings stand, in the overall argument, under premises (1) and (2). That is, *if we presuppose the PoH*, then all feelings are of the same kind with respect to their motivational role and further distinctions as to their origins cannot be taken to be relevant to this role. "*If* the determination of the will rests on the feelings of agreeableness or disagreeableness which he expects from any cause, it is all the same to him through which kind of representation he is affected" (5: 23; my emphasis). *If* it is "the agreeableness and enjoyment which one expects from the object which impels the activity toward producing it," then "however dissimilar the representations of the objects ... the feeling of pleasure, by virtue of which they constitute the determining ground of the will ... is always the same" (5: 23). This has to be so because the PoH requires that all incentives be *comparable* with respect to their degree or intensity; they cannot qualitatively differ from each other, which would render them incomparable.[10] The obvious differences, for example, between the pleasures from reading a book and from going hunting are made, as it were, inoperative so as to allow comparison of them, as determining grounds of desire, under the PoH. Pleasures of taste, for instance, could well contribute to one's overall happiness but *how much* they contribute, in comparison to other pleasures, can only be

---

[9] Cf. also the Preface to GMS (4: 390f.) where a similar objection is raised against Wolff and his followers who accept the PoH as basic.

[10] More precisely, what matters is "how great, how long-lasting, how easily obtained, and how often repeated this agreeableness is." (5: 23)

assessed once they have been rendered comparable, that is, once a 'common currency' has been introduced. Only then can a ranking of alternatives be established to which the PoH can be applied.[11]

Since the homogeneity or qualitative sameness of pleasures follows from the requirements of the principle of choice, nothing can be said about the nature of pleasures if the principle is *not* assumed at the start. And since Kant rejects this assumption (in contrast to the philosophers addressed in the passage), he should not be understood as embracing the pleasure-as-sensation view in the KpV.

If we go further back than 1788, we find numerous *Reflexionen* in which Kant makes it clear that feelings are different from sensations. In 1776/78, for instance, Kant noted that "feelings [*Fühlungen*] are distinguished from sensations" and that the former are "the subjective in my representations that cannot be objective" (R 552; 15: 240; cf. R 551; 15: 240, and R 1884; 16: 140).[12] This is the distinction he also uses in KU when he concludes our section by pointing out that if "the feeling of pleasure and displeasure is called sensation, then this expression means something entirely different than if I call the representation of a thing (through sense . . .) sensation." He suggests capturing the former sense with the label "subjective sensations," which can never become an ingredient in cognitions, and opposes it to "objective sensations," which do contribute to cognition (5: 206).[13]

The choice of the term "subjective sensation" is, however, not fortunate. It encourages the impression that whatever problem Kant might have found to result from treating pleasure as a sensation, calling pleasure a subjective sensation "only aggravates [the problem]; it simply confirms the view that pleasure consists in a special kind of sensation."[14] It is indeed hard to see how Kant's argument that treating feelings as sensation leads to the collapse of all sorts of pleasure into the agreeable could be blocked by labelling feelings "subjective sensations." As long as they are a kind of sensations, our liking of them will be a liking of the agreeable.

---

[11] Cf. Reath (2006: 50f.) who claims that Kant is explicit about this requirement but actually does not need it.
[12] One should also point out that Tetens had made the distinction of sensation (*Empfindung*) and feeling (*Gefühl* or *Empfindnis*) explicit in 1777. See Tetens (1777: e.g., 181).
[13] Pollok (2006) argues that Kant's distinction of feelings and sensations in KU is meant to emphasize his rejection of the *Prolegomena* notion of 'judgments of perception,' a need he felt after Johann Schultz (1785/86) had pointed out the conflict this notion generates with the project of the KrV. While this may be correct, it does not seem to help in understanding the moral argument in our section.
[14] Guyer (1997: 153).

Although Kant during the 1770s denied that feelings are sensations, it is also clear that during this time he held on to the view (mentioned in the KpV passages discussed above) that practical deliberation required feelings to be qualitatively the same, that is, that a 'common currency' is needed in order to perform such deliberations. Even though pleasures are "of different kinds, even when they are sensual," he noted, they "subjectively ... agree among each other because each kind moves the subject's desire; objectively [however] they cannot be compared, e.g., a meal and a virtuous action" (R 591; 15: 255; 1771/72?). And a few years later he claimed that all gratifications and pains are "equal [*gleichartig*] insofar as they contribute to the unity of life; in themselves, however, they are unequal .... Gratification in sensation (subjective satisfaction) and satisfaction (objective) in judgment [*in der Beurtheilung*] are completely different kinds of pleasure" (R 1488; 15: 728; 1775/79?).

If my reading of the KpV passages is correct, Kant must have changed his mind about the homogeneity of pleasure at some point after those notes were written. This can be explained with a change in his doctrine of the incentives of the moral law, which was officially presented in the GMS of 1785.[15] Until that time, he distinguished the law as the *principium diiudicationis*, the principle according to which we make moral evaluations, from its *principium executionis*, the principle that governs how the law becomes binding for us. Moral laws, according to the KrV of 1781, can be "commands," that is, binding for us, only if they "connect appropriate consequences with their rule a priori, and thus carry with them promises and threats," which would be the prospect of happiness in a future life and the threat of divine punishment (A 811). Thus, with respect to the 'execution' of the law, the PoH was still the relevant principle, although it was clearly distinguished from the moral law itself. The PoH, however, requires the qualitative sameness of pleasures and displeasures for its operation. Once Kant arrived at the new doctrine of incentives in GMS, where the law itself becomes empowered to provide its own incentive in the form of the feeling of respect, the difference between a principle of moral judging or discrimination and a principle of execution became moot. Kant could now allow that feelings *in general* are not homogeneous and restrict the requirement of qualitative sameness to non-moral practical contexts – the view he expressed in KpV.

---

[15] For more on this, see Section 5.2.2.

4.1 What Pleasure Is Not

Kant's insight from the mid-1780s, that the moral law generates its own incentive and does not have to rely on "promises and threats" from other sources, returns us to Rehberg, the acute reviewer of the KpV, who thought Kant was mistaken in not treating the feeling of respect as a sensation. Since Kant was aware of the review and respected its author,[16] it is perhaps not unlikely that he responded in § 3 to this particular line of criticism. An action, argued Rehberg, cannot be regarded as the effect of reason; to claim this would mean to commit the very mistake Kant had diagnosed in the Amphiboly section of the KrV. The transition from reason to action rather has to be mediated through 'something' that is homogenous with sensibility so as "to subject pure reason to the determination of time, without reason becoming thereby sensible," that is, what is required here is something analogous to the schematism in the first *Critique*. This mediating instance is

> moral feeling, respect for the law. But is this [feeling of] respect not a sensation? Kant twists and turns in the 3. chapter of the Analytic [of KpV] in order to show that this sensation is not a sensible feeling. But here he is completely unconvincing.[17]

Kant "accuses those of enthusiasm who take this feeling of pleasure in the law to be the moral incentive while the incentive has to consist of the law itself." But, Rehberg concludes,

> the idea that the law itself rather than the delight [*Vergnügen*] in the law has to be the incentive for morality is itself enthusiasm [*Schwärmerei*]. For what else than enthusiasm (which consists in the invention of supersensible objects) is the idea that respect for the law is supposed to be a feeling but not a sensation [*sinnliche Empfindung*]?[18]

Rehberg's criticism of the way Kant treats the feeling of respect culminates in the accusation that denying it the status of a sensation (as Kant appears to do) amounts to "enthusiasm" because enthusiasm is the claim that we have an unmediated experience of the intelligible realm.[19] Kant's response to this, in § 3 of the KU, may well have consisted in pointing out that the identification of feeling and sensation would not prevent enthusiasm but lead to hedonism, to precisely the scenario where rational beings are incapable of experiencing that feeling by which the law "immediately influences ... [us] to obedience" (5: 452).

---

[16] See di Giovanni (2005: 134f.).   [17] Rehberg (1975: 187).   [18] Rehberg (1975: 188f.).
[19] Cf. KpV: to regard the law "as an object of sensation" is to regard "as an object of sensation, what can only be thought through reason" – "a plain contradiction" (5: 38f.).

4.1.3 If Pleasure Is a Sensation, Hedonism Results

I have argued that we cannot extract from the KpV passages any commitment on Kant's part to the view that all pleasures are sensations. But even if this is granted, it does not shed light on his claim in the KU that assuming pleasures are sensations would lead to hedonism. After all, the KpV argument *presupposed* the PoH while the KU discussion is supposed to show that the PoH *follows* from the assumption about pleasure.

The second step in Kant's argument starts from the result that under (A), all pleasure is pleasure in the agreeable.

> But if this is conceded, then impressions of the senses, which determine inclination, or principles of reason, which determine the will, or merely reflected forms of intuition, which determine the power of judgment, are all entirely the same as far as the effect on the feeling of pleasure is concerned. For this would be the agreeableness in the sensation of one's state, and, since in the end all the effort of our faculties is directed to what is practical and must be united in it as their goal, one could not expect of them any other assessment of things and their value than that which consists in the gratification [*Vergnügen*] that they promise. In the end, how they achieve this does not matter at all, and since the choice of means alone can make a difference here, people could certainly blame one another for foolishness and incomprehension, but never for baseness and malice: for all of them, each seeing thing his own way, would be after one goal, which for everyone is gratification. (5: 206)

Although the argument here proceeds from the result of the first step (all pleasures are pleasures in the agreeable) to the PoH as the only practical principle for the subjects, Kant is not narrowly concerned with moral deliberations. The somewhat obscure phrase that "in the end all the effort of our faculties is directed to what is practical and must be united in it as their goal" suggests that the discussion is more generally concerned with the ways in which the deliverances of the faculties motivate us to engage with objects or actions in different contexts.[20] In the *actual* world – as opposed to the counterfactual scenario that Kant describes – the response to what is agreeable motivates us to procure the agreeable objects or to prolong their effect; in taste, the pleasure of taste induces us to continue contemplation of, or "linger" over, the beautiful object (5: 222); and in moral contexts, the feeling of respect motivates us do what is morally good.

---

[20] 'Motivate to engage' is chosen here to indicate that the discussion is not meant to be restricted to determinations of the faculty of desire, which would exclude the case of aesthetic response.

Our conduct with respect to these different contexts can be assessed and we assign value to what we engage in or accomplish. In the cases of taste and moral conduct, we evaluate our engagement in terms of whether we appreciate the (form of) the object for its own sake and whether we perform an action that is judged to be morally good for its own sake and not as a means for some further end.

These are, for Kant, the standard ways of assessment. What happens to these practices when we assume (A) and its consequence? If the pleasures that motivate our engagement are all sensations, then what we immediately or intrinsically like are these (pleasure) sensations while the objects that occasion them are liked only as means; liking of an object or action for its own sake is ruled out. This is the consequence of the separateness claim in (A). Assuming (A) makes it effectively impossible in the counterfactual scenario to draw the crucial distinctions of our actual evaluative practices between the agreeable, the beautiful, and the good:

> In the case of the good there is always the question whether it is merely mediately good or immediately good (whether it is useful or good in itself), while in contrast this cannot be a question at all in the case of the agreeable, since the word always signifies something that pleases immediately. (This is exactly the same in the case of that which I call beautiful.) (5: 208)

Under the assumption that pleasure is a distinct sensation, the pleasure in the good in itself and in the beautiful could not be immediate kinds of satisfaction in some representation R. In each of these cases, what we would like immediately is the pleasure sensation rather than the having of R. The same holds for the agreeable itself: the taste sensation of the wine would not be the object of our immediate liking but rather the further pleasure sensation, produced by the taste sensation.[21]

Furthermore, according to the sensation claim in (A), pleasure is now supposed to be a sensation and from this Kant concludes that the pleasure sensations are 'homogenous,' that is, differences between them (if there are any) cannot be indicated by their different sources, which, Kant says, "are all entirely the same as far as the effect on the feeling of pleasure is concerned." This does not exclude, of course, differences in intensity of the pleasure sensations. In fact, such differences – quantitative differences – seem to be the only feature that allows for discrimination of pleasures and

---

[21] This is the reason why I understand Kant's rejection of 'all pleasures are sensation' not as 'there are at least some pleasures that are not sensations' but as the stronger claim that 'no pleasures are sensations.' The agreeable itself cannot be a distinct sensation because this would entail that agreeable objects or representations do not please immediately.

for their comparative assessment. That intensity or degree of sensations is the only standard for assessment Kant had already argued in the passage from KpV discussed above (cf. also 5: 266). But how is this claim to be defended in the present context? In the KpV, he had argued that such homogeneity is required by the PoH, which, so I claimed, was the premise of the whole discussion. In the KU argument, however, this presupposition is not made; the PoH as the only practical principle is rather supposed to be the conclusion of the argument. Kant, therefore, needs a different reason (independent of the PoH) for the homogeneity of pleasures – which he does not provide.

I suggest that as a sensation that is occasioned by some other representation, pleasure shares with all sensations a lack of transparency as to its source (what Guyer called its "opaqueness"). A sensation, for Kant, does not have an intentional object,[22] nor does it somehow represent the object that causes it. It is a perception that "refers merely to the subject as a modification of its state" (A 320) and only in conjunction with a concept can it become an "objective perception," a representation of an object. But if neither causal origin nor intentional object can discriminate between the pleasure sensations, then it is hard to see what other standard for our liking could be applied than intensity or degree of the sensations.[23]

From the homogeneity of pleasures, Kant concludes that the subjects in the scenario under (A) can have only "one goal" and that "one could not expect of them any assessment of things and their value than that which consists in the gratification that they promise." The subjects can evaluate their conduct only with respect to the goal of maximized gratification, that is, in terms of how adept they are in procuring whatever means are suitable to reach that goal. In such evaluations, "the choice of means alone can make a difference" and the subjects "could certainly blame one another for foolishness and incomprehension, but never for baseness and malice." Thus, engagement with the beautiful could be assessed, as a means, for what degree of the pleasure sensation it provides but not in terms of whether somebody has taste or not. Telling a lie could be evaluated as a means for the same goal but not as an intrinsically malicious act.

In the light of these results, how should we understand Kant's explicit claim that in the counterfactual scenario "principles of reason" have an effect on feeling? Under (A), such principles occasion sensations of pleasure or displeasure, feelings of the agreeable or disagreeable. The moral law

---

[22] I should note that this is a traditional but not an uncontroversial interpretation.
[23] Cf. Zuckert (2007: 242–44).

4.2 An Alternative Theory of Pleasure

might be one of these principles. The subjects then are aware of the moral law (the imperative to choose maxims that are universalizable); but they do not feel respect for the law, that is, they do not feel that the law obliges unconditionally, that they are to execute actions for the sake of duty alone. Instead, under some circumstances, the subjects might feel pleasure in obeying the law but this pleasure would have to be weighed against the pleasure associated with alternative options for actions. If it so happened that the pleasure attained from acting on principles of reason is larger than what the alternatives can deliver, then the subjects obey the law – not, however, for its own sake, as the concept of duty requires, but for the sake of the agreeable state of mind that they expect from such obedience. The subjects would act in accordance with what moral duty requires but not from duty. In short: under (A), the moral law would lack its appropriate incentive.[24] This result – derived from the claim that pleasures are sensations – is evidently a scenario in which subjects have reason (they calculate their maximal expected pleasure and are aware of the content of the moral law) but their actions cannot be imputed to them since they lack the feeling of respect for the moral law that would let them experience the obligating force of the law.[25]

4.2 An Alternative Theory of Pleasure

If pleasure is not to be considered as a distinct sensation, what is it then for Kant? Section 3 does not contain further information about his positive view about feelings; but in light of the maintenance definition and the achievement principle we can reconstruct such a view – which is, in fact, recognizably close to some theories of pleasure in contemporary philosophy. Although such a reconstruction is inevitably anachronistic, it will allow me to draw conclusions that shed light on several issues concerning the pleasure of taste in the KU.

4.2.1 Pro-attitudes and Desire Satisfaction

Pleasure, we recall, was by Kant defined in terms of the *influence* or effect that a pleasurable representation has on the activity of the mind, namely,

---

[24] Zuckert (2007: 245–48) has argued in a somewhat similar way in her interpretation of § 3.
[25] In the terms of the later MS, these subjects possess reason (they are *vernünftige Wesen*) but they are not intelligible beings (they are not *Vernunftwesen*) (6: 418; cf. also *Religion*, 6: 26). See Chapter 9 for further discussion.

the tendency of such a representation to maintain itself in the mind; pleasure is "the consciousness of the causality of a representation with respect to the state of the subject, for maintaining it in that state" (5: 220; cf. 20: 230). This can be understood, in anachronistic terms, as attributing a functional role to pleasure: Being in a state of pleasure means that upon becoming aware of a representation, it tends to cause its own maintenance in the mind. The definition was intended by Kant to assist in identifying the sense in which the concept of pleasure has "an affinity with the pure faculty of cognition a priori" (5: 177n). I suggested that this affinity can be recognized once we introduce interests, in particular, interests of the higher faculties. The fact that a representation R satisfies such an interest then causes R's preservation in the mind.

With this move from the functional role definition to a specification of what realizes or fills the role, we have imitated the way functionalists in philosophy of mind connect a mental state or property, defined in terms of their functional roles, with physical states or properties that realize or fill these roles. More precisely put:

> Being in a state of pleasure (about R) = being in a state that has property P, where P is the (second-order) property of having a property F(R) so that F(R) causes the maintenance of R.

The (first-order) property F(R) – that R satisfies an interest F – fills the characteristic role of pleasure. Note that on this view, pleasure is not identified with interest satisfaction but *supervenes* on the latter.[26]

In the philosophical literature on pleasure, a theory of this kind is usually classified as an 'attitudinal' view, which holds that a pleasurable representation R is one toward which we adopt a (pro-)attitude that is variously described as 'preferring to have R,' or 'wanting R to continue,' or 'desiring to have R.'[27] Twentieth-century characterizations of the various pro-attitudes read very much like the eighteenth-century examples mentioned in Section 3.2: "an experience is pleasant if and only if it makes its continuation more wanted." Or, in terms of a preference rather than continuation: "to get pleasure is to have an experience which, as of the moment, one would rather have than not have."[28] Such views usually deny that pleasure is a distinct kind of sensation.

---

[26] It is, however, controversial whether the supervenience relation can really be prevented from collapsing into identity. See, e.g., Kim (1998) for a brief overview of an extended discussion.
[27] For helpful overviews of such theories see, e.g., Wolfsdorf (2013: ch. 9) and Aydede (2018).
[28] Alston (1967: 345); Brandt (1979: 40f.).

4.2 An Alternative Theory of Pleasure

Although his theory is not strictly speaking an attitudinal approach, the basic intuition underlying such theories is nicely brought out by a famous illustration Gilbert Ryle used to motivate his own view:

> To say that a person has been enjoying digging is not to say that he has been both digging and doing or experiencing something else as a concomitant or effect of the digging; it is to say that he dug with his whole heart in his task, i.e. that he dug, wanting to dig and not wanting to do anything else (or nothing) instead. His digging was a propensity-fulfillment. His digging was his pleasure, and not a vehicle of his pleasure.[29]

For Ryle, pleasure is not a sensation distinct from the activity and the latter is not a means for achieving a distinct state of having the pleasure sensation. The activity itself is an occurrence (an episode) and hence is "clockable," but Ryle denies that pleasure itself is an occurrence (otherwise it should be clockable independently of the activity). It is, rather, a *disposition* we have for remaining in the state of activity.[30]

Although attitudinal theories characterize the relevant attitude in different ways, they make no attempt to identify a special quality of feeling common to all pleasurable experiences or to define a distinct pleasure sensation. In fact, the perceived implausibility of postulating a felt quality shared by experiences as different as the one of Ryle's man who enjoys digging and, say, of sexual pleasure was the original motivation for attitudinal theories. The widely held opinion among eighteenth-century philosophers that there cannot be a proper definition of pleasure also may well be the result of failing to identify such a common feature of all pleasures.[31] Attitudinal theories respond to this 'heterogeneity problem' by postulating that what is common to them as pleasures is our pro-attitude towards having the relevant representations or engaging in some activities. The price for this resolution of the problem, however, is that, according to such theories, there is no further 'phenomenology' to pleasure, no characteristic way it feels.[32]

---

[29] Ryle (1949: 108).
[30] For discussions of problems with Ryle's theory, see, e.g., Aydede (2000) and Wolfsdorf (2013).
[31] See Guyer (2018) for further discussion of this with reference to Kant.
[32] There have been attempts to combine an attitudinal approach with a view that ascribes a phenomenology to pleasures. Such proposals hold that the pro-attitude is constituted in part by the way the attitude feels (e.g., Aydede 2000; Lin 2020). This feeling is construed not as a distinct sensation but rather as a 'hedonic tone.' It is, of course, incumbent on these approaches to come up with their own solution to the heterogeneity problem and to explain why such a solution does not make the attitudinal machinery superfluous in the first place. Without going into further details, I mention this possibility of a 'hybrid theory' because one might worry whether Kant – notwithstanding the plausible reasons for attributing an attitudinal theory to him, given the

A typical formulation of a contemporary view, in which the pro-attitude is taken to be one of desiring, for the case of sensory pleasure,[33] looks like this:

> A sensory experience (having a sensation S) is a sensory pleasure iff having S is contemporaneously desired for its own sake.[34]

The desire for S can, of course, precede the experience. But what is relevant is the fact that at the time of the experience there is a desire for S that the experience of S simultaneously satisfies. This excludes counterexamples to the definition, based on desires had in the past but not (any more) at the moment of the experience. The qualification that S be desired for its own sake prevents experiences from counting as pleasurable even though they are not because we desire them only in the interest of satisfying a desire for certain consequences of having S. If S is, for instance, the taste of wine, the pleasantness of the sensation is a desiring of the wine in the very act of sensing it. It might seem to follow that whenever I desire to have a certain representation, it must be pleasurable for me. This is obviously not correct since I can desire S in order to achieve an aim, without S being pleasurable at all: I might not like the taste of wine but desire it nonetheless because I want to get drunk. In order to avoid this problem, attitudinal theories are often phrased in terms of 'intrinsic desire': in Alston's words, for S to be a pleasurable experience, one has to desire S, "apart from any further considerations regarding consequences."[35] When I desire the taste of wine, despite my finding it disagreeable, it is because I consider the desired consequences. With the restriction to intrinsic desires, we can desire the means to an end without the means themselves being pleasurable because we desire them non-intrinsically, that is, only in respect to their consequences.

With some adjustments, this basic desire-satisfaction model can be mapped onto Kant's theory.[36]

---

transcendental definition and the achievement principle – really joined attitudinalists in omitting a phenomenology of pleasure.

[33] That is, pleasure in having a sensation: my pleasure in having the sun shine on my skin, as opposed to the propositional pleasure: my being pleased *that* my children are doing well.

[34] This is a slightly simplified version of Heathwood (2007: 32).   [35] Alston (1967: 345).

[36] Paul Guyer has recently made a pioneering attempt to employ Ryle's theory for a new way of understanding Kant's view. Although he does not discuss § 3 of the KU, he argues that the pleasure of taste is not a "separate and unique sensation" but a *disposition* we have: to remain in the state in which we have the representation of something beautiful. Where Guyer's proposal significantly differs from what I argued is that he thinks the disposition to remain in a state refers to the state of the free harmonious play of the faculties, a play that manifests itself in a distinct "sensation of

(a) The definition of sensory pleasure above corresponds to what Kant calls the pleasure in the *agreeable*, which is idiosyncratic, that is, it cannot make a claim to being valid for everybody. The relevant faculty is the *lower* faculty of desire, which has no a priori principle; it is rather the collection of pre-existing dispositions, appetites as it were, for certain *sensations* – a collection that varies from person to person. Kant distinguishes several types of these desires: "propensities" (*Hang*) that are the "possibilities [or pre-dispositions] for the formation of desires," "instincts" that are "actual desires without a clear cognition of the object," and "inclinations" as "habitual desires."[37] At least the first two of these humans share with animals. Their satisfaction constitutes a kind of pleasure that is a pleasure in a sensation without consideration of consequences.[38]

(b) Kant's category of pleasure in the *useful* or *instrumentally good* is not covered by the definition of sensory pleasure. For this, he explains, "the agreeable, which as such represents the object solely in relation to sense, must first be brought under principles of reason through the concept of an end [purpose] before it can be called good as an object of the will" (5: 208). The agreeable, one could say, is the 'matter' to which the concept of a purpose gives 'form.' Once this transformation has taken place, a means–end structure becomes possible: having a representation (which may itself be agreeable or not) can be such that a consequence of such possession can satisfy a

---

'animation'" of the mental powers; and it is *this sensation* – not the initial representation of an object's form – that we want to continue having (Guyer 2018: 161). But is it really the "sensation" of harmony from the state of free play that we want to continue in our mind, or is it the state of having a representation of an object's form (which somehow occasions the free play)? Guyer's proposal has much textual support. For instance: In the First Introduction to KU, the free play "produces ... a sensation that is the determining ground of a judgment which for that reason is called aesthetic and as subjective purposiveness (without concept) is combined with the feeling of pleasure" (20: 224). This sounds – confirming Guyer's view – as if we take pleasure in the 'sensation of harmony'; it is this sensation that we are, in Ryle's sense, "disposed" to continue having.

But if we keep the argument of § 3 in mind, it should be clear that, on Guyer's view, it would be the *sensation* of harmony that we like immediately, not the representation of the form of an object that occasions it. The immediate liking of a sensation, however, is a case of the agreeable, not the beautiful. On Guyer's proposal, we would like the representation of the object's form only as a means – "a vehicle", as Ryle said – for attaining what we immediately like, namely, the sensation of harmony. Furthermore, I think an attitudinal interpretation of Kant's view of pleasure can be more plausibly combined with Guyer's earlier and – to me – eminently plausible suggestion that pleasure for Kant consists in the satisfaction of a faculty interest.

[37] *Anthropologie Mrongovius* (25: 1339); cf. also *Religion* (6: 28f.n.).
[38] Desires in the form of inclinations are somewhat ambiguous because Kant uses the term not quite consistently (see Allison 1990: 108f.). At (25: 1339), for instance, instincts differ from inclinations in that the latter presuppose a purpose, that is, a concept of the desired object.

further desire or purpose (as in the above example of the wine) – the representation then "pleases as a means to some agreeableness or other." This is the pleasure in the "mediately good" (5: 209).

Judgment of the determining kind is involved in the determination of an appropriate means, given that we have a certain purpose (something agreeable or other). But since the choice of purpose is arbitrary, the pleasure in the useful cannot claim universal validity.[39]

With the other two kinds of pleasure, that in the morally or absolutely good and the pleasure of taste, the interests of *higher* or intellectual faculties come into play as well as the power of judgment that establishes whether having a given representation indeed satisfies the relevant interest of the faculty. The representations involved in these cases are not sensations but either conceptual representations (in the case of the good) or the forms of objects (in the case of taste). The adjusted definition for these cases could therefore look like this:

Having representation R is pleasurable for subject N iff there is a principle F such that it is the case that

(i) N is having R
(ii) while having R, N comes to
    (a) judge that R falls under F
    (b) desire having R (under F)
(iii) N desires having R (under F) for its own sake.[40]

The 'principle F' is the principle of the relevant faculty that expresses its interest or desire. Clause (ii)(b) identifies F, and hence having R, as a desire of the subject. As before, the desire for R is simultaneously satisfied by actually having R.

(c) In the case of *moral pleasure*, the relevant principle that expresses the interest of the higher faculty of desire is the moral law, or, rather the categorical imperative. If the representation of a proposed maxim or action – a *conceptual* representation – agrees with, or can be subsumed under, the principle, then the faculty's "exercise is advanced" (5: 119) because such subsumption means a determination of the will to adopt the maxim. The subsumption itself is a (moral) judgment about the 'absolute goodness' of the

---

[39] The choice of purposes can be guided by the PoH. But this principle cannot confer universal validity to the choices since different subjects understand the notion of happiness differently.
[40] This is inspired by Warner (1980).

representation. The power of judgment is involved in the subsumption but, just like in the case of theoretical cognition, it is determining judgment, which does not require a principle of its own.[41] Since the principle here is a universally valid law, the pleasure from its satisfaction itself is "determined through a ground that is a priori and [the pleasure is therefore] valid for everyone" (5: 187).

Although the case of the pleasure of taste will have to be discussed in more detail in subsequent chapters, we can see that it also fits the desire–satisfaction definition of pleasure:

(d) The pleasure of taste responds to a representation of the *form* of an object that satisfies what Kant calls 'the principle of the power of judgment.' This principle is supposed to be an a priori principle, and hence the pleasure in its satisfaction can claim universality. Clause (iii) of the definition obviously applies here: the faculty interest is not supposed to be satisfied by a consequence of having the representation. Since determining judgment does not have its own principle, the principle that promotes the interest of the faculty has to be the principle of the *reflecting* power of judgment. In the KU, pronouncements like the following clearly support the suggestion that the pleasure of taste *consists in* (and is not a causal consequence of) the satisfaction of the interest of the power of judgment, if we read (as suggested in Section 3.2) 'purposive' as 'satisfying a (faculty) interest':

> The object is ... called purposive in this case only because its representation is immediately connected with the feeling of pleasure; and the representation itself is an aesthetic representation of the purposiveness. (5: 189)

> The pleasure can express nothing but its [the object's] suitability [*Angemessenheit*] to the cognitive faculties that are in play in the reflecting power of judgment ... and thus merely a subjective formal purposiveness of the object. (5: 189f.)

> Thus nothing other than the subjective purposiveness in the representation of an object without an end ... can constitute the satisfaction that we judge, without a concept, to be universally communicable. (5: 221)

---

[41] The details of the subsumption operation are, of course, more complicated than described here. In the theoretical case, the power of judgment provides a 'schema' in order to subsume an intuitive representation under concepts; in the moral case, it is the 'typus' of the moral law that facilitates the subsumption (cf. 5: 69ff.).

In judgments of taste the power of judgment operates "for the sake of perceiving the suitability of the representation for the harmonious (subjectively purposive) occupation of both cognitive faculties in their freedom, i.e., to sense the representational state with pleasure." (5: 292)

The representation of a subjective purposiveness of an object is even identical with the feeling of pleasure. (20: 228)

(e) Kant's characterization of practical pleasure[42] in the KpV clearly belongs into the class of desire–satisfaction theories: "*Pleasure* is the representation of the agreement of an object or an action with the *subjective* conditions of life, i.e., with the faculty of the causality of a representation with respect to the reality of its object (or with respect to the determination of the powers of the subject to action in order to produce the object)" (5: 9n.). Pleasure so defined – which can motivate to action – is nothing but the representation that an object or action satisfies the 'subjective conditions of life,'[43] that is, the interests, inclinations, or desires connected with the higher and lower faculty of desire. This interpretation seems to be in line with the way Reath understands the definition from KpV:

the pleasure taken in the representation of the object indicates that the object answers to existing susceptibilities and dispositions, or to existing inclinations in the subject. We might say that the resulting interest in the object is mediated by the feeling of agreeableness that represents the fit between the object and the dispositions and desires of the subject.[44]

Reath accordingly writes of a "functional equivalence" of pleasure and desire, and even though he does not mention desire *satisfaction*, it is hard to see how Kant's 'agreement' could mean anything else.[45]

Representation of the object (before its realization) 'promises' pleasure or is itself pleasant. (This leads to 'determination' of desire, to an active interest, to realize the object.) In the former case, the promise or expectation of pleasure is equivalent with the promise of satisfaction of a desire: if the object existed, it would answer to the desire. Thus we actually have to distinguish, with Heathwood, "prospective desires" and "non-prospective desires," where only the satisfaction of the latter constitutes pleasure.

---

[42] Practical pleasure is "that pleasure which is necessarily connected with desire (for an object whose representation affects feeling in this way)" (6: 212).

[43] "*Life* is the faculty of a being to act in accordance with the laws of the faculty of desire. The *faculty of desire* is a being's faculty to be by means of its representations the cause of the reality of the objects of these representations" (6: 212). See also MS (6: 211).

[44] Reath (2006: 58).

[45] For further discussion and criticism of Reath, cf. Morrisson (2008) and Höwing (2013).

When Ryle's enthusiastic gardener imagines (represents) himself digging, he prospectively desires to start digging; when he actually starts, his pleasure consists in the satisfaction of his non-prospective desire for digging. Thus, he can say "I want (desire) to dig because it is pleasurable," even though such an answer would at first seem uninformative on the desire–satisfaction theory ("I desire to dig because I desire to dig"). His claim should be understood as a shorthand for: "I prospectively desire to dig because digging will produce a non-prospective intrinsic desire."[46]

I have so far ignored the crucial distinction Kant insists on *within* the concept of practical pleasure. In the case of 'pathological' practical pleasure, he says, the pleasure "precedes" the determination of the faculty of desire, while in the moral case the pleasure is supposed to "follow" upon the determination (e.g., MS 6: 378; 399). Since pleasure, according to the general theory advertised here, consists in satisfaction of desire, it would seem that this theory cannot reproduce Kant's distinction of precedence and subsequence. I shall discuss this further below (Section 5.1).

4.2.2 *The Contingency Clause*

I have been arguing that pleasure consists in desire or interest satisfaction, without paying attention to the modality of the satisfaction, even though, when introducing the achievement principle (S), I emphasized that for Kant the satisfaction of an interest or the achievement of an aim is pleasurable only if it is not guaranteed but in some sense *contingent*. This contingency clause is of crucial significance for Kant's theory of pleasure – both, for making it cohere with other doctrines he holds and for blocking empirically implausible consequences.

The contingency clause is derived from Kant's view about (i) purposes and purposiveness, as laid out in KU and (ii) the principle (S) that connects the achievement of a purpose with pleasure. In the teleological (rather than etiological) sense that is relevant in this context, a purpose is an aim that a subject tries to achieve. Some object or activity is purposive with respect to the purpose if the object or activity achieves the aim. If the attainment of the aim, however, is guaranteed according to general laws of nature, that is, if it is necessary rather than contingent with respect to these laws, then the terms purpose and purposiveness, on Kant's view, are misapplied. In that case, the 'mechanism' of nature would account for what is happening in the realization of the (misleadingly so called) aim; the

---

[46] See Heathwood (2007: 38).

notion of a teleological causality (causation through a concept) would be superfluous. In a draft of the First Introduction, Kant explains that "purposiveness is a lawfulness which is at the same time contingent with respect to general laws of nature that are necessary for experience" (20: 217).[47] In other words, if the laws of nature suffice to explain how some state of affairs comes about, then it is a mistake to invoke the language of purposes and teleological causation. (This is, of course, why Kant is entitled to call organisms "natural ends.")

Pleasure in X indicates the purposiveness of X for an aim of ours, that is, that X attains this aim. But this general claim holds only if the notions of purposiveness etc. are legitimately applied – in which case the attainment of the aim is contingent in the sense explained. Kant himself draws an important consequence from the contingency clause in the Introduction: the clause explains why we do not experience pleasure when the interest of the faculty of understanding – cognition of objects – is satisfied. In the cognition of objects there is "concurrence of perceptions with laws in accordance with universal concepts of nature (the categories)," but here "we do not encounter the least effect on the feeling of pleasure in us nor can encounter it, because here the understanding proceeds unintentionally [*unabsichtlich*], in accordance with its nature" (5: 187). This can be paraphrased as follows: Since the laws of the understanding are *constitutive* for experience, and hence for objects of experience, such objects cannot be said to be purposive for their own constitution. *What* is given in intuition to the understanding is, of course, contingent; but once it is given, it is no longer contingent that the given appears to us in the form of objects of experience. Thus, we also cannot say that nature is purposive for our interest in cognition because nature organizes itself in accordance with the principles of the understanding because these laws themselves are conditions of the possibility of nature in the first place. The situation is different with respect to the empirical (or particular) laws of nature, those laws that are left undetermined by the transcendental laws. From the viewpoint of the latter, our success in organizing the empirical laws into a system of more and more general laws is contingent since it is not implied by the principles of the understanding. In cases where we succeed in systematizing a group of empirical laws, we can therefore say that nature is purposive for us; in § VI of the Introduction, Kant explains our pleasure in systematization in precisely these terms. (We'll revisit this in Chapter 6.)

---

[47] In the final draft this was changed into: "purposiveness is a lawfulness of the contingent as such." Cf. also (5: 404).

The contingency requirement for pleasure is also crucial for the pleasure in beautiful objects. The representation of such objects is found to be in agreement with the interest of the power of judgment; and Kant adds: "since this agreement ... is contingent, it produces the representation of a purposiveness of the object with regard to the cognitive faculties of the subject" (5: 190). The consciousness of such purposiveness is the pleasure of taste.

With respect to moral pleasure, Kant claims that the determination of the will (the higher faculty of desire) by the moral law is felt as a pleasure (5: 222; 20: 207).[48] Here as well, the contingency clause seems important because such determination, in human beings, is not guaranteed. This is evident from the fact that the law for us is an imperative, that is, it does not describe how the will operates always and everywhere but prescribes choices of maxims. In the human being, there are hindrances to the exceptionless operation of the law because we are influenced by sensible desires and our will is determined by the law only once such hindrances have been overcome – a success that is registered in the (pleasurable aspect of the) feeling of respect.

I tentatively suggest a further consequence of the contingency clause. In the *Anthropologie* (and long before in his notes and lectures)[49] Kant "fully subscribes" to the view that pain, at least in the case of the agreeable, has to precede pleasure: "Pain is always first" (7: 231f.). I am not sure that the claim that "gratification is nothing but ceasing of a pain and [therefore] something negative" is consistent with other aspects of Kant's theory.[50] But in light of the contingency requirement it certainly follows that a continuous, uninterrupted satisfaction of an interest or desire – a "continuous promotion of the vital force" (7: 231f.) – would be indistinguishable from a guaranteed satisfaction of the interest or desire (as in the case of the understanding) and hence could not be manifested in a feeling of pleasure. The requirement of interruptions, that is, episodes of pain, which Kant believes are necessary could plausibly be interpreted as evidence that the contingency clause is satisfied.

4.2.3 Intentionality of Pleasure

Pleasure understood as a pro-attitude we take towards having certain representations is clearly intentional – it is *about* (having) a representation

---

[48] Cf. also, e.g., KpV (5: 116f.).   [49] See Shell (2003).
[50] Cf. Zuckert's discussion of this doctrine (2007: 272ff.).

or about the object represented. This is in contrast to pleasure as a sensation, which could not be intentional insofar as it has no intentional object (see Section 4.1). But it is not *representational* in the sense that we are entitled to attribute the pleasantness to an object as one of its properties; the feeling, as Kant defines it in § 3, cannot contribute to the cognition of the object. Adoption of a pro-attitude towards a representation, however, indicates that the representation is purposive for us, that it satisfies a desire or faculty interest. In this sense, at least, Kant seems to exaggerate when he claims that pleasure "does not serve for any cognition at all, not even that by which the subject cognizes itself" (5: 206).

5

Consequences of the Theory

Without having yet identified the interest of the power of judgment, the theory of pleasure as the satisfaction of faculty interests leads to several important results. In this chapter, I argue, first, that in the light of this theory we can understand Kant's famous claim that in judgments of taste the judging of the object has to "precede" the feeling of pleasure – a claim that seems to conflict with his insistence that pleasure is the determining ground of those judgments. Second, I show that the theory allows an inference from the (assumed) characteristics of the pleasure of taste to the existence of a faculty that is distinct from the other two higher faculties, understanding and reason. This inference is the basis for a conjectural reconstruction of Kant's path to the KU after 1784.

5.1 'Judging Precedes Pleasure' and the Determining Ground of Judgments of Taste

The basic structural feature of Kant's mature moral philosophy – that the representation of the moral law, which means a moral judgment, cannot be based on a 'feeling for morality' but only gives rise to such a feeling (as its own incentive) – is to some extent reflected in the theory Kant develops in KU about judgments of taste. This is evident in § 9 where the question is posed: "Whether in the judgment of taste the feeling of pleasure precedes the judging of the object or the latter precedes the former." And Kant adds: "The solution to this problem is the key to the critique of taste" (5: 216),[1] because, he argues, only if the judging "precedes" the pleasure can there be any hope for establishing that such judgments have universal validity.

---

[1] Actually, one of *two* official keys: cf. (5: 341) and Section 7.3.

5.1.1 The Determining Grounds of Judgments of Taste

The question and Kant's answer in the KU are parallel to the problem he discussed in the KpV under the title of the "paradox of method in a critical examination of practical reason" (5: 62). The supposedly paradoxical feature in Kant's procedure is that he wants to establish the moral law *before* he can say what is (morally) good and bad. Critics like Pistorius had pointed out that this sequence borders on the absurd because only our idea of the good can enable us to set up a law that tells us what we have to do in order to achieve what is good. Kant replied that if the moral law is to be absolutely binding (i.e., if it is supposed to be a categorical imperative), such a law has to determine what is good because our only criterion for what is good in the *absence* of a universal law would be the feeling of pleasure and displeasure (presumably, in the agreeable and disagreeable). A law with the required characteristics cannot be based on such feelings "since only through experience can we find out what is in accordance with the feeling of pleasure"; a law based on them could therefore not be an a priori law (5: 63). Put differently: If pleasure is the basis for the concept of the good, and this concept informs moral judgments, then these judgments could be universally and necessarily valid only if the pleasure itself is correspondingly universal and necessary. But this could be shown only if the pleasure itself results from, or is identical with, the satisfaction of an a priori principle.[2]

Similarly, in KU, Kant argues that the pleasure reported in a judgment of taste could never make a claim to universality if the pleasure "preceded" the judgment, arising, as it were, from sources that are independent of the judging itself. And again he claims that such an 'independent' pleasure could only be the "mere agreeableness in sensation" (5: 217).[3] Since the attitudinal theory of pleasure identifies pleasure with the satisfaction of a desire or faculty interest, it is prima facie mysterious (i) how such satisfaction could "precede" the feeling in the cases of moral pleasure and the pleasure of taste and (ii) how these cases can be distinguished from other pleasures if *all* pleasure consists in the satisfaction of some desire. A closely related question pertains to Kant's obvious intention to construe the cases of moral and aesthetic pleasure analogously. This analogy, however, seems

---

[2] Cf. also Kant's argument against moral sense theories (5: 38): such theories claim that a special sense enables us to feel pleasure in virtuous conduct; but, says Kant, this is a deception because the concept of virtue (or morality or duty) has to be presupposed in order to assume that we feel pleasure in its fulfillment; hence, this concept cannot be derived from that feeling. This means that Kant thinks that there has to be an aim, the satisfaction of which results in pleasure.

[3] See also (20: 224f.).

to be misconceived because he claims that the "determining ground" (*Bestimmungsgrund*) of moral judgments is the moral law, not any kind of feeling, while the judgment of taste, by contrast, is an aesthetic (that is, not concept-based) judgment and its determining ground therefore has to be the feeling of pleasure (rather than a concept). How can this be reconciled with the claim that "judging the object" precedes the feeling?

Taking the moral case as the starting point, it is plausible to identify the recognition that a proposed action or maxim agrees with the moral law, that is, that the representation of the action or maxim satisfies the interest of the higher faculty of desire, as a *judgment* (about the action or maxim). Since the power of judgment is the capacity for "thinking the particular as contained under the universal" (5: 179), it is employed in order to find out whether an action or maxim can be subsumed under the moral law and thus whether they satisfy the interest of practical reason. According to the attitudinal theory, this satisfaction *is* the moral pleasure but it is established through the exercise of judgment. The judging, however, cannot be said to 'precede' the pleasure in a *temporal* sense since it consists in the satisfaction of the interest. But the attitudinal theory gives satisfaction (and thereby the judging) *logical* precedence over pleasure because it defines the feeling in terms of satisfaction, which is taken to be the more basic notion.

Does it then follow from the theory that judgment, in *all* cases of pleasure, 'precedes' the feeling, including the cases that Kant classifies as pathological pleasures and for which he claims that pleasure precedes? No, because an act of judging, in which an item is subsumed under a general principle or interest, takes place only in the case of the higher or intellectual faculties. In the lower faculty of desire, satisfaction of the various desires, dispositions, etc., which are idiosyncratic to different humans, constitutes the pleasure of the agreeable (see Section 3.2). But no satisfaction of an intellectual interest or principle is involved and no check is required on whether a given representation of an object indeed falls under the principle. With the desires of the lower faculty, the 'fit' of representation and desire is detected, as it were, passively; no operation of a spontaneous faculty is required. In other words: with respect to the satisfaction of those desires we operate like non-rational animals: we "physically differentiate" the agreeable and the disagreeable (like a dog "differentiates the roast from the loaf") but as beings with intellectual faculties we can also "differentiate logically," by judging that an action is morally good or not.[4]

---

[4] The terms and the example are from Kant's "False Subtlety" from 1762 (2: 60).

Once an object has been represented as satisfying a desire of the lower faculty, it can become an object of the will if the agreeable is "brought under principles of reason by the concept of a purpose" (5: 208). At this point, the intellectual faculty becomes involved: we deliberate which agreeable objects to procure, or to produce, etc. Such deliberation is indeed guided by a principle – the principle of happiness – but satisfaction of this principle does not consist in a pleasure of its own because the principle operates on options of (prospective) pleasures of the agreeable that have been established before our deliberation. That is, the judgment that some course of action for producing or procuring certain objects should be realized comes 'after' the (prospective) pleasures.[5]

I summarize: For moral pleasure and the pleasure of taste, the satisfaction of the principles of the respective higher faculties – the subsumption of some representation under their principles – amounts to a "judging of the object," which in a *logical* sense precedes the pleasure because we take the notion of a faculty interest as fundamental and define pleasure in terms of its satisfaction.

Although Kant's intention in his "key" argument in § 9 concerning the precedence of judging over pleasure is clear enough – to employ the parallel with the moral case in order to secure universal validity for judgments of taste – it has given rise to an extended debate that focused on the issue of how many distinct acts of judging are involved in the 'judgment precedes pleasure' view. According to a 'two-act' interpretation, a prior act of judging the object results in pleasure; this is followed by a further judgment about the pleasure, that is, a judgment about whether the pleasure indeed arose from the prior judging and not, say, from some agreeable feature of the object. Only if the pleasure has (been found to have) the right pedigree can an explicit and prima facie correct judgment of taste 'this object is beautiful' be made. The main advantage of a 'two-act' view is that it can explain how mistaken judgments of taste are possible: they are those judgments where we went wrong in establishing the right pedigree for the pleasure. And we can be wrong about this because reflecting on the causal history of the feeling – the pleasure is here the causal effect of the prior judging – is fallible, like all judgments about causal connections.[6]

---

[5] Cf. the discussion in KpV (5: 60–62).
[6] The two-act view is Guyer's (1997: 97–105; 140–47). For a recent criticism and defense, see Guyer (2017) and Ginsborg (2017). In Guyer's revised interpretation of Kantian pleasure, the two acts are still retained (2018). Cf. also Ginsborg (2003); Allison (2003); and Longuenesse (2003).

5.1 'Judging Precedes Pleasure'

In the desire–satisfaction theory I attribute to Kant, there is of course no causal connection between the judging of the object and the feeling of pleasure. The pleasure of taste consists in the satisfaction of the interest of the power of judgment (whatever that may turn out to be; see Chapter 4) and this satisfaction – the subsumption of a representation under the a priori principle of the faculty – involves an exercise of judgment. There is only one act of judging the representation of an object to be purposive for the power of judgment and the "consciousness" of this purposiveness, as Kant says, "is the pleasure itself." (5: 222) It also seems that Kant's rejection of the view that pleasure is a sensation, separate from the representation of a pleasurable object, makes a causal connection between judging the object and the feeling unlikely – quite independently of ascribing an attitudinal theory to him.[7] (The desire–satisfaction interpretation obviously shares with other 'one-act' views the challenge to account for the possibility of erroneous judgments of taste. See Section 6.5 for discussion.)

The two-act interpretation receives motivation from apparently confusing statements Kant makes about the "determining ground" of judgments of taste. On the one hand, he emphasizes that such judgments are distinguished, as *aesthetic* judgments, from logical judgments because their determining ground is the feeling of pleasure. On the other hand, he insists that the judging of the object 'precedes' the pleasure, which qualifies judgments of taste as "aesthetic judgments of reflection" rather than "aesthetic judgments of sense" (20: 224f.).[8] On a two-act interpretation, such statements can be reconciled because the 'original' judging causes the feeling, which in turn is the determining ground of the 'final' judgment (about the pedigree of the pleasure).

By paying attention to a distinction within the notion of a determining ground – a distinction that Kant had been employing through much of his career – I think the seemingly contradictory statements can be plausibly interpreted within a one-act, desire–satisfaction theory. The judging of the object (or its given representation), I suggested above, is the subsumption of the representation under the interest of the faculty of judgment, thus stating the satisfaction of the faculty's a priori principle, which satisfaction

---

[7] Unlikely but perhaps possible: see Guyer (2018).
[8] Cf. Guyer (1997: 99): "The necessity of distinguishing two acts of judgment might be most simply demonstrated by pointing to the fact that Kant describes the feeling of pleasure as both the product of judgment and the ground of determination for judgment; yet of aesthetic judgment resulted from a single act, this would be to say that the same feeling of pleasure both succeeded, as its product, and yet preceded, as its evidence or ground, a single judgment. This is clearly absurd."

constitutes the pleasure of taste. At the same time, this pleasure is the only criterion for the satisfaction; no feeling-independent check or confirmation is possible (see Section 5.1.2). In this sense of a (or *the*) criterion, the pleasure is what Kant in the *Nova Dilucidatio* called the "consequently determining reason" or ground of a judgment: the "reason *that* or reason of knowing [*rationem quod sive cognoscendi*]." He distinguished this from the "antecedently determining reason" or "reason why [*rationem cur sive rationem essendi vel fiendi*]" (1: 392). Thus, while the former ground gives us the reason for *holding* a judgment to be true, the latter is the ground for the judgment's *being* true.[9] In the KpV, this distinction is famously employed when Kant tries to clarify the relation of freedom and the moral law:

> though freedom is certainly the *ratio essendi* of the moral law, the latter is the *ratio cognescendi* of freedom. For had not the moral law already been distinctly thought in our reason, we would never have been justified in assuming anything like freedom, even though it is not self-contradictory. But if there were no freedom, the moral law would never have been encountered in us. (5: 5n.)

It is our consciousness of the moral law, our awareness of duty, that allows us to regard ourselves as free; but the law is possible only if freedom is presupposed. The relation of pleasure and judgment in KU is construed in analogous fashion: the principle of the faculty of judgment is the *ratio essendi* of the pleasure (and judgments) of taste; the principle is supposed to be constitutive of the feeling and makes possible its claim to universal validity. The pleasure itself is the *ratio cognoscendi* of the principle; we become aware of the existence of a faculty with its own a priori principle only through the experience of this pleasure (see Section 4.1.2).[10] Even though this distinction is clearly employed in the KU, Kant does not explicitly acknowledge it and consequently induces some confusion in the reader. For instance:

> A judgment can be called aesthetic, i.e., sensible (as far as its subjective effect, not its determining ground is concerned), although judging (that is, objectively) is an action of the understanding (as the higher cognitive faculty in general) and not of sensibility. (20: 223)

Here the "subjective effect" is sensible, that is, the feeling of pleasure as the consequently determining ground of the judgment, while the antecedently

---

[9] See Longuenesse (2005: 120f.). [10] This has also been suggested by Ted Cohen (1993).

determining ground is intellectual, that is, the satisfaction of an a priori interest of the power of judgment.

Similarly, in the following notorious passages, both notions of a determining ground are involved: If an aesthetic judgment

> carries such a claim [to universality and necessity] with it, then it [the judgment] also makes a claim that its determining ground must lie not merely in the feeling of pleasure and displeasure in itself alone, but at the same time in a rule of the higher faculty of cognition, in this case, namely, in the rule of the power of judgment. (20: 225)

Here, the first occurrence of 'determining ground' is the 'consequently determining ground'; the second the 'antecedently determining ground.' They are not the same, and keeping them conceptually distinct prevents confusion.

In a related passage of the First Introduction, Kant seems to suggest that a judgment of taste actually involves two separate judgments, one that reports pleasure about an object and one that makes a claim *about* this pleasure[11]:

> the faculty of aesthetic reflection judges only about the subjective purposiveness ... of the object: and the question arises whether it judges only *by means* of the pleasure or displeasure which is felt in it, or whether it even judges *about* these [feelings], so that the judgment at the same time determines that pleasure or displeasure *must* be combined with the representation of the object. (20: 229*)

Again, I submit that distinguishing the *ratio cognescendi* from the *ratio essendi* resolves the puzzle and makes a multiplication of judgments superfluous: we judge "by means" of, or through, pleasure that the object is purposive for us, that is, *that* a faculty interest – of the power of judgment – is being satisfied. At the same time, the reason *why* a pleasure with the characteristics of universality, necessity, etc., is possible, is this faculty's own a priori principle; we therefore also judge, at least implicitly, "about" the pleasure: that it ought to be shared by everybody (cf. 20: 229).

5.1.2 An a priori Principle That Is Constitutive for Pleasure

The determining ground of a judgment of taste, in the sense of its *ratio essendi*, is the principle of the power of judgment, which is said to be

---

[11] This is how Longuenesse (2005: 278–80) interprets the passage and thereby concurs with a two-act interpretation, although not with Guyer's. See also Longuenesse (2003: 151; 153).

constitutive for the pleasure of taste. And we saw in Chapter 2 that this constitutive role is a necessary condition for a power of the mind to qualify as a faculty of its own. But what does it mean for a principle to be constitutive of pleasure, especially within a desire–satisfaction theory of feeling? If pleasures other than that of taste consist in the satisfaction of faculty interests, shouldn't the moral law, in particular, also count as constitutive of moral pleasure?

Since determining judgment does not have its own principle, in this case the reflecting power is operating. With all higher faculties, judgment is involved in establishing that a faculty's interest is being satisfied by a given representation. The pleasure of taste, however, is distinguished from moral pleasure because in this case the interest being satisfied is the power of judgment's *own*, not a principle 'foreign' to this faculty. We can in this way understand why the moral law, despite the fact that it occasions, as Kant says in GMS, the "self-wrought" moral feeling of respect (4: 401n.), cannot be regarded as constitutive for feeling. As the more detailed discussion of respect in KpV shows, the law operates directly on the will and only *indirectly* on the faculty of feeling.[12] Hence, the moral law is constitutive of (rational) desire, it determines the will; and such determination, Kant says, is *eo ipso* accompanied by pleasure or is identical with it (20: 221f.). In other words, the feeling is here connected with the satisfaction of a 'foreign' principle, not a principle that is 'native' to the faculty of feeling. Even though this is an instance of the achievement principle (S) – moral pleasure *is* the satisfaction of the a priori principle of the faculty of desire – a *direct* influence of an a priori principle on the faculty of feeling is reserved for the power of judgment in its employment in taste. Only in this case – so Kant claims – is there an a priori principle that can be said to be constitutive of feeling: "It is ... properly only in taste ... in which alone the power of judgment reveals itself as a faculty that has its own special principle and thereby makes a well-founded claim to a place in the general critique of the higher faculties" (20: 244).

Although a discussion of 'the principle of judgment' still lies ahead (see Chapter 5), it is relevant here to point out the contrast of the pleasure of taste with another feeling of satisfaction that Kant analyzes in § VI of the Introduction (5: 186–88). This section announces "the combination [*Verbindung*] of the feeling of pleasure with the concept of the purposiveness of nature" and it was from here that I extrapolated the achievement principle. Kant claims that "the discovered unifiability of two or more

---

[12] See, e.g., Engstrom (2010: 97f.).

empirically heterogeneous laws of nature under a principle that comprehends them both is the ground of a very noticeable pleasure" (5: 187). This feeling indicates the (however partial) success in systematizing nature with respect to its empirical (or particular) laws, which are not themselves laws of the understanding and which therefore appear contingent to it. The contingency clause in Kant's theory of pleasure is therefore fulfilled and Kant identifies the a priori principle that is being satisfied as 'the' principle of the reflecting power of judgment, which says (in one of several formulations) "that nature specifies its universal laws," that is, the laws of the understanding, into particular laws that are arranged in a system, in a hierarchy of (particular) laws in which more concrete laws are ordered under more general ones, without gaps.

The message is clear enough: satisfaction of 'the' principle of systematicity constitutes a pleasure that inherits its universal validity from the a priori character of that principle (5: 187). But it is equally clear that this pleasure cannot be identified with the pleasure of taste since the delight we take in systematicity is obviously based on concepts and hence it lacks one of the defining features of the pleasure of taste: the former feeling is not aesthetic.

Although § VI is obviously not discussing the pleasure of taste, could one not still say that with respect to the described 'pleasure of systematicity' the power of reflecting judgment is constitutive? After all, the principle that it satisfies is judgment's own, not a 'foreign' principle as in the case of moral pleasure. Two considerations, I suggest, speak against this possibility.

The first concerns an ambivalence Kant displays in §§ V and VI – an ambivalence that I will try to understand in subsequent chapters and merely mention here. The reflecting power of judgment, according to these sections, seems to be employed in the service of the understanding: it assists the understanding in achieving "an end that is necessary for it [the understanding], namely to introduce into it unity of principles" (5: 187), that is, the systematization of the particular laws of nature. We are "delighted ... when we encounter such a systematic unity among merely empirical laws" because it (partially) achieves "a necessary aim (a need) of the understanding"; our feeling delighted, therefore, means "strictly speaking [that we are] relieved of a need" (5: 184). Thus, there is at least some vagueness concerning the origin of the pleasure of systematization.[13]

---

[13] Kant seems to confirm this later when he mentions the task of "grasping [an] object in a single representation" – presumably in the process of forming an empirical concept – as "an end with

Second, and more relevantly, it seems obvious that the success or failure of an attempt at systematizing empirical laws of nature, which we delight in, can be determined or checked quite independently of the feeling that accompanies it. It is a conceptual matter, a matter of establishing inferences between empirical laws or of discovering relations between species and genera of such laws. Such checking has nothing to do with our feelings; they are quite dispensable in the pursuit of the task. And this would seem to be the case with all conceptual principles, including the moral law. Whether a maxim satisfies the moral law can be decided on grounds that do not involve the feeling of respect or moral pleasure. If the categorical imperative is understood as a test for maxims, the test makes no reference to feelings but instead considers possible 'contradictions' that can be established conceptually if the maxim is universalized.

The pleasure of taste provides a contrast. If the pleasure consists in the satisfaction of the interest of the (reflecting) power of judgment, the characteristics of the pleasure impose constraints on any checking of such satisfaction: it cannot be done independently of the pleasure itself. Since Kant denies that judgments of taste can be derived from (and hence checked by) any concepts or rules, the only criterion (the "subsequently determining ground") for the satisfaction of the – so far still elusive – principle of judgment is the pleasure, or its absence, itself. There is no other way of finding out whether the aim of the power of judgment has been achieved: its principle or

> rule itself is only subjective and correspondence with it can be recognized only in that which always merely expresses relation to the subject, namely sensation [i.e., feeling], as the criterion and determining ground of the judgment. (20: 226)

In this respect, there is a similarity between the pleasure's role and the way Kant characterized the "dynamical" principles of the understanding in KrV, in particular, the causal law, as "constitutive in regard to experience," although they are "merely regulative ... of intuition." These principles are constitutive, he says, because "they make possible a priori the concepts without which there is no experience" (A 664). Although these principles themselves cannot be derived from concepts or other, higher principles,[14]

---

regard to cognition," the achievement of which is "always connected with satisfaction (which accompanies the accomplishment of any aim). But then it is merely the approval of the solution that answers a problem," not the pleasure characteristic of taste (5: 242).

[14] "A priori principles bear this name not merely because they contain in themselves the grounds of other judgments, but also because they are not themselves grounded in higher and more general cognitions. Yet this property does not elevate them beyond all proof. For although this [proof] could not be executed objectively, but rather grounds all cognition of its object, yet this does not

they are still in need of justification (they "must be proved"). But they have the "special property" that they "first make possible [their own] ground of proof, namely experience, and must always be presupposed in this" (A 737).[15]

Similarly, the principle of the power of judgment that is constitutive of pleasure can "not be derived from concepts a priori; for they belong to the understanding, and the power of judgment is concerned only with their application." And for this there cannot be a further principle, on pain of an infinite regress (5: 169; 20: 239). Like the principles constitutive for experience, the principle of judgment makes possible its 'ground of proof' – the existence of the pleasure of taste – and the proof, just like in the case of the causal law, has to consist in showing that without the principle such pleasure would not be possible.

5.2 From the Pleasure of Taste to a New Faculty

5.2.1 An Inference to a New Faculty

In Kant's theory of pleasure as desire–satisfaction, there is a correspondence between the interests of various faculties and their characteristic pleasures. We have seen this already in the metaphysics lectures of the 1770s. If the characteristic features of these pleasures were uniquely correlated with its respective faculty, it should therefore be possible, with the help of the achievement principle in its necessity version, to infer from such a pleasure to its associated faculty. In particular, *if we were assured* that some kind of pleasure has characteristics that qualify it as corresponding to a higher faculty (that is, universal validity) and if those features could not be accounted for by the faculties we are familiar with, we should be entitled to infer to the existence of a new faculty, distinct from the familiar ones.

Employing this possibility and returning to the topics discussed in Chapter 1, I want to suggest a route by which the new faculty of (reflective) judgment can be introduced into the system of faculties as a genuine member. This route is conjectural: there is no decisive evidence that Kant actually followed it, but he at least hints at this strategy in the First Introduction. If we take seriously that judgments of taste make a

---

prevent a proof from the subjective sources of the possibility of a cognition of an object in general from being possible" (A 148f.*).

[15] For discussion, see Cramer (1985: 64–66).

claim to universality and necessity – that is, if we grant that they claim "that everyone *ought* to so judge" – then there must be an underlying a priori principle that alone can account for such a claim. "It is only such a claim and its possibility that is at issue here, for it is precisely that which causes a critique of reason to search for the principle itself which does ground it [the judgment] even though it [the principle] is indeterminate" (20: 239). Adding the further characteristics of the pleasure of taste identified in the First and Second Moment of the KU Analytic: non-conceptuality and disinterestedness, it can be excluded that the a priori principle underlying the pleasure is a principle either of the understanding or of practical reason. Thus, the critical investigation could start from the (at least provisional) assumption that judgments of taste have universality and necessity and proceeds to identify the faculty (and its a priori principle) that makes this feature of the judgments – and correspondingly of the pleasure – possible.[16] I suggest that § 11 of the KU can be read along these lines, keeping in mind that, according to the Preface, it is only with reference to taste that the power of judgment can be established as a separate faculty with its own a priori principle; only in this way can the "phenomenon of the power of judgment be deduced" (5: 170).

In § 11, Kant wants to establish that the pleasure of taste, which we express in judgments of taste, is sui generis, that is, that it is a kind of pleasure distinguished from the other kinds, the satisfaction in the agreeable and in the good. If it can be shown to be unique in this sense, it could not be accounted for, according to (S), by the achievement of the faculty interests that are relevant for the other pleasures. And assuming that the pleasure of taste makes a legitimate claim to universality (as Kant does here, even though this claim has not yet been justified by a deduction but is just extracted, in the Second Moment, from the phenomenology and common practice of making judgments of taste), it would follow that a separate faculty has to be postulated, with its own interest, expressed in an a priori principle in order to account for the universality of the pleasure.

To the extent that Kant's argument in § 11 relies on the first two Moments and proceeds by elimination, it seems at first glance straightforward. The pleasure of taste cannot come from the achievement of

---

[16] I note that there is an ambiguity about the characterization of the principle as "indeterminate." This could merely mean that it is not determined at the beginning of the investigation. More likely, however, Kant means to indicate that the principle is indeterminate even as the result of the discussion. In the context of the quote from (20: 239), he points out that judgments of taste "cannot be in any way grounded on concepts and therefore cannot be derived from any determinate principle, since they would otherwise be logical." We will return to this issue in Chapter 7.

5.2 From the Pleasure of Taste to a New Faculty

"subjective purposes" since it is disinterested. It cannot be grounded on "objective purposes" either because it is aesthetic, that is, not based on concepts. Apparently assuming that this division of purposes is exhaustive, Kant concludes that the pleasure of taste, can be "nothing other than the subjective purposiveness in the representation of an object without any end [purpose] (objective or subjective)" (5: 221). Rephrased in our framework of faculty interests, the argument thus excludes the interests of the lower and higher faculty of desire (corresponding to the agreeable and the instrumental and absolute good). In an aside, Kant also excludes "the representation of the perfection of the object," on grounds of the non-conceptual nature of the pleasure of taste, which could be read as the elimination of the interests of the higher faculty of cognition, understanding and (theoretical) reason. Thus, if there really is a pleasure with the assumed characteristics, in light of (S) it would be orphaned and to account for it would require the introduction of a new faculty.

This apparently straightforward reading of §11, however, encounters difficulties that have been discussed by commentators. Although he had just given the etiological definitions of purpose and purposiveness in § 10, Kant switches in the first sentence of § 11 to the teleological notion:[17] "Every end [purpose], if it is regarded as a ground of satisfaction, always brings an interest with it, as the determining ground of the judgment about the object of the pleasure" (5: 221). This is irritating but, as I suggested earlier, the switch between the notions is not troublesome, at least in this context, if we assume faculty interests. To recall: In § 10, 'purpose' is defined as an object that is produced (caused) by a concept. A concept that causes an object is called 'purposive.' Pleasure then was explicated as our awareness of the purposiveness of a representation (not necessarily a concept) to maintain itself in the mind. I suggested that this can be glossed as: the state of mind in which I have R causes the state of mind in which I still have R at a later time; hence, the later R would qualify as a purpose because it is caused by the earlier R. In this special case, the etiological purpose can then be identified with a teleological one, namely a faculty interest.

Kant's talk of subjective and objective purposes in § 11 fits into this reconstruction if we assume that 'subjective' and 'objective,' in this context, refer to representations that are sensations and concepts, respectively. The elimination argument then excludes subjective purposes, that is,

---

[17] See the discussion in Section 3.2.

sensations as the source of the agreeable, because they excite the lower faculty of desire (and are therefore inducing an interested pleasure); and it excludes objective purposes, that is, concepts as the source of the pleasure in the good, because they are the objects of the interest of the higher faculty of desire.

Another concern raised about this section is that the division of subjective and objective purposes may not be exhaustive, as the argument requires. Kant only excludes agreeable objects as subjective purposes but ignores ruling out the possibility that the pleasurable state of mind, on occasion of a beautiful object, could itself be a subjective purpose.[18] Since this pleasure is disinterested and non-conceptual, so the objection, it is not captured by Kant's argument. Could the pleasure of taste itself be a subjective purpose? In the 1770s, Kant had explicitly denied this on the grounds that pleasure signifies only the relation of an object, a purpose, to our capacity for feeling and is not itself an object that we attempt to achieve: "One must never say that one takes pleasure as one's purpose; but rather: that which pleases us immediately is our purpose. Because pleasure is merely the relation of a purpose to our feeling" (R 6881; 19: 190*; from 1776–78?). In the KpV, he still holds this view when he characterizes (practical) pleasure as "the relation ... [of an object] to the subject, through which the faculty of desire is determined to realize [the object]" (5: 21).[19] Furthermore, if pleasure consists in the achievement of an aim, according to (S), the feeling itself cannot be regarded as an aim since this would reduce (S) to a tautology: 'the attainment of pleasure is combined with pleasure.'[20]

The disjunction of subjective and objective purposes that Kant assumes in the exclusion argument in § 11 is therefore indeed exhaustive. Insofar as we are conscious, in the pleasure of taste, of the purposiveness of a representation, this purposiveness must be different from the subjective purposiveness of representations of agreeable objects (because of taste's disinterestedness) and from the objective purposiveness of representations of the good or perfect (because of taste's non-conceptual nature). According to (S), aesthetic purposiveness, therefore, cannot be related to

---

[18] This is Fricke's criticism (1990, 108).
[19] This does not mean that hedonism has been excluded by a mere terminological maneuver. The hedonist, in Kant's view, chooses objects of her desire according to the amount of pleasure they promise. But she chooses the *objects* as her purposes of action, not pleasure as a purpose.
[20] Alternatively, if we were to distinguish pleasures of different orders – so that the pleasure we aim at (our subjective purpose), once achieved, results in a further pleasure – a regress of pleasures would result.

the interests of the lower or higher faculty of desire; nor can it be directly related to the interest of the understanding or theoretical reason because these faculties deal with conceptual representations. If the pleasure of taste indeed is characterized by a claim to universality that is not grounded on concepts or desires in the narrow sense (as Kant assumes here), then the interest (or desire in the wide sense) of another faculty has to be postulated in order to account for this pleasure, a faculty that makes possible the "subjective purposiveness in the representation of an object without any (objective or subjective) purpose" (5: 221).

The argument of § 11 does not go beyond the postulation of a new faculty. It does not identify this faculty as the power of reflecting judgment, nor does it contain information about an a priori principle that would have to characterize the new faculty. The argument does, however, shed more light on Kant's claim in the Preface, viz., that in order to resolve "what is puzzling" about the pleasure of taste – the apparent connection of a feeling with an a priori principle – indeed "makes a special division for this faculty necessary in the critique" (5: 169f.).

5.2.2 Kant Is Planning to Publish "Something about Beauty": A Historical Conjecture

The premise in the sketched argument, leading to the stipulation of a new faculty, is that there is indeed a pleasure that has the characteristics ascribed to the pleasure of taste, including the claim to universality and necessity. In order for the argument to have even merely heuristic value, such a pleasure has to be assumed as at least possible, that is, its possibility does not have to be ruled out by other considerations.

In the lectures and notes from the 1770s, Kant held, by and large, a view that is summarized in the famous footnote in the KrV of 1781: "The putative rules or criteria [of aesthetics] are merely empirical as far as their sources are concerned, and can therefore never serve as a priori rules according to which our judgment of taste must be directed" (A 21n.). And in the absence of such a priori principles, the pleasure of taste could not make a legitimate claim to universality. In other words, given this view, a transcendental investigation of judgments of taste would lack the motivation essential for it; in particular, there would be no reason for postulating a new higher faculty. The situation obviously must have changed for Kant at some point between 1781 and 1787, when he wrote a letter to Karl Leonhard Reinhold, in which he announced the discovery of a new faculty with its own a priori principle that would account for the universal validity of judgments of taste.[21] I suggest that there are two pieces of evidence that indicate (however inconclusively) that the change in Kant's view happened in early 1784. First, Kant wrote down, perhaps in February of that year, a note in which he asked: "How is an objectively valid judgment [the judgment of taste] possible which is not determined by any concept of the object?" and he gave the sketch of a deduction of such judgments' claim to universality and necessity.[22] Second, in February 1784, Johann Georg Hamann reported to a correspondent that Kant intended to publish "something about beauty" in the newly founded *Berlinische Monatsschrift*[23] – clearly somewhat remarkable news since Kant had not published anything relating to aesthetics in twenty years.

All of this indicates that Kant must have looked at the possibility of universally valid judgments of taste more confidently around the time. What may have precipitated the change in his views? Given the sparsity of documents, I can again only offer a conjecture: by early 1784, an obstacle had been removed that had prevented Kant so far from considering taste's claim to universality more seriously; and the removal of the obstacle was made possible by a development in Kant's moral philosophy during the same time.

In the spring of 1784, he was working on a book that would soon turn into the *Groundwork of the Metaphysics of Morals* (GMS) and which he finished in September of the year (cf. 4: 626–28). The innovation that is of interest in our context is not the formulation of the categorical imperative (which preceded the 1780s) but rather the doctrine of the incentives of morality that Kant presented in the GMS, the claim that the motivation for morality, its executive power, could not come from any other source than the moral law itself. My conjecture, in short, is that morality first had to become fully autonomous in order to allow aesthetics to be recognized as a subject for a transcendental investigation.

As we saw in Section 2.7, in the lectures of the 1770s, Kant assigned different kinds of pleasure to different faculties, where each pleasure indicated the agreement of a representation with the principles of the respective faculty. Among the pleasures Kant listed, only the satisfaction in the good is distinguished as universal and necessary[24] because only the good satisfies "according to concepts of the understanding" (28: 252),

---

[21] Kant to Reinhold, late December 1787 (10: 514f.).
[22] R 988 (15: 432f.). According to Reicke (1889: 112), this note is written on a letter from Count Keyserling to Kant from 7 February 1784 (see 10: 364).
[23] Hamann to Scheffner, 18 February 1784. See Hamann (1965: 130).
[24] "Good is what must please everyone necessarily" (28: 249).

where the understanding is taken in a wide sense that includes reason; it is the faculty of universal laws or rules. Although the pleasure of taste assumes a middle position between the idiosyncratic gratification of the agreeable and the universal satisfaction in the good, Kant insists that taste "is still always only a judging through the relation of the senses" (28: 249) and although agreement with the "laws of sensibility" results in a pleasure that is occasionally characterized as "universal" and "objective" (28: 248; 252f.), he points out that "the beautiful does not please everyone necessarily, rather the agreement of the judgment is contingent" (28: 249). Such contingent consensus among subjects on what they judge to be beautiful allows for rules of taste – presumably associated with the "laws of sensibility" – but they "are not a priori ... but empirical"; they concern "order, proportion, symmetry, harmony in music" (28: 251; cf. 253).[25]

In the *Metaphysik Mrongovius* of 1782/83, Kant takes the further step of allowing the understanding some role in judgments of taste: "with taste, *sensibility and understanding* are connected in judging." He now claims that since taste "rests on general [*allgemeine*] rules, the understanding must provide these" (29: 892; my emphasis).[26] Since the understanding is the source of universally valid judgments, one might have expected the status of judgments of taste to be elevated and the pleasure of taste to achieve a universality similar to that of the satisfaction of the principles of morality. In fact, based on the agreement of sensibility and understanding in taste, it might have been possible to design an argument analogous to the one Kant gave in the L_1 lectures for the universality of moral judgments. He there argued that "all morality is the harmony of freedom with itself .... Whatever harmonizes with freedom agrees with the whole of life. Whatever agrees with the whole of life, pleases" (28: 250).[27] Using the agreement of sensibility and understanding in taste, an analogous argument could have been made at that point for the universality of the pleasure in the beautiful. But Kant does not attempt such an argument

---

[25] Guyer interpreted similar passages in the anthropology lectures of the 1770s as indicating that Kant, at that time, was already convinced that judgments of taste make a legitimate claim to universality because the "laws of sensibility," on which they are supposedly grounded, are as universally valid as any laws of the understanding. See Guyer (2005: 171). This interpretation assumes that there is a fairly tight connection between the "laws of sensibility" with "order, proportion, symmetry, harmony," for which Kant, as Menzer (1952: 73f.) noted, does not provide any argument.

[26] Guyer has traced this change to the earlier anthropology lectures of 1775/76 and 1777/78. See Guyer (2005: 173f.). Some *Reflexionen* from around 1770, however, already mention that beauty requires correspondence of sensibility and understanding: cf. R 1797 and R 1798 (16: 119).

[27] Kant adds that this moral pleasure "is only a reflective pleasure" and is thereby distinguished from the agreeable.

and even the inclusion of the understanding into the pleasure of taste does not lead him to accord universality and necessity to judgments of taste; the moral pleasure retains this monopoly.

According to my conjecture, Kant changed his mind about these issues in early 1784, when he attempted a deduction of judgments of taste and must have told his friends that he intended to publish "something on beauty." Why was he, apparently somewhat abruptly, now willing to grant universal validity to judgments of taste? My proposal is that he had at this time, while working on the GMS, realized that there is no competition between a universal feeling for beauty and the universal feeling that is involved in moral judgments, a competition that, up to this point, would have been a threat to the 'purity' of morality.

This purity, the independence of the moral law from anything like moral feeling or moral sense, Kant had defended at least since the *Inaugural Dissertation* of 1770. In the lectures from the 1770s, he employed for this purpose the distinction between the law and its incentives as the distinction of the *principium diiudicationis* (henceforth PD) – the ground of moral judgment or insight – and the *principium executionis* (PE) – the ground on which the moral insight can be connected with an incentive for action (e.g., 28: 318). Until the GMS, he had tried to identify the incentives (the PE) in feelings that had sources other than the law itself. This strategy seemed inevitable since he regarded it as impossible that the understanding, or reason, could directly induce feelings of pleasure or displeasure. His view on this matter is summarized in the Canon of the KrV of 1781: although the moral law is absolutely obligating, it is, by itself, not (yet) practical, that is, emotional and prudential factors are necessary to motivate a human agent to act on the law's obligation. Moral laws could not be regarded as "commands ... if they did not connect appropriate consequences with their rule a priori, and thus carry with them promises and threats" (A 811). Without such promises and threats, "the majestic ideas of morality are, to be sure, objects of approbation and admiration but not incentives for resolve and realization" (A 813). The metaphysics lectures of 1782/83 agree with this view (e.g., 29: 777). In the *Moral Mrongovius II* of 1784/85, however – a lecture that follows the completion of the GMS – reason is now seen to be practical in the sense of the GMS and KpV: "If reason determines the will through the moral law, it has the force of an incentive, and in that case has, not merely autonomy, but also autocracy. It then has both legislative and executive power. The autocracy of reason ... would then be the moral feeling" (29: 626). This is, obviously, the doctrine Kant had arrived at in the GMS, according to which moral actions "need no recommendation from any subjective disposition or taste, regarding them with immediate favor and satisfaction, and no immediate propensity or feeling for them" (4: 435). Instead, the "moral feeling" is to be regarded as "the *subjective* effect that the law exercises on the will" (4: 460). All morally relevant feelings, therefore, have to *succeed* – and hence originate from – the representation of the law in our consciousness rather than precede and occasion such representations.[28]

In the 1770s, Kant had sometimes distinguished the moral feeling and the incentives for moral action.[29] The former was the satisfaction that follows on moral judgments and with respect to such feeling, the priority of judgment over feeling was clear to Kant, for example, in 1772: "The moral judgment does not arise from the feeling but rather the latter from the former. All moral feeling presupposes a moral judgment by means of the understanding" (R 6760; 19: 152). From this, the universality and necessity of moral satisfaction derives but because it was parasitical on judgment according to moral principles, the feeling itself, despite its universality, could not serve as a replacement of the PD in the way in which moral sense theories had claimed that a universal feeling provided the ground for the validity of moral laws. But although the existence of moral feeling could therefore not endanger the purely rational nature of morality, in Kant's view before the GMS, the incentives for moral action, the PE, had in general *non-moral* sources, as the above quotations from the Canon of KrV make clear. With respect to the incentives, however, Kant could not see, before 1784, how they themselves could follow from the moral law and hence have a rational origin. If there were universal feelings that could serve as incentives, the danger that they might usurp the role of the PD could not be ruled out and the argument against moral sense theories would have been seriously obstructed. For this reason, it must have been important to Kant to deny that there could be such universal feelings that did not arise from moral grounds.

With the realization, in GMS, that the moral law itself provides the required incentive, this threat was ruled out. Feelings of non-moral origin could now be allowed to have universal validity without endangering the purity of morality. The full autonomy of the moral law – in the sense that it is not only based on reason alone but also independent of any incentives

---

[28] For the change in the doctrine of incentives, cf., e.g., Henrich (1960: 106; 112); Allison (1990: ch.3); Kuehn (2004).
[29] See, e.g., R 6864 (19: 184; from 1776–78).

it does not produce itself – now enabled Kant to consider seriously the possibility that the pleasure of taste can make a legitimate claim to universal validity.

In a *Reflexion* from early 1784, Kant indeed undertook a first attempt at giving what in the KU he called a deduction of judgments of taste (R 988; 15: 432f.).[30] The question he tried to answer was: "How is an objectively valid judgment possible which is yet not determined through any concept of the object?" Although the details of the answer are not completely clear, they do seem to anticipate features of the later deduction. Such judgments, he suggested, must be "related to the object in general through the mental powers of cognition in general." In that case, the "ground of the judgment" must be "contained ... only in the feeling of a movement of all the cognitive powers," that is, of imagination and understanding, and it is the power of judgment that "makes possible the agreement of the two [powers] in a case *in concreto*." This "movement" or "play of the cognitive powers" is supposed to be experienced with pleasure, that is, the pleasure of taste.

The most interesting part of the *Reflexion* for my purposes is the last paragraph in which Kant tried to explain why the occupation of the cognitive powers thus characterized is pleasurable. He employed here an analogy with the doctrine of moral incentives of the GMS. The autonomy of the moral law, he said in GMS, requires (and hence makes it the case) that reason "have the capacity to induce a feeling of pleasure ... in the fulfillment of duty" (4: 460). In R 988, he paraphrased this: "it is analytically certain that if freedom exists as a property of the will such a pleasure will be presupposed." Analogously, Kant claims, in the case of taste: "Likewise ... it follows of itself [i.e., analytically] that if cognition in itself has incentives [*Triebfedern*], then a movement [*Bewegung*] of the cognitive powers will produce pleasure" (15: 433). The incentives of "cognition in itself," I think, refer to a desire or interest of the cognitive faculty; and the satisfaction of such an interest by some representation is registered with pleasure in the same sense in which Kant had discussed the 'harmonizing' of representations with faculties in the lectures from the 1770s. One could speculate that once he had accepted the existence of a universal aesthetic feeling as the result of the satisfaction of an interest of our higher faculties, Kant could have gone on to compare the established

---

[30] R 988 has been discussed before by, among others, Menzer (1952: 115) and Dumouchel (1994: 429f.). Giordanetti (1999) is the first who emphasized the innovation and significance of the *Reflexion*.

characteristics of the pleasure of taste – disinterestedness and non-conceptual origin – with the interests of the extant faculties, that is, the understanding, theoretical and practical reason. The result would have been the sort of regressive argument for the existence of a new faculty, as outlined above.

6

The Principle(s) of the Power of Judgment

The need to introduce a new faculty into the system of the powers of the mind, I have argued, can be motivated from (i) a theory of pleasure as satisfaction of an interest and (ii) a provisional acceptance of the pleasure of taste as a pleasure that makes a claim to universality and necessity and yet cannot be grounded on concepts. These premises let us infer to a (higher) faculty with an interest and an a priori principle that must be different from the other faculties. Neither the content of the interest nor that of the principle emerge from this inference.

In the Introductions to KU, however, Kant seems to proceed differently when he justifies the power of judgment as a separate faculty. There he motivates – and even gives a deduction of – the a priori principle of the new faculty from the "unity of experience (as a system in accordance with empirical laws)." Such a principle is required, he says, "for otherwise no thoroughgoing interconnection of empirical cognitions into a whole of experience would take place" (5: 183; cf. 20: 232). This is the principle of the systematicity of nature in its empirical laws, a principle that, despite its similarities with the "maxims of reason" in the KrV (A 666; cf. A 699), Kant does not assign to theoretical reason but to the new faculty of reflecting judgment. In the First Introduction, he indeed claims that it is this principle on which the "introduction of the power of judgment into the system of the pure faculties of cognition through concepts rests entirely" and that this "is what first gives us the concept of an objectively contingent but subjectively (for our faculty of cognition) necessary lawfulness, i.e., a purposiveness of nature, and indeed does so a priori." Given this a priori principle, he continues, we can then see that "an aesthetic reflecting judgment can be regarded as resting on a principle a priori" (20: 242f.) This statement Kant apparently thought to be compatible with the remark a page later (which I have referred to before) that "it is ... properly only in taste, and especially with regard to objects in nature, in which alone the power of judgment reveals itself as faculty that has its own special

6.1 Two Versions of One Principle

principle and thereby makes a well-founded claim to a place in the general critique of the higher faculties of cognition" (20: 244).

It would be natural to assume a division of labour here: The inference from the pleasure of taste justifies the introduction of a new faculty (as *constitutive* for feeling), while the deduction of the principle of systematicity (as *regulative* for cognition) identifies the content of the new faculty's a priori principle, which the previous inference left completely open. This proposal, however, is problematic – as I mentioned before – because it is hard to see how the principle of systematicity itself could be constitutive for the pleasure of taste, despite Kant's attempt to connect the principle with feeling in § VI of the introduction.

In this chapter, I shall discuss the status and the justification of this principle. Since it is not clear how it could be relevant for taste, it would seem that there are in fact two principles of the reflecting power of judgment (Section 6.1). A further, well known issue concerns Kant's claim that the principle of systematicity is a transcendental principle, which, on the usual understanding of 'transcendental,' means that it is a condition of the possibility of experience. But if this sense of the term is adopted, it becomes puzzling why Kant insists that we cannot assert that nature is systematic but only presuppose or postulate it to be so. A condition of the possibility of experience, like the causal principle, should not be a postulate but be true of the world of experience. I shall try to spell out in what (weaker) sense the principle can be regarded as transcendental by explaining the role it plays in our quest to find new, more general empirical laws and concepts on the basis of already available laws and concepts (Section 6. 2). This reconstruction of the role of the principle is then extended to the case that is most relevant for my purposes: the formation of new empirical concepts *ab initio*, from perceptions rather than from previously available concepts (Section 6. 3).

6.1 Two Versions of One Principle?

Rather than simply identifying the principles of systematicity and of taste, it has been suggested[1] that Kant has in mind a 'general' principle of the purposiveness of nature, which manifests itself in two versions: the "discursive" principle of systematicity and the "intuitive" principle of taste.[2] This suggestion captures a change in the relation of the notions of a systematicity of nature and of its

---

[1] Allison (2001: 63f.). Düsing (1968: 81–85) had earlier taken the principle of systematicity as a version of a general principle of purposiveness but identified the latter with the principle of taste.
[2] This contrast is taken from Kant's letter to Johann Friedrich Reichardt of 15 October 1790 (11: 228): "The ability to make judgments of taste, though not founded on objective concepts of

purposiveness that has been observed in the transition from the treatment in KrV to that in KU.³ While in the first *Critique* the systematic organization of nature is the genus and purposiveness a species (namely, the highest form of systematicity),⁴ the relation seems reversed in KU: here systematicity becomes a species of purposiveness because nature shows itself subjectively purposive in the systematic arrangement of its particular laws but also in beautiful forms of natural objects. This reversal thus allows for two species of the genus purposiveness, one governed by the principle of taste, and one by the principle of systematicity, or for two ways of applying the genus concept.

If this reconstruction of Kant's view is accepted, we can see a close analogy or correspondence with the rationalists' construal of two ways in which perfection – the agreement of a manifold with respect to a purpose⁵ – can be perceived, namely, either through clear and distinct concepts, or through clear but indistinct concepts, in which case it is called beauty. In Kant's framework, the two versions of perceiving perfection correspond to judging (subjective) purposiveness in a conceptual manner, through the principle of systematicity, and to judging it non-conceptually, through the pleasure of taste.

perfection

/ \

perceived   perceived

distinctly   indistinctly (beauty)

purposiveness of nature

/ \

principle of   principle of

sytematicity   taste

("discursive")   ("intuitive")

---

reason ... is still founded on an a priori principle of judgment (albeit an intuitive and not a discursive one)." For further discussion of this, see Chapter 7.

[3] See Allison (2004: 513 n. 33).

[4] "This highest formal unity that alone rests on concepts of reason is the *purposive* unity of things; and the speculative interest of reason makes it necessary to regard every ordinance in the world as if it had sprouted from the intention of a highest reason. Such a principle, namely, opens up for our reason, as applied to the field of experience, entirely new prospects for... attaining to the greatest systematic unity among [things]" (A 686f.).

[5] "Complete purposive unity is perfection (absolutely considered)" (A 694).

6.1 Two Versions of One Principle

Further support for this analogy is found in the Preface where Kant laments the difficulty of finding an a priori principle for the power of judgment. The problem he outlines at first seems to pertain to the power of judgment in general, that is, determining and reflective judgment:

> It can, however, easily be inferred from the nature of the power of judgment ... that great difficulties must be involved in finding a special principle for it ... which nevertheless must not be derived from concepts a priori; for they belong to the understanding, and the power of judgment is concerned only with their application. It therefore has to provide a concept [or principle] itself ... which only serves as a rule for it, but not as an objective rule to which it can conform its judgment, since for that yet another power of judgment would be required in order to be able to decide whether it is a case of the rule or not." (5: 169)

But from the KrV, we know that the determining power of judgment is not in need of a principle of its own – objective rules are provided to it by concepts of the understanding under which it subsumes intuitions or other concepts (A 133f.) – the focus obviously is on the reflecting employment of judgment, which, in its task of subsuming particulars under not yet known general concepts, is in need of a principle of its own. The Introductions identify this as the principle of systematicity. The real target of Kant's lament, therefore, turns out to be the principle of judgment that is operating in judgments of taste: "The embarrassment about a principle (whether it be subjective or objective) is found chiefly in those judgings that are called aesthetic" (5: 169).

Indeed, the First Introduction's § X is addressed to the question about "the search for a principle of the technical power of judgment" (20: 237). And here the focus is exclusively on the aesthetic case. There must be an a priori principle underlying such aesthetic reflecting judgments because they make a claim to universal and necessary validity. The "difficulty" here is that these judgments "cannot in any way be grounded on concepts and therefore cannot be derived from any determinate principle, since they would otherwise be logical; the subjective representation of purposiveness, however, should not in any way be a concept of a purpose" (20: 239*). Later on, the sought-for principle is characterized as one that "grounds" judgments of taste "even though it [the principle] is indeterminate." Even though these claims could suggest that there is a separate 'principle of taste,' Kant insists that the judgment of taste's claim to universality relies on "the *Beziehung* of the subjective purposiveness of the given representation [of a form] for the power of judgment to that a priori principle of the power of judgment, of the purposiveness of nature in its empirical lawfulness in general" (20: 243), that is, to the principle of systematicity.

The latter principle may well be called 'indeterminate' because of its regulative status; but it is "grounded on concepts" and therefore cannot "ground" judgments of taste. Thus, everything depends on how we can understand what that *Beziehung* between the "discursive" principle of judgment (systematicity) and the "intuitive principle" of taste is supposed to be. This contrast is also displayed in the Introduction where the *aesthetic* power of judgment is characterized as "a special faculty for judging things in accordance with a rule but not in accordance with concepts" (5: 194). The employment of the reflecting power of judgment under the principle of systematicity, however, is clearly a judging in accordance with – however indeterminate – concepts.

It seems to me that Kant is referring to the difficulty of identifying a connection between a conceptual principle and a non-conceptual or intuitive one, where both are somehow supposed to belong to the same faculty, in a passage at the end of the Preface:

> The great difficulty in solving a problem which nature has made so involuted, may, I hope, serve to excuse some not entirely avoidable obscurity in the solution, as long as it can be shown clearly enough that the principle has been correctly stated; granted that the way in which the phenomenon of the power of judgment has been derived from it [the principle?] does not have all the distinctness that one can rightly demand elsewhere, namely from a cognition in accordance with concepts, which I also believe myself to have achieved in the second part of this work. (5: 170*)

This "obscurity" pertains to the first, aesthetic part of KU and has supposedly been avoided in the second, teleological part – presumably because the first part had to deal with a non-conceptual principle and its relation to the principle of systematicity.[6]

6.2 The Principle of Systematicity: Its Introduction and Function

Since the Preface mentions only the contrast in clarity between the teleological part and the aesthetic part of the KU, we cannot be sure that Kant meant to include the introduction and justification of the principle of systematicity in the Introductions as belonging to the non-obscure aspects.

---

[6] In his *Encyclopaedisches Wörterbuch der Kritischen Philosophie*, Mellin (1798) devoted a long entry to this remarkable admission of Kant's and came to the conclusion that the "obscurity" is unavoidable because the judgment of taste's claim to universality ultimately rests on a concept of the supersensible (cf. the resolution of the antinomy of taste in § 57, esp. 5: 340). This seems implausible because the second part of KU invokes the supersensible as well in the resolution of the teleological antinomy (§ 78, esp. 5: 412ff.).

6.2 The Principle of Systematicity

But since the principle, at least in the published Introduction, is officially given a transcendental deduction, it would be plausible to assume so. In the First Introduction, this justification proceeds in a way that is, apparently, similar to the transcendental deduction of the categories and principles of the understanding in KrV. According to the latter, an object can become an object of possible experience only if its representation is part of a single unified experience:

> There is only *one* experience, in which all perceptions are represented as in thoroughgoing and lawlike connection .... The thoroughgoing and synthetic unity of perceptions is precisely what constitutes the form of experience, and it nothing other than the synthetic unity of appearances in accordance with concepts. (A 110)

Cognition is possible only insofar as appearances have "connection in accordance with universal and necessary laws" (A 111), which is to say, we have to represent objects as standing under a system of laws (the principles of the understanding) so that the object's relations with other appearances are determined within a single space and time:

> All appearances lie in one nature, and must lie therein, since without this a priori unity no unity of experience, thus also no determination of the objects in it, would be possible. (A 216)

Similarly, the justification of the principle of systematicity refers to the unity of experience and argues that such unity would be impossible unless we presuppose that nature arranges its empirical (as opposed to the transcendental) laws in the form of a system:

> Unity of nature in time and space and unity of the experience possible for us are identical, since the former is a totality of mere appearances (kinds of representations), which can have its objective reality only in experience, which, as itself a system in accordance with empirical laws, must be possible if one is to think of the former as a system (as must indeed be done). Thus it is a subjectively necessary transcendental *presupposition* that such a disturbingly unbounded diversity of empirical laws and heterogeneity of natural forms does not pertain to nature, rather that nature itself, through the affinity of particular laws under more general ones, qualifies for an experience, as an empirical system. Now this presupposition is the transcendental principle of the power of judgment. (20: 209)

Without going into further details of the version of Kant's argument in the published Introduction,[7] I want to highlight some peculiar features of the

---

[7] For which, see, e.g., Allison (2001: ch. 1).

relation of the deduction of a transcendental principle in KU and the deduction of the pure concepts and principles of the understanding in KrV.

What is peculiar is that the unity of experience secured by the principles of the understanding does not by itself imply the unity of experience in accordance with empirical laws of nature. Although Kant had insisted already in KrV that the latter laws cannot be derived from the former (B 165), one might have thought that the unified framework established by the understanding is robust enough to assure us that whatever may happen within the framework happens in an orderly, that is, law-governed, fashion, even though we may not know (or never will know) all of the empirical laws governing nature at a less abstract level. For instance, we might expect that the Second Analogy guarantees that *there must be* empirical causal laws, even though it does not tell us what these are. But Kant does not seem to allow us to draw this conclusion: although the deduction in KrV establishes the fundamental laws of nature in a fashion that allows us to assert their truth, when it comes to the claim that the unity of experience requires that nature specifies its empirical laws in a certain order, we are only allowed to "*presuppose*" this claim, not assert it (20: 209, quoted above). Put differently, the KrV transcendental deduction shows the principles of the understanding to be necessary for (the unity of) experience and thereby entitles us to assert them as the basic laws of nature; the principle of systematicity is likewise argued to be necessary for the unity of experience, but we cannot assert it on this basis as a truth about nature. Kant, of course, emphasizes this difference by labelling the principles of the understanding as "constitutive" for the experience of objects and the principle of the power of judgment as (merely) "regulative" for cognition, or, apparently equivalently, by declaring the former as "objectively necessary" for experience while the latter is (merely) "subjectively necessary" (e.g., 20: 214; 219; 5: 385; 457).[8]

Kant attributes our lack of insight into the necessity of the particular laws to "the constitution and the limits of our faculties of cognition" (5: 183). For the "manifold of forms in nature," he says,

> there must nevertheless also be laws ... which, as empirical, may seem to be contingent in accordance with the insight of *our* understanding, but which,

---

[8] In First Introduction Kant seems to imply the existence of a *subjective* transcendental philosophy: Since the power of judgment has a transcendental principle and since, as he says, "despite its a priori principle [it] provides no part of transcendental philosophy as an objective doctrine," one might infer that there is also transcendental philosophy as a subjective doctrine (20: 242).

6.2 The Principle of Systematicity

if they are to be called laws (as is also required by the concept of a nature) must be regarded as necessary on a principle of the unity of the manifold, even if that principle is unknown to us. (5: 179f.)[9]

Consequently, we have to think of an understanding, different from and superior to ours, that would be in possession of "that principle" and therefore be able to grasp the empirical laws as properly necessary, just as we grasp the general laws of nature as necessary because they are the principles of our understanding: "the particular empirical laws ... must be considered in terms of the sort of unity they would have if an understanding (even if not ours) had likewise given them for the sake of our faculty of cognition, in order to make possible a system of experience in accordance with particular laws of nature" (5: 180).[10]

With the reference to a superior understanding, Kant is following a maxim that he had already applied in the KrV and will apply again in the teleological part of the KU: "One cannot think of a mode of representing [*Vorstellungsart*] as restricted with respect to a certain principle without opposing it to another mode that is general in this respect," that is, that does not suffer the same limitation (R 6358; 18: 685; from 1797). Given that our way of intuiting is sensible, the KrV had claimed, we cannot have access to noumena (in the positive sense) but at the same time we have to think of a being with a "non-sensible" or "intellectual intuition" that would have such access (B 307). Through such a merely thinkable contrast, the limitation of our intuitive capacity comes into sharp relief. Likewise, in § 77 of the KU, an "intuitive understanding" is introduced that has no need – in contrast to our "discursive" understanding – to employ the concept of (natural) purpose in the consideration of organisms (5: 406). The superior understanding of the Introduction, analogously, has no need for a principle of the subjective purposiveness of nature, because it can apprehend the necessity of the empirical laws directly.[11]

The principle of purposiveness, in our mind, substitutes for the insight such a superior understanding would have, just as the concept of a natural purpose is a stopgap we have to use because our understanding is not

---

[9] There is controversy about whether the 'unknown principle' should be identified with the principle of systematicity that Kant is about to introduce in the text (see Allison 1996: 90f.). I do not think this is a plausible reading because I do not take Kant to claim that with the principle humans can grasp the necessity of the particular laws just as the superior understanding can (see below in this section).

[10] This superior understanding does not figure in the First Introduction.

[11] I do not mean to claim that the higher understanding in the Introduction can be identified with the intuitive understanding of § 77.

intuitive. From the perspective of *our* cognitive capacities, all we can say is that we have to *presuppose* that the empirical laws are arranged *as if* a different understanding had done so with the benefit our power of judgment in mind, just as we judge that the forms of beautiful objects in nature are *as if* they had been designed with the same intention (5: 245).

I understand Kant's claim that the particular laws are contingent for our understanding as a categorical claim: it is *in principle* not possible for us to grasp the laws as laws, that is, as necessary. No amount of cognitive progress can overcome those limitations – just as little as we can 'improve' our sensibility so as to bring it close to an intellectual intuition or just as little as we can ever come to explain organisms mechanically.[12] What we can and should do is extend our knowledge of nature by unifying or specifying existing laws and strive to discover new ones, thereby filling in more and more of the system of laws. From this it follows that the principle of systematicity has the same status – that of a regulative or heuristic principle – as the maxims of reason in KrV. As a regulative principle, it instructs us to search for and form new, more general empirical laws that enable us to unify already known laws (the principle of homogeneity or generality), to form more specific laws to differentiate known laws (the principle of specification), and to search for laws intermediate between more specific and more general ones (the principle of affinity or continuity).[13] The ideal outcome of a process of inquiry along these lines would be a representation of nature as a system with respect to its empirical laws.

But what does it mean that the principle is transcendental though not constitutive for cognition? If a principle is transcendental, as Kant explains in the Introduction (5: 181), if it pertains to the possibility of the experience of objects, how could such a principle fail to be constitutive of such experience?[14] And how could it help in addressing this issue to say that such a principle is merely 'subjectively necessary,' that is, necessary for the possibility of cognition but not for the possibility of objects?[15] After all, "the conditions for the possibility of experience in general are at the same time conditions of the possibility of the objects of experience" (A 158).

---

[12] The notion of a substitute or stopgap is therefore not to be understood in the sense of a provisional tool that could ultimately be replaced by a superior one.

[13] See (A 654–60); similarly, e.g., (5: 186), (20: 210).

[14] This question has occupied many commentators; for a brief overview of some views on offer, see Willaschek (2018: 110–12).

[15] But see above, n. 8.

6.2 *The Principle of Systematicity*

There is a curious contrast between the epistemic urgency with which Kant insists on the principle of systematicity as required for experience and the nonchalance with which he describes our response to apparent failures of the principle in inquiry. The prospect of finding more and more unified laws pleases us, he says; conversely, if we were "foretold that even in the most minor investigation of the most common experience we would stumble on a heterogeneity in [nature's] laws that would make the unification of its particular laws under universal empirical ones impossible for our understanding," we would be "thoroughly displease[d]" because "this would contradict the principle of the subjective-purposive specification of nature."

This sounds like the characterization of an annoyance, not like an epistemic catastrophe or the outbreak of lawless empirical chaos. Kant goes on to diagnose our comparatively mild response to such failures as due to the fact that the presupposition of systematicity

> is so indeterminate on the question of how far that ideal purposiveness of nature for our faculty of cognition should be extended that if someone were to tell us that a deeper or more extensive acquaintance with nature through observation must finally stumble upon a multiplicity of laws that no human understanding can trace back to one principle, we would be content with this. (5: 188)

This emphasis on the indeterminacy of the principle of systematicity is prefigured in the KrV, where Kant classifies the maxims of reason as "objective but indeterminate (*principium vagum*)" (A 680; 664f.). In light of these pronouncements, a deflationary interpretation of 'transcendental' in KU seems advised.[16]

I shall first discuss the operation of the principle in the formation of new laws and concepts on the basis of already available laws and concepts and then look at the case of concept formation *ab initio* in Section 6.3. As a regulative principle, the principle of systematicity is first of all a *prescription*: "It is a command of our power of judgment to proceed in accordance with the principle of the suitability of nature to our faculty of cognition as far as it reaches, without (since it is not a determining power of judgment that gives us this rule) deciding whether or not it somewhere has its boundaries" (5: 188). But when Kant claims that the principle's status is

---

[16] In what follows, I draw on Willaschek's interpretation of 'transcendental' in the Transcendental Dialectic of KrV (2018: chs. 4 and 5). He does not claim that this proposal also applies to Kant's use of the term in KU but I regard it as the most plausible interpretation so far when extended to the third *Critique*.

transcendental, it takes on the form of a *descriptive* statement, namely the presupposition: "there is in nature a subordination of genera and species that we can grasp" and these divisions "in turn converge in accordance with a common principle, so that a transition from one to the other and thereby to a higher genus is possible" (5: 185); or: "Nature specifies its general laws into empirical ones, in accordance with the form of a logical system" (20: 216); and finally: "for all things in nature empirically determinate concepts can be found" (20: 211f.; cf. 5: 187). While the prescriptive form of the principle is not a claim about nature at all (since it is an imperative), the descriptive versions are such claims, even though we cannot affirm them as truths about nature but can only presuppose them.

The systematization of existing knowledge (concepts, laws) is to some extent a purely logical matter. In the KrV, Kant distinguishes a logical from a real, or transcendental, use of reason's principles (A 305f.). In its "merely formal, i.e., logical use" reason "abstracts from all content of cognition" (A 300) and thus, if we take the homogeneity maxim as an example, it instructs us to find for any two species concepts a common genus concept: given a concept A, with marks a, b, c, and a concept B with marks c, d, e, we can form a new concept C with mark c that subsumes A and B. All this is done without the need to consider the content of the concepts. But from such merely logical operations, no extension of our knowledge results. The intent of the principle of the power of judgment, however, is to expand the known system of particular laws or concepts more and more, to fill in gaps, to find new laws, etc. This task requires more than logic, namely, empirical inquiry. Here we have to take into account not only logical relations between concepts but also causal and explanatory relations. Without paying attention to the latter, mere logic can give us incorrect hierarchies of genera and species. For instance, if the concepts of two properties, M and H, are co-extensive (they apply to the same class of objects), we cannot logically determine their place in the hierarchy of concepts, that is, whether M should stand under H, or H under M, or whether neither of these possibilities obtains. Insight into the causal relations, however, can reveal which concept is basic and which one should be considered as derived. An illustration is provided by the co-extensive concepts 'is a mammal' and 'has hair': in the correct hierarchy we have to take the former as basic and treat the latter as derived.[17]

How does the principle of systematicity in its 'real' use, that is, as a transcendental principle play out? It enables us to generate empirical

---

[17] The example is from Willaschek (2018: 128).

6.2 The Principle of Systematicity

hypotheses (concerning laws or concepts) that can be subjected to testing. For this, the principle first of all and obviously has to be taken in its descriptive form; a prescription ('Find an X such that ...') does not generate a testable hypothesis ('There is an X such that ...'). Second, the hypotheses we come up with should expand our knowledge of nature in the sense outlined above. And third, the hypotheses have to satisfy minimal rational constraints: we must not have reasons to believe that they cannot possibly be true. All three aspects of the 'real' use of the principle are illustrated in a case Kant briefly discusses in the First Introduction (20: 216n.): Suppose a group of rocks have previously been classified as belonging to different species (e.g., according to where they tend to be found). The rocks share surface properties, a,...,d, and are sufficiently different from other rocks. Should we classify them as members of a (new) genus of rocks? The descriptive version of the principle of systematicity – the presupposition that *there are* genera in nature for species that show commonalities – allows us to form the hypothesis

(G) Rocks with a,...,d belong to the species 'granite.'

(G) can be subjected to tests, for example, we could try to find more commonalities among a larger group of objects with a,...,d. If we are successful, the hypothesis can be inductively confirmed in the way Kant described in the KrV under the title of the "hypothetical use of reason."[18] The point of the discussion of this case in the First Introduction, however, is that (G) involves more than a merely logical operation. It also presupposes (defeasibly) that the surface properties correspond to a shared "inner constitution" or nature of the rocks in our group and that the shared properties therefore constitute not merely accidental similarities between internally quite different objects. In the latter case, Kant says, we would "find ... always individual things, as it were isolated for the understanding, and never a class of them that could be brought under concepts of genus and species" (20: 216n.).[19] Such a correspondence would mean that the

---

[18] Here "the universal is assumed only problematically ... the particular being certain while the universality of the rule [the hypothesis] for this consequent is still a problem; then several particular cases, which are all certain, are tested by the rule, to see if they flow from it, and in the case in which it seems that all the particular cases cited follow from it, then the universality of the rule is inferred... this use of reason is only regulative, bringing unity into particular cognitions as far as possible and thereby approximating the rule to universality" (A 646f.).

[19] The same concern is expressed in the KrV: "If among the appearances offering themselves to us there were such a great variety – I will not say of form (for they might still be similar to one another in that) but of content, i.e., the manifoldness of existing beings – that even the most acute human understanding, through comparison of one with another, could not detect the least similarity ...

surface properties are connected to the internal constitution by (particular) laws. Since at this stage of inquiry we do not have insight into the inner nature of the rocks, (G) is in need of further testing – in analogy to the case, discussed above, of the correct relation of the concepts 'is a mammal' and 'has hair.'

In this way, the principle functions like the traditional assumption of the 'uniformity of nature,' which, if we knew it to be true, would turn inductive inferences into deductive ones. Since we do not have this knowledge, Kant treats the principle as a presupposition that is indispensable in inquiry. As Allison has noted,[20] there is a connection between the principle of systematicity in KU with what Kant calls in the *Logik* the "principle of the inferences of the reflecting power of judgment," which says: "that the many will not agree in one without a common ground, but rather that which belongs to the many in this way will be necessary due to a common ground" (9: 132).[21] From the result of a comparison – that some forms share a set of properties – we are entitled to infer, defeasibly, that the commonality is not accidental but has a ground that makes such commonality necessary and that it can therefore be projected onto other objects that share those properties.

If the principle of systematicity plays the role I ascribed to it, it should be clear that presupposing it is not (i) an assertion that nature is in fact systematically organized, nor is it (ii) the assumption that our efforts at systematization are guaranteed to succeed. The principle rather presupposes merely that such efforts, in the form of hypotheses about particular

---

then the logical law of genera would not obtain at all" (A 654). I take this to mean that similarity of form – surface similarity – is not enough to ground the existence of genera; agreement in respect of "inner nature" is required.

Cf. also the 1788 essay on the use of teleological principles (8: 136n) where Kant distinguishes a classification of natural objects into "orders and classes" as merely logical, in contrast to a classification into "genera and species," which refers to how nature orders itself.

[20] See Allison (2001: 34f.). There is, however, a problem with this connection because in the *Logik* Kant seems to restrict the principle of inductive (and analogical) inferences to objects *of one kind*. Thus, induction is characterized as based on the principle: "What pertains to many things of a kind [*Gattung*], pertains to the rest of them" (9: 133). With this restriction, it is not clear how the principle can assist in forming concepts of *new* kinds.

[21] This principle is related to what Baumgarten identified as the principle of the *Beurtheilungsvermögen*: The "law of the capacity to judge is: if the manifold of a thing is recognized either as agreeing or as disagreeing, we recognize its perfection or imperfection" (1783, § 452). And: "If many things together contain the sufficient reason [ground] of One, they agree to this One. This agreement itself is the perfection, and the One to which they agree, is the determining ground of the perfection" (1783: § 73). As Wolff had pointed out (see Section 3.1), there are two ways of judging perfection: (i) infer from agreement to a (previously unknown) purpose and (ii) infer from a known purpose to the functioning of the manifold. (i) is clearly similar to Kant's principle of the inferences of the power of judgment.

6.2 The Principle of Systematicity

laws and concepts, are not ruled out as impossible. This is a minimal constraint on the rationality of our cognitive pursuit of expanding knowledge of nature that the hypotheses generated on the basis of the principle have to satisfy. It does conform to the plausible view that "to rationally undertake some pursuit, success in which would clearly be valuable, it may be enough to lack any reason to believe it must fail"; and it is not committed to the implausible postulate "that the efforts of reflective judgment will be rational only if we have a guarantee that nature itself is fully systematic."[22]

The presupposition of systematicity thus allows us to generate testable hypotheses concerning more general laws and concepts, more specific ones, and interpolating laws and concepts. It is also evident that even though the generated hypotheses, like (G), can be confirmed or disconfirmed by observations, the presupposition of systematicity itself is not affected by the way the evidence turns out to be.[23] However, if we are successful in our inquiry under the constraint of the principle, any law or concept formed will be such that it fits into the presupposed hierarchy of genera and species, that is, into the view of nature as a system.

This deflationary interpretation of the sense in which systematicity is a transcendental principle is in conflict with other proposals – most recently Geiger's (2022) – that hold onto the understanding that 'transcendental' means a principle is a condition of the possibility of experience. Insofar as the principle is required to form new empirical concepts and such concepts are a condition of the experience of objects, it satisfies the criterion of being a 'condition of the possibility of experience.' But the fact that the hypotheses generated with its assistance are defeasible, that is, not guaranteed to be satisfied, distinguishes it significantly from other transcendental principles. It is regulative but not constitutive for experience. In this respect, the principle fails to qualify the power of judgment as a faculty (see

---

[22] This is Guyer's well-known criticism (1997: 44). It is perhaps of interest to note that Fichte, when he planned to publish a commentary on the KU that would help readers to penetrate the occasional "obscurity" of the text in 1790/91 (a plan he never completed), understood the role of the principle of systematicity in the way I suggested: The reflecting power of judgment, he wrote, has to find the universal to a given particular but it "cannot find it except through trials, i.e., through provisionally assuming some principle as an empirical law of nature and attempting to order particular cases under it until the principle either shows itself to be universally applicable and is thereby confirmed [as a law], or proves itself to be unsuitable because it suffers frequent exceptions, in which case the power of judgment is forced to come up with a different principle. In this trial-and-error procedure, the reflecting power of judgment is therefore guided by the presupposition that *some* principle it [hypothetically] adopts *could* be a law of nature; and that repeated observations must show whether it actually is a law or not" (1962: 336) .

[23] See again (5: 188), quoted above.

Chapter 2); only the still elusive principle of taste can convey this status to judgment.

6.3 The Power of Judgment and Rules of Apprehension

In the First Introduction, Kant emphasizes the use of the principle of systematicity in the formation of concepts, that is, the case where we arrive at a new concept, starting from intuitions, instead of from logical and explanatory relations between established concepts (which was the focus of the previous section):

> For those concepts which must first of all be found for given empirical intuitions, and which presuppose a particular law of nature, in accordance with which alone *particular* experience is possible, the power of judgment requires a special and at the same time transcendental principle for its reflection, and one cannot refer it in turn to already known empirical concepts and transform reflection into a mere comparison with empirical forms for which one already has concepts. (20: 213)

As is well known, Kant never elaborated much on this process of concept formation. But in the quote, he emphasizes the difference between the task of forming new concepts out of existing ones and the task to form concepts, as it were, *ab initio*, from perceptions, and claims that here, in particular, the principle has to play an indispensable role. It is worth noting that the maxims of reason from the KrV could not have functioned in this way since they could operate directly only on products of the understanding, not on the imagination (A 643f.). But the reassignment of the maxims to the reflecting power of judgment makes their role in the imagination's operations at least possible.

For insight into this case, we have to first look at the procedure by which *determining* judgment applies given concepts to manifolds of intuition and thereby subsumes the latter under the former, making cognition of objects possible.

While the understanding is the "faculty of rules," the power of judgment "is the faculty of *subsuming* under rules, i.e., of determining whether something stands under a given rule" (A 132). How is such subsumption of intuitions under (pure and empirical) concepts possible, given that concepts are a completely different kind of representations than intuitions?

Kant mentions the example of the concept of a dog. It "signifies a rule in accordance with which my imagination can specify the shape [*Gestalt*] of a four-footed animal in general, without being restricted to any single particular shape that experience offers me or any possible image that

6.3 Power of Judgment and Rules of Apprehension

I can exhibit *in concreto*." Thus, under the guidance of the concept, the imagination is provided with a "rule for the determination of our intuition in accordance" with the given concept (A 141). This rule, the "schema," instructs the imagination in apprehending a manifold of intuition to search for and select those features that are required for an instance of the concept 'dog,' like four-legged, etc. Selecting the relevant features also means ignoring irrelevant details that do not affect the classification of the object, for example, the colour. The (determining) power of judgment then compares the result of the imagination's apprehension with the "shape" outlined in the schema; in case of (sufficient) agreement, it then *subsumes* the object under the concept 'dog.' The result, in this case, is an agreement or harmony of concept and intuition, which is the condition of any cognition.[24]

When Kant considers the *reflecting* employment of judgment in KU, he starts out with the general characterization: "The power of judgment in general is the faculty for thinking of the particular as contained under the universal" (5: 179). 'Thinking the particular as contained under the universal' obviously means: thinking of it as subsumed under the universal. Since the universal is not given in the case of reflecting judgment, the characterization then has to read: the faculty for subsuming particulars under a not-yet-given general rule or concept. If a concept is not yet available, it becomes of course mysterious how the imagination could come up with a schema, understood as a rule for apprehending the given manifold. Although Kant never worked out a detailed suggestion of this process in which the imagination has to engage in something that can only be characterized as "schematizing without a concept" (5: 287),[25] I propose to understand the procedure in analogy with what I explained above with respect to the formation of new concepts and laws out of existing ones. There the maxim of homogeneity (or generality) instructs us to find a law or concept that unifies more specific laws or concepts that we already know. The maxim is turned into a hypothesis that asserts that some candidate law is the unifying one and this hypothesis can then be tested. At the level of the operations of the imagination, what is at issue is the task of forming a new rule of apprehending a given manifold that can then be

---

[24] The doctrine of the schematism is notoriously difficult but the sketch given should suffice for my purposes. For more detailed overviews, cf., e.g., Allison (2004: ch. 8) and Matherne (2014, 2015).

[25] See Fricke (1990: 119) and Allison (2001: 171). For attempts to reconstruct a Kantian account of concept formation, see Longuenesse (1998: 115ff.); Zuckert (2007: chs .1 and 2); Schlösser (2013); Anderson (2015: 336ff.); Ginsborg (2015: 69–76 and ch. 7). For doubts about the reliability of some of the textual basis in Kant's *Logik*, see McAndrew (2021).

'reflected' in a new concept. That is, the imagination has to be provided with a rule, a selection criterion, that is not informed by the concept-to-be-formed.

Suppose we encounter an object for which the understanding has no concept yet. Kant describes a scenario like this in the *Logik*: He compares the apprehension of the manifold of an object by a "savage," who has no concept of the object, with the apprehension by someone who is already in possession of the concept, say 'house' (9: 33). In the case of the house expert, if the imagination, while going through the manifold, can identify the features that are specified in the schema of the concept 'house,' she will cognize the object as a house. She is in possession of a rule that instructs the imagination in apprehending the manifold of intuition to search for and select those features that are required for an instance of the concept 'house' and ignore irrelevant 'details' that do not affect the classification of the object, for example, the colour. If the "savage," however, engages in the process of *forming* – instead of applying – the concept 'house,' the situation is different. He, though of course bound by the categories and whatever empirical concepts he has, will try out several rules of apprehension and, under the right circumstances, probably arrive at such a rule that can be reflected in the concept 'house.'[26] Longuenesse put the point this way: "Only ... the gradually dawning consciousness of a 'rule of apprehension' common to the representation of various objects serving the same purpose, would pick out analogous marks and bring forth the concept of a house."[27] 'Picking out analogous marks' corresponds to following the maxim of homogeneity and leads to a hypothesis about the genus to which the object might belong.

But more must be involved in the formation process so that any concept that results will satisfy the formal requirements imposed on all concepts we use. Concepts have to have a form (namely, generality) so that they can (i) figure as the matter in judgments which are ways of subordinating concepts; judgments, in turn, have to have a form so that they can (ii) figure in syllogisms as their matter; and (iii) syllogisms have to have a structure so that they can fit, as its matter, into a system. Thus, concepts are formed in the first place 'with a view towards' this hierarchy of roles, that is, with a view towards a system.[28] Concepts contain marks by which

---

[26] "This general validity [of a conceptual representation] presupposes a comparison, not of perceptions, but of our apprehension, insofar as it contains the presentation of an as yet undetermined concept" (R 2883, 16: 558, from 1776–78; quoted in Allison [2001: 28]).
[27] Longuenesse (1998: 118).
[28] Longuenesse (1998: chs. 4–6); a convenient summary is found in Longuenesse (2005: 186ff.), which I paraphrase in the text.

6.3 Power of Judgment and Rules of Apprehension

we recognize the class of objects that fall under a concept. In the collection of marks a,...,d that make up, say, the concept 'granite,' a judgment is implicit: 'Everything that has a,...,d is a sample of granite' (and conversely). This judgment, in turn, can form the major premise of a possible inference by which we conclude that 'this rock is a sample of granite.' And judgments and inferences can be ordered into a system that represents a hierarchy of genera and species. This implies that the maxims of the power of judgment must be involved in the very formation of concepts: concepts must be general ('pick out analogous marks'), they must be specifiable (by adding further marks), and they must be specifiable in a way that makes possible affinity or continuity with other concepts under the same genus. So if everything goes well, the "savage" in the example above will come up with a rule of apprehension that incorporates the principle of systematicity and finally results in a concept of the object that satisfies the power of judgment's requirements for all concepts that are to be used in judgments.

This brief sketch of the process of concept formation in terms of trying out different candidate rules of apprehension is no doubt too simple and does not address all the objections that have been raised since Longuenesse first made a similar proposal.[29] Whatever the details of the process, however, may turn out to be, the important point for us is this: In the *application* of a concept the imagination schematizes – apprehends the manifold – under the guidance of the concept. The manifold is subsumed by the determining power of judgment that uses the extant concept as its rule. In concept *formation*, the manifold is apprehended without such guidance; there is only the instruction, given by the reflecting power of judgment, to arrive at a rule of apprehension that, when reflected in a concept, satisfies the maxims. Compared to the application case, here the imagination has a sort of *freedom* – namely, from a concept prescribing the rule of apprehension – but its operation is, of course, bound by what is given in intuition and by the constraints of the power of judgment. Kant described this in the First Introduction: in concept formation, the reflecting power of judgment

> proceeds ... not as it were merely mechanically, like an instrument, under the direction of the understanding and of the senses, but *artistically*, in accordance with the general but at the same time indeterminate principle of a purposive arrangement of nature in a system, as it were for the benefit of our power of judgment, in the suitability of its particular laws (about which the understanding has nothing to say) for the possibility of experience as a system. (20: 213f.*)

---

[29] For an overview of such objections, see, e.g., Schlösser (2013).

'Artistically' here must mean 'schematizing without a concept,' that is, the terms refer to an activity that generates schemata *ab initio*.

The operations of concept application and formation – that is, the operation of the determining as well as of the reflecting power of judgment – can both be characterized in terms of 'subsumption,' as Kant does in what its editor called a "forgotten" *Reflexion* from the time of the KU or later:[30] "The power of judgment in general is the faculty for determining the general rule with respect to the condition of the particular that stands under it (subsumption)."[31] Although this definition at first glance looks as if it covers only the reflecting power of judgment, it actually is a general characterization because 'to determine the general rule' can mean (i) applying the rule to a particular (making the rule, as it were, concrete) and (ii) finding the general rule from the particular.[32] Kant then goes on to explain the difference between the determining and the reflecting case in terms of two ways in which subsumption can proceed: first, "through schemata that ... are designed [*entworfen werden*] in accordance with concepts of the understanding" or, second, "through schemata that ... are designed in accordance with the understanding in general."[33] The latter case, I suggest, should be understood as covering the formation of concepts *ab initio*, that is, as the activity in which the power of judgment settles on a rule of apprehension that satisfies the constraints imposed on all empirical concepts – constraints that the principle of systematicity imposes and that the understanding requires in order to use concepts.

In Chapter 7, I shall discuss in what ways the design of schemata "in accordance with the understanding in general" is related to the case of the *aesthetic* employment of reflecting judgment. This will allow us to identify the interest of the faculty of judgment, the satisfaction of which is registered in feeling, according to the theory of pleasure and displeasure developed in Chapter 3, and return us to the question, raised above, about the relation between the principle of systematicity and the principle of taste.

---

[30] "Forgotten" because it is not contained in the *Akademie* edition and was published only in Bayerer (1968).
[31] Bayerer (1968: 272).
[32] Cf. the two senses of 'condition' in Kant that Longuenesse has identified (1998: 94f.).
[33] In each case, Kant emphasizes that the schemata are designed "*allgemein*," "because the power of judgment is a higher cognitive faculty." That is, the schemata have – in contrast to an intuition or an image – generality qua *rules* of apprehension. Cf. again R 2883 (16: 558), quoted above in n. 26.

7

The Interest of the Reflecting Power of Judgment and the Deduction of Judgments of Taste

The doctrine of faculty interests and the associated theory of pleasure as satisfaction of such interests were the basis of all our previous discussion. We saw that there were reasons for Kant to postulate a faculty whose interest was the source of the pleasure of taste. Like any other higher faculty, the new candidate had to be assigned an a priori principle, which, in the Introductions, turned out to be the principle of systematicity. But it seemed obvious that this principle could not be the one that Kant claims is constitutive for the pleasure of taste, even though the satisfaction of the presupposition of systematicity among empirical laws is accompanied by pleasure, just not the pleasure of taste. The task in this chapter is twofold: I will identify the interest or aim of reflecting judgment and on this basis suggest how the relation between the principle of systematicity and the principle of taste should be understood; this leads to an interpretation of the deduction of judgments of taste.

7.1 What Is the Interest of the Faculty of Reflecting Judgment?

The a priori principle of a faculty is not to be identified with the interest or aim of that faculty. A faculty has an interest in representations agreeing with its principle; but this is because satisfaction of the principle is a (or the) means to attain the aim of the faculty. In Kant's official explication of faculty interests in KpV, this distinction of means and ends is somewhat obscured. He there defined the interest of speculative reason as "a principle that contains the condition under which alone [the faculty's] exercise is promoted" (5: 119). This does not agree with the other characterization of speculative reason's interest as "cognition of the object up to its highest a priori principles" (5: 120).[1] The apparent conflict between the two

---

[1] Willaschek (2010: 172 n. 7) has noticed this discrepancy.

characterizations of interest, however, can be resolved if we take whatever principle 'promotes the exercise' of the faculty as a means for attaining the aim of 'cognition of the object up to its highest a priori principles.' Similarly with practical reason, where the aim is "determination of the will with respect to the final and complete end," while the principle that determines the will is the moral law.

For the reflecting power of judgment, if we assume its principle to be that of systematicity, this means that the aim of the faculty is not systematicity of empirical laws and concepts itself; this regulative principle rather has to be regarded as a means to achieve the aim of the faculty. What should this aim be? In the KrV, the role of the (then not so labelled) *determining* power of judgment is to establish the agreement of given concepts and the manifold of intuition by subsuming the latter, the product of the imagination, under concepts provided by the understanding and thereby make cognition of objects possible. While the understanding is the "faculty of rules," the power of judgment "is the faculty of *subsuming* under rules, i.e., of determining whether something stands under a given rule" (A 132). Such agreement or harmony of understanding and imagination can be identified as the aim of the *reflecting* power as well, if we regard it in its role in concept formation, which is obviously necessary for establishing the harmony of concepts and intuitions. And although the principle of systematicity, in the formulation that pertains to empirical laws, at first does not seem to contribute to the relation of understanding and imagination – but rather, as in KrV, concerns the relation of understanding and theoretical reason – it is clear from the principle's role in concept formation (see Chapter 6) that it is, after all, a means for attaining the aim of harmony.

But is this harmony not the same as cognition itself? In this case, the aim of reflecting judgment would turn out to be the same as the interest of the understanding. The 'new' faculty, then, would lack an interest of its own – something one should not expect from a separate higher faculty. In the case of determining judgment, as discussed in KrV, this result was plausible: no principle of its own was needed for subsumption under concepts provided by the understanding and there was no claim that this power of judgment was a separate member in the system of the higher faculties of cognition. In the KU, accordingly, Kant characterizes the status of determining judgment as "heteronomy" because it "has to conform to the laws given by the understanding (whether general or particular)." For reflecting judgment, however, Kant claims "autonomy" because it has a principle "which is valid merely subjectively for the use of reason in regard to the particular laws of experience" (5: 389).[2]

The role of reflecting judgment in concept formation, therefore, suggests a further distinction within the overall characterization of the aim as harmony: (i) a harmony 'imposed' by the understanding through a given concept that is applied to intuition and (ii) a harmony that is not (yet) imposed but established by the imagination under the guidance of the reflecting power of judgment – a preliminary agreement, as it were, in the phase of concept formation that, of course, ultimately results in case (i), once a concept has been established.

The significance of this distinction becomes clear when we consider the feeling of pleasure that, on Kant's theory, consists in the satisfaction of faculty interests. Such pleasure results only when the attainment of an aim is *contingent*, that is, when it is not guaranteed by the operation of the faculty alone, as was the case with the application of the categories.[3] An act of cognition, where determining judgment applies an empirical concept and thereby a rule of apprehending the manifold, is likewise not experienced with pleasure because the subsumption, which establishes harmony of understanding and imagination, is not contingent, given that the manifold can be apprehended according to the rule. *That* we experience an object, and *which* one, is of course contingent; Kant writes accordingly of the "intrinsic contingency [*innere Zufälligkeit*]" of empirical judgments, that is, of the contingency of their content (5: 191). But *given* a concept and its schema, the apprehension of manifolds is no longer contingent. That is, every object, insofar as we can have cognition of it, *has to* agree with this concept-determined harmony of imagination and understanding (cf. A 111). This lack of contingency in the fit of an empirical concept and an apprehended manifold is the reason why an object, under these conditions, cannot be said to be purposive for its cognition (since only contingent agreement of the faculties "produces a representation of purposiveness" [5: 190]) and therefore cognition is not pleasurable.[4]

---

[2] In the Introductions, he labels this "heautonomy" (20: 225; 5: 186). The phrase "for the use of reason" here has to be understood in the sense in which reason includes the understanding.

[3] Cf. (5: 187; 190) and Section 4.2.2.

[4] Kuhlenkampff (1978: 129). Cf. also Guyer: "A beautiful object is pleasurable precisely because it seems like the satisfaction of our fundamental cognitive aim for unity but also seems contingent because it is not produced by the application of any determinate concept to the manifold which would guarantee the unification of the manifold" (1993: 10). And "if the unification of the manifold presented by a beautiful object were thought to contain sufficient conditions for knowledge, there would not be any ground for a specially noticeable pleasure in it" (1993: 399 n. 17).

In the illustration from Chapter 6, the subject who is in possession of the concept 'house' will not experience pleasure when she sees a house; the 'savage,' however, who is in the process of forming this concept, could fail in his attempts and the process would have to start again. Should he succeed, the aim of harmony has been attained in a contingent way and the satisfaction of the interest is registered as a feeling of pleasure – "just as if it were a happy accident which happened to favor [his] aim" (5: 184). At the end of the reflecting power of judgment's process of finding a rule of apprehension, the 'preliminary' harmony has to be ratified by a determining judgment, the subsumption of the intuition under the newly formed concept. At this point, the contingency of the process of 'schematizing without a concept' ends and, with the contingency, ends the pleasure:

> To be sure, we no longer detect any noticeable pleasure in the comprehensibility of nature and the unity of its division into genera and species, by means of which alone empirical concepts are possible through which we cognize it in its particular laws; but it must certainly have been there in its time, and only because the most common experience would not be possible without it has it gradually become mixed up with mere cognition and is no longer specially noted. (5: 187)[5]

I have previously emphasized that the pleasure that, according to the Introduction (§ VI), is "combined" with systematization and concept formation is not the pleasure of taste. Although the former shares the claim to universal validity with the latter, the fact that the principle of systematicity, as a ground of pleasure, is a principle in conceptual form rules out the suggestion that it could be identical with the essentially non-conceptual pleasure of taste. The inference I discussed in Section 4.2, from a pleasure with certain characteristics to the satisfaction of the interest of some faculty, would not, in the case of the pleasure of systematization or concept formation, justify the introduction of a new faculty because the pleasure, in this case, is not sufficiently distinguished from other pleasures that are also conceptually based (the pleasure in the good).

---

[5] In contrast to my interpretation, Merritt (2014) takes this pleasure to be a "pleasure of the understanding" rather than resulting from attaining the aim of the reflecting power of judgment. Furthermore, she suggests that the pleasure is not forgotten or ceases when a concept has been formed; instead she claims that the feeling merely goes "unnoticed" and is, in this unnoticed state, always present in acts of cognition. When we experience beauty, our attention is re-directed onto this feeling and the pleasure of taste ultimately turns out to be a pleasure of the understanding. In my view, this consequence is implausible (see Section 7.4) as is the notion of unnoticed feelings, at least within Kant's framework.

7.1 Interest of the Faculty of Reflecting Judgment

These considerations notwithstanding, there are obvious *similarities* of this pleasure with the way Kant characterizes how the pleasure of taste comes about. In both cases, the imagination, together with the power of judgment, 'schematizes without a concept' and the harmony of understanding and imagination is described as one in which the understanding does not impose a (previously established) empirical concept. In both cases, the apprehension of a manifold by the imagination agrees with the presentation or exhibition of a concept of the understanding – "indeterminate which one" for taste and as yet indeterminate for concept formation.[6] Such phrases characterize a certain *freedom* that is accorded to the imagination, where the sense of 'freedom' here derives from what Kant sometimes describes as a "burdensome constraint [*lästiger Zwang*]," which the understanding, by providing a concept, imposes on the activity of the imagination (5: 243). Its freedom terminates once a concept is formed; in the case of taste, however, the freedom lasts, as it were, indefinitely in what Kant describes as a "free play" of the imagination and the understanding. (I'll come back to this shortly.)

To fix the distinction within the aim of harmony terminologically, I'll use the terms 'unfree' and 'free' harmony.[7] The former is attained, by the determining power of judgment, in the application of previously established concepts and is not accompanied by pleasure; the latter is achieved by reflecting judgment in the moment of concept formation and in taste and results in a 'momentary' or lasting pleasure, respectively. This notion of a free harmony has to be further specified in order to distinguish between the case of concept formation and that of taste. In both cases, the imagination operates freely in the sense of not following a rule prescribed by the understanding in the form of an empirical concept (although the categories presumably are involved).[8] One might further differentiate the cases by saying that in the process of concept formation there is, trivially, an intention to arrive at a concept – the imagination is still somehow "in the service" of the understanding (cf. 5: 242) – whereas Kant denies this intention for the imagination's role in taste.[9]

---

[6] "If, then, the form of a given object in empirical intuition is so constituted that the apprehension of its manifold in the imagination agrees with the presentation of the concept of the understanding (indeterminate which one), then in the mere reflection understanding and imagination mutually agree for the advancement of their business, and the object will be perceived as purposive merely for the power of judgment" and this subjective purposiveness is registered as the pleasure of taste (20: 221). Cf. also R 2883 (16: 558), quoted in Chapter 6.

[7] Cohen (2017) uses these terms too. For discussion of her proposal, see the end of this section.

[8] Whether this is so, is a controversial issue, which I will ignore here; cf., e.g., Ginsborg (2015: ch. 3).

[9] In an "aesthetic judgment of reflection," "no determinate concept of the object at all is required nor is one thereby generated" (20: 221).

I prefer, for reasons that will become clear shortly, to characterize the difference in this way: in concept formation, the imagination is free in the sense mentioned but it is obviously bound by what is given in intuition, the 'material' for which a rule of apprehension has to be found. The imagination does not create or produce what is to be apprehended but "runs through" it (cf. A 99). I'll call this its *'reproductive freedom.'* In the aesthetic case, however, Kant claims a stronger sense of freedom for the imagination:

> if in the judgment of taste the imagination must be considered in its freedom, then it is in the first instance taken not as reproductive, as subjected to the laws of association, but as productive and self-active (as the authoress of voluntary forms of possible intuitions). (5: 240)

At this point, it is not at all obvious how such a *'productively free'* employment of the imagination could coexist with the need to apprehend a *given* object for aesthetic appreciation and what Kant means when he defines the "aesthetic power of judgment" as the capacity to detect "in the apprehension of an object agreement of the imagination in its freedom with the laws of the understanding in general."[10] The clarification of this notion of productive freedom is the task taken up in Section 7.3 and in Chapter 8.

At this preliminary stage, I suggest that free harmony in the productive sense of freedom should be identified as the genuine aim or interest of the power of reflecting judgment because it is this aim with which the new faculty establishes itself as separate – in some sense 'autonomous' – and not merely as operating "in the service" of the understanding. And if the pleasure of taste consists in the attainment of this aim – which is, for us, accidental and not guaranteed by the workings of the faculties involved – then we can see indeed a connection between a unique kind of pleasure and a unique faculty interest. Furthermore, it should be obvious, even before further clarifications, that the productively free harmony involved in judgments of taste is not a necessary condition for cognition of objects. If it were, the notorious problem of 'everything (that is, every cognized object) is beautiful' for Kant's theory would arise. The reproductively free harmony, aimed at by reflecting judgment, of course, is such a necessary condition but this does not imply that the productively free harmony has to play the same role. If we were to identify the two aims,[11] we would have to say that in some cases the effort to attain the aim comes to a halt when a

---

[10] Bayerer (1968: 272).   [11] As Longuenesse has suggested (1998: 164; 2003).

concept has been formed and the 'momentary' pleasure ceases, while in other cases (the experience of beauty) the same activity is allowed to continue indefinitely, without issuing in a concept but is still experienced as pleasurable instead of as frustrating.[12]

An interpretation that is at first glance very similar to mine has been suggested by Alix Cohen.[13] She understands harmony of the faculties as the source of pleasure and distinguishes the unfree harmony in concept application (or at the moment when a new concept has been formed) from the free harmony in "aesthetic reflection" and both kinds are registered with pleasure. She takes both forms of harmony ultimately to be the interest of the understanding – in contrast to my view, according to which only the unfree version could be said to be the aim of the understanding – and interprets the free case, in the usual way, as a "free play" of the faculties. As I shall discuss in more detail below, this leads to the problem of what such a free play can contribute to the source of pleasure, that is, the satisfaction of the interest of the understanding, since the play is to be distinguished from cognition (unfree harmony). Cohen's answer is that even though the play does not directly make such a contribution, it functions as a "booster," a sort of exercise or training of the faculties in the service of the understanding. With the different interpretation of the free play I suggest in Sections 7.3 and 7.5, I hope to provide an account that does more justice to the autonomy of taste, without severing all ties to cognition.

7.2 "Cognition in General"

In § 9 of KU, this free harmony is further described. If the pleasure of taste with its claim to universal validity is not based on a concept of the object, Kant argues, then its determining ground

> can be nothing other than the state of mind that is encountered in the relation of the powers of representation to each other insofar as they relate a given representation to *cognition in general*. The powers of cognition that are set into play by this representation are hereby in a free play, since no determinate concept restricts them to a particular rule of cognition. Thus the state of mind in this representation must be that of a feeling of the free play of the powers of representation in a given representation for a cognition in general. (5: 217)

---

[12] Cf. Ginsborg (2015: 98ff.).   [13] See Cohen (2017).

Talk about a free harmony of the faculties is here replaced by their "free play," a phrase that perhaps suggests an even stronger sense of freedom than the notion of free harmony. But Kant restricts this association of freedom by giving the play a direction towards – a *Beziehung* to – the aim of "cognition in general." Because of this relation, the "freedom in the play of our cognitive powers" is "yet at the same time ... purposive" (5: 306). Kant's intention that underlies this construction is clear enough: the claim to universality that judgments of taste make is ultimately to be justified through the relation of the free play to "cognition in general."

This is, prima facie, a paradoxical notion since cognition always requires agreement of a concept with intuition, while cognition 'in general' seems to exclude the employment of concepts – like in the following passages that all emphasize this feature:

(a) In the free play, the cognitive faculties are engaged in "an activity that is indeterminate but yet, through the stimulus of the given representation, in unison [*einhellige Tätigkeit*], namely that which belongs to a cognition in general." (5: 219)
(b) The relation of the faculties in this play is one "that is not grounded in any concept (like that of the powers of representation to a faculty of cognition in general)." (5: 219)
(c) The judgment of taste is "still related to concepts, although it is indeterminate which." (5: 244)
(d) The aesthetic power of judgment "relates the imagination in its free play to the understanding, in order to agree with its concepts in general (without determination of them)." (5: 256)

Apparently, Kant is not claiming that the free harmony or play is a relation of the faculties that does not involve concepts at all (even though they are not the determining ground of the pleasure and judgment of taste). But the notion of a "concept in general" or of an "indeterminate concept" is still obscure enough. My suggestion is to understand these claims – in order to preserve any semblance of 'cognition in general' with cognition – as attempts to characterize a relation of the faculties that involves (determinate) concepts but nothing in the analysis of free harmony depends on *which* concepts they are, that is, this case does not depend on how the concepts are empirically determined (i.e., which marks they contain etc.). I try to motivate the suggestion by taking a closer look at the technical term 'cognition in general.'

Since Kant nowhere seems to give a more detailed explication of the concept, we should take a clue from similar terms Kant uses in many places, that is, terms of the form "... in general" and focus on "sensation in general" and "thing in general."

The first of these is mentioned in the *Prolegomena to Any Future Metaphysics*, where Kant discusses the derivation of further a priori concepts, the "predicables" of the KrV (A 82), from the categories by connecting the latter with either the pure forms or the matter of appearances. While it may seem unproblematic to form a priori concepts by invoking the *pure* forms of sensibility, space, and time, it is prima facie surprising that a connection with the *matter* of sensibility – which, if it is considered apart from its form, is sensation – could result in a priori concepts since sensation is a posteriori; it always has to be given in empirical intuition. Kant therefore explains that what he has in mind is "the matter [of an appearance] insofar as it is not yet empirically determined (object of *sensation in general*)" (4: 324) – that is, a notion of this matter in which one abstracts from any only empirically determined differences within the matter. Later, Kant puts a further gloss on an "object of sensation in general": in this concept, he explains in *Fortschritte*, nothing empirical, that is, empirical determinations of the object, is presupposed, only *that* something like this exists (20: 285). In the KrV, he handles in an analogous fashion the concept of a "thing in general," which he claims to be an a priori concept even though it requires reference to "the matter of appearances through which things are given to us in space and time," that is, to something that can only be given empirically (A 720). The idea is again that we can legitimately talk about a "thing in general" by abstracting from all empirical differentiations in what can be given.[14]

If we try to understand "cognition in general" along such lines, we have to say: since all cognition requires intuition and concept and the agreement of both, in the notion of "cognition in general," we abstract from all that is empirically determined in given intuitions and concepts; instead, we focus on the fact of their agreement. Employing the phrase from the *Prolegomena*, we consider cognition, as the agreement of empirical intuition and concept, insofar as the intuition "is not yet empirically determined" by a concept. This, in turn, can be read – with another, potentially misleading phrase – as "agreement of the imagination with the understanding to a cognition in general, *prior* to any concept" (R 1935, from 1790s; 16: 161; my emphasis). Similarly, in the Introduction, Kant writes about the agreement of an object's "form in its apprehension ... *prior* to any concept with the faculties of cognition, in order to unite the intuition with

---

[14] Cf. the discussion of these passages in Cramer (1985: 206–12).

concepts for a cognition in general" (5: 192; my emphasis). 'Not yet determined' and 'prior to determination' are plausibly equivalent expressions; but in both cases, one has to avoid associating a misleading temporal sense. What is at issue in these constructions is abstraction from any empirical determinations in what is (and can only be) empirically given. 'Cognition in general' thus refers to an *actual* relation of a determinate concept and intuition where we are not interested in those actual determinations; all that matters is "that something like this exists."

This explication of 'cognition in general' can be further illustrated by considering an important passage from the first Introduction where Kant argues that the relation of imagination and understanding can be regarded in two ways:

> In the power of judgment understanding and imagination are considered in relation to each other, and this can, to be sure, first be considered objectively, as belonging to cognition (as happened in the transcendental schematism of the power of judgment); but one can also consider this relation of two faculties of cognition merely subjectively, insofar as one helps or hinders the other in the very same representation and thereby affects the state of mind, and [is] therefore a relation which is sensitive [*empfindbar*]. (20: 223)

I take it that Kant is here considering the *same*, given relation of the faculties in two ways; he is not talking about two kinds of relation, one in which intuition is subsumed under a concept and one in which it is not. This granted, one might still try two possible readings: (i) in the given relation there is no objective determination of the intuition by a concept but there is a feeling induced by the relation; and (ii) there is an objective relation (a case of cognition) and the question is whether this relation also has a feeling aspect. I think alternative (i) can be rejected because it would be hard to see how it could qualify as a case of cognition in general. According to (ii), we would have to say that even though the faculties stand in the subsumption relation required for cognition of an object, this relation can have – in some cases – a feeling associated with it, a feeling, however, that does not depend on the particular concept that subsumes the intuition; it is only based on whether or not the objective relation of the faculties qualifies, *at the same time*, as one of free harmony.

This at first glance paradoxical and implausible reading, I submit, is further confirmed by Kant's claim, a few pages earlier in the First Introduction, "that in a merely reflecting judgment imagination and understanding are considered in the relation to each other in which they *must* stand in the power of judgment in general, as compared with the relation in which they *actually* stand in the case of a given perception" (20: 220; my emphasis). This passage is often read as suggesting a comparison of an 'ideal' relation of the faculties with an actual one. Pleasure would then arise when the actual relation 'comes close' to the ideal norm: we judge the object's form as purposive for the power of judgment or as 'especially suited' for conceptualization.[15] But the passage can also – and, as I argue in the sequel, more plausibly – be read as comparing the relation in which the faculties 'must,' or 'ought to,' stand in the cognition of an object (their objective relation), which is not accompanied by feeling, and their 'actual' relation, in which such feeling may or may not occur.[16]

7.3 The Comparison Model

It sounds implausible, I said, to entertain that one and the same relation can be, at the same time, unfree and free, constrained by a concept and not be so constrained. And this reading seems to contradict what Kant emphasizes in the preparation for the Deduction of Judgments of Taste where he explicitly distinguishes the subsumption of intuitions under concepts in cognition from what the aesthetic power of judgment does in judgments of taste: it "contains a principle of subsumption, not of intuitions under concepts, but of the faculty of intuitions or presentations (i.e., of the imagination) under the faculty of concepts (i.e., the understanding), insofar as the former in its freedom is in harmony with the latter in its lawfulness" (5: 287).

Thus, if we want to hold on to the suggestion that the relation of the faculties in a cognition can at the same time qualify as one of free harmony, we have to assume that the comparison of intuition and concept (or schema) that results in the subsumption of the former under the latter (the business of the determining power of judgment) can be accompanied by a further comparison (by the aesthetic power of judgment) that, depending on the case, can result in the verdict that the given, actual relation, unfree as it is, also qualifies as a relation in which the imagination is free. This, in turn, is possible only if the comparison involves, besides the given and conceptually determined form of the object, a form that the

---

[15] More on this in Section 7.6.
[16] The two passages from the First Introduction can be compared to how Kant, in the KpV, considers the moral law objectively, as determining the will as it ought to be determined, and subjectively, as it actually determines, in the form of an incentive, the feeling of respect (e.g., 5: 72; 76). Cf. Engstrom (2010: 93).

imagination could have apprehended if it were free from conceptual constraint. In other words, we have to invoke a *counterfactual* scenario in which the imagination is free (contrary to what is the case in the given relation) and then compare the given, conceptually determined form with the counterfactual form. If there happens to be agreement, we can say that the unfree relation of imagination and understanding – the "objective" relation – also happens to be a case of free harmony and therefore is accompanied by pleasure.

Kant actually presents exactly this view in the General Remark to the First Section of the Analytic, a passage that commentators have not been paid enough attention to:[17]

> If in the judgment of taste the imagination must be considered in its freedom, then it is in the first instance taken not as reproductive, as subjected to the laws of association, but as productive and self-active (as the authoress of voluntary forms of possible intuitions); and although in the apprehension of a given object of the senses it is of course bound to a determinate form of this object and to this extent has no free play (as in invention [*wie im Dichten*]), nevertheless it is still quite conceivable that the object can provide it with a form that contains precisely such a composition of the manifold as the imagination would design in harmony with the lawfulness of the understanding in general if it were left free by itself. (5: 240f.)

Thus, in a judgment of taste, we compare the actual, objective relation of the faculties on occasion of a given form with a counterfactual, freely produced form. If the comparison is successful – if actual and counterfactual form agree – the aim of the aesthetic power of judgment – free harmony – has been attained and is manifested in the pleasure of taste.

It is not that the given form in such cases is somehow especially suited to conceptualization, or 'invites concepts,' or that the understanding 'tries out' many concepts, etc.[18] Such interpretations place the emphasis, as it

---

[17] Exceptions are: Henrich (1992: 51f.); Budd (2002: 32); Rueger/Evren (2005); Rueger (2008); Vogelmann (2018); Williams (2021).

[18] Cf., e.g., Allison (2001: 171): The imagination, when it schematizes without a concept, "yields ... the exhibition of the form of a concept in general (but not any concept in particular)." The intuitive representation of an object "simulates the exhibition of a concept, or, equivalently ... its 'form' as apprehended immediately suggests a rule-governedness, albeit no rule in particular .... In that case, as Carl Posy has put it, the experience of the object 'invites the application of a concept' (though, again, no concept in particular)" (2001: 188). According to Rush (2001: 58), the imagination ranges "over the manifold of intuition ... engaged in the activity of modeling it as unifiable in any of the multifarious ways that the spatial and temporal properties of that manifold permit." See also Guyer's overview and criticism of such approaches (2005: 77–109).

7.3 The Comparison Model

were, on the wrong side of the comparison. What matters, rather, is that the imagination can produce forms, without constraint by the understanding, that satisfy the requirement of subsumption under a concept. And since the concept that subsumes the given intuition, by assumption, does not play a role in the (counterfactual) free production of the imagination, it does not matter *which* concept happens to fulfill the subsuming function. All that is relevant here is *that* there is such a concept, but with respect to the relation of free harmony this concept can be left "indeterminate."

Kant continues the previous quote:

> Yet for the imagination to be free and yet lawful by itself, i.e., that it carry autonomy with it, is a contradiction. The understanding alone gives the law .... Thus only a lawfulness without law and a subjective correspondence of the imagination to the understanding without an objective one – where the representation is related to a determinate concept of an object – are consistent with the free lawfulness of the understanding (which is also called purposiveness without an end) and with the peculiarity of a judgment of taste. (5: 241)

The correspondence of imagination and understanding – their free harmony – is "subjective" because the (counterfactual) free form is produced without a concept (and it is this correspondence that can be felt); and for the same reason, it is also "without an objective" correspondence, even though in actuality there is such an objective relation. The imagination displays a "lawfulness without law" because it happens to produce a (counterfactual) form, without guidance by a law (from the understanding), a form that agrees with a 'lawfully' apprehended actual form.

I understand the last sentence of the quotation as saying that the free harmony requires that the autonomy of the understanding (its "free lawfulness") has to be compatible with the freedom of the imagination; this is possible only when the imagination, without being constrained by a law, nevertheless, on its own, can produce forms that satisfy the lawfulness of the understanding. This special compatibility of the faculties is "called purposiveness without an end [purpose]," or, equivalently, the forms that allow such free harmony are purposive without a purpose.

Although this interpretation of the free harmony and the free play of the faculties – I call it the *comparison model* – relieves the commentator from having to make sense, for example, of a given form 'inviting the application of concepts,' many questions are still to be addressed. Prominent among these, of course, is: How are we to understand what the imagination does 'on its own'? This is the topic of Chapter 8.

7.4 The Deduction of Judgments of Taste

In the Introduction, Kant gives a deduction of the principle of systematicity or of "the formal purposiveness of nature," which he announces as the "transcendental principle of the power of judgment" (5: 181); he does not there provide a separate section in which "the principle of taste" is deduced. In preparation for the official "deduction of judgments of taste" in § 38, however, he entitles the crucial § 35 "The principle of taste is the subjective principle of the power of judgment in general" (5: 286) and he announces, in § 31, that he is about to give "the deduction of this unusual faculty [*dieses sonderbaren Vermögens*]" (5: 281), that is, of taste as the aesthetic power of judgment.[19] Thus, the aim of the deduction, as it is usually stated – to give "a legitimation" of the judgment of taste's "presumption [*Anmassung*]" to "universal validity for every subject" (5: 279) or to provide "the guarantee of the legitimacy" of the judgment (5: 280) – is at the same time to establish the power of judgment as a faculty.

We recall, furthermore, from the First Introduction, that the "introduction of the power of judgment into the system of the pure faculties of cognition through concepts rests entirely on its transcendental principle, which is peculiar to it." Since this principle, however, does not "determine anything with regard to the particular forms of nature" (since it concerns the comparison of groups of forms and particular laws), whether such individual forms are subjectively purposive for us has to be determined empirically, from case to case. Judgments about the subjective purposiveness of individual forms are judgments of taste but, despite being empirically conditioned, they can make a claim to universality and necessity "through the relation [*Beziehung*] of the subjective purposiveness of the given representation for the power of judgment to that a priori principle ... of the purposiveness of nature in its empirical lawfulness in general." In virtue of this relation, judgments of taste "can be regarded as resting on a principle a priori (although it is not determining)" (20: 243). The expectation is that the official deduction of judgments of taste will finally shed more light on these cryptic remarks.

In the preparatory sections, Kant emphasizes that the deduction has to be conducted only on the basis of the "logical peculiarities, in which a judgment of taste differs from all judgments of cognition" (5: 281; 287). These formal features are familiar from the Four Moments: besides the fact that judgments of taste are *singular* judgments, that is, they concern only

---

[19] Cf. also the Preface's talk of "deducing the phenomenon of the power of judgment" (5: 170).

7.4 The Deduction of Judgments of Taste

"a given singular empirical representation" (5: 289), the two peculiarities are: (1) judgments of taste make a claim to universal validity – they claim to hold for all judging subjects – "as if" they were *objective* judgments; and (2) they cannot be derived from concepts and through them the object is not subsumed under a concept, that is, they do not allow of proofs, just "as if" they were merely *subjective* judgments. The deduction has to show how judgments with these logical features are possible, even though none of the extant faculties (understanding and reason) can account for these features.

The focus on formal features means that we abstract from the "content" of judgments of taste (5: 281; 287). The *first step* of the argument then is supposed to lead to the result that what is relevant for making a judgment of taste is nothing but the (reflecting) power of judgment itself; no concepts or principles of other faculties are involved. What underlies such judgments, therefore, can be nothing but the power of judgment's own principle. They are, as it were, a (or even *the*, unique) *pure* case of the operation of this faculty. The *second step* is intended to show that this principle is required for all cognition and hence can be assumed to be available to all cognizers. Finally, in a *third step*, Kant re-introduces the "content," namely that the judgments make a claim about a felt pleasure (5: 289): If somebody experiences a pleasure with the characteristics of the pleasure of taste, it can only be the pleasure in the satisfaction of the power of judgment's interest or principle; and since the latter is universally shared, so should be the pleasure.

In more detail, § 35 argues by elimination: Since in a *logical* sense (that is, ignoring the feeling expressed), the content of judgments consists in the concepts that are used in them and since judgments of taste are not determined by any concepts of objects, such judgments have no content (in the logical sense) at all. They must therefore be "grounded only on the subjective formal condition of a judgment in general," in contrast to cognitive judgments where the concept of an object provides an objective condition. This subjective formal condition can only be the power of judgment itself (5: 287), since the "logical peculiarities" exclude any other faculty's concepts or principles to be involved. Thus, we have a 'pure' case of the employment of the power of judgment – a result that is obviously important if the task is "a deduction of this unusual faculty" (5: 281).

Any employment of this faculty – here Kant seems to extrapolate from the case of determining judgment – "requires the agreement" of imagination ("for the intuition and the composition of the manifold of intuition") and the understanding ("for the concept as representation of the unity of this composition") (5: 287). Kant is thereby stating the interest or aim of the power of judgment 'in general' to be the harmony of imagination and understanding. This interest, however, has to be modified in the case of reflecting judgment: since in judgments of taste "no concept of the object is ... the ground of the judgment," the aim has to be what I called 'free harmony': "the subsumption of the imagination itself ... under the condition that the understanding in general advance from intuitions to concepts."[20] That is, the aim cannot be, as in the case of determining judgment, "the subsumption ... of intuitions under concepts" (this would require to consider more than merely the subjective conditions of judgments), but rather the subsumption "of the *faculty* of intuitions or presentations (i.e., of the imagination) under the *faculty* of concepts (i.e., the understanding)." In this sort of subsumption, the imagination "in its freedom is in harmony with the [understanding] in its lawfulness." The free harmony of the faculties consists in the imagination composing the manifold of intuition, that is, schematizing it, without guidance from a concept of the understanding – "the freedom of the imagination consists precisely in the fact that it schematizes without a concept" – but nevertheless arriving at a composition that satisfies the requirements of the understanding.

In sum: the argument up to § 35 aims to show that, given the logical features of judgments of taste, the interest of the faculty of judgment has to be specified as the free harmony of the cognitive faculties. Since this interest is different from that of determining judgment, a further version of the power of judgment – the reflecting kind – has to be introduced. Kant does not give any more information on what the "condition that the understanding in general advance from intuitions to concepts" might be. But it is natural to associate this with the transcendental principle of the power of judgment from the Introductions, especially the version emphasized in the First Introduction: "The principle of reflection on given objects of nature is that for all things in nature empirically determinate concepts can be found," which Kant at this point equates with the principle of systematicity: "which is to say the same as that in all of [nature's] products one can always presuppose a form that is possible

---

[20] These considerations contain a reply to Rind's acute observation that "when we take the idea of a harmonious relation [of the faculties] and subtract from it the idea of a harmony of intuition and *concept*," Kant "offers no reason why the difference should be anything greater than zero" (2002: 28; my emphasis). If there is a pleasure with the characteristics of the pleasure of taste, then Kant's theory of pleasure requires that some relation of the faculties (purposive for the power of judgment) is left after we 'subtract' concepts from the harmonious relation necessary for cognition; that is, *some* aim must still be attained after such subtraction and it is here identified as free harmony.

7.4 The Deduction of Judgments of Taste

according to general laws cognizable by us" (20: 211*). If he is indeed referring to this principle in § 35, we would have an explanation for the title of this section: "The principle of taste is the subjective principle of the power of judgment in general" (5: 286). But since we already know that the (transitory) pleasure that results from concept formation does not coincide with the pleasure of taste, we can anticipate that following the deduction along these lines cannot ultimately be successful. The attempt to do so is nevertheless worthwhile.

We reflect on objects in nature under the guidance of the principle "that for all things in nature empirically determinate concepts can be found" in the process of concept formation, which, as we have seen (Chapter 6), is a process in which the imagination schematizes without a concept (i.e., the concept yet to be formed). At the end of this operation, a (short-lived) free harmony of the faculties is established; the aim of the reflecting power of judgment is achieved and we can say that nature has shown itself to be subjectively purposive for the power of judgment. It might seem at this point that in this employment of the faculty we have again a 'pure' case.

In § 38, Kant re-introduces the content of judgments of taste, from which the earlier discussion had abstracted, that is, the claim they make about the feeling of pleasure. From the general theory of pleasure we know that pleasure indicates subjective purposiveness, the satisfaction of an interest. This is how Kant starts:

> If it is admitted that in a pure judgment of taste the satisfaction in the object is combined with the mere judging of its form, then it [the satisfaction] is nothing other than the subjective purposiveness of that form for the power of judgment that we sense as combined with the representation of the object in the mind. (5: 289f.)

The qualification that the pleasure be connected only with the form of the object is obviously meant to exclude the other kinds of pleasure from consideration (the agreeable and the good). Under this restriction and drawing on the results of § 35, the pleasure in question must be in the free harmony of the faculties, that is, in the satisfaction of what had been identified as the interest of the power of judgment. In this case – as Kant has argued in § 35 (5: 287) – the employment of judgment "can be directed only to the subjective conditions of the use of the power of judgment in general," without restrictions arising from ("particular") sensations or concepts. These subjective conditions, Kant then claims, are "that subjective element that one can presuppose in all human beings (as requisite for possible cognitions in general)." With the identification of the subjective conditions with "the faculty of judging itself, or the power of judgment" (5: 287), the deduction seems to issue in the claim that (i) judgments of taste employ only the (reflecting) power of judgment (they are the 'pure' case of such employment) and (ii) this faculty is a necessary condition for possible cognition and hence can be presupposed in all human beings capable of cognition.[21] These subjects then can also be expected to be able to register the satisfaction of the faculty's aim, free harmony; therefore, "the agreement of a representation with these conditions of the power of judgment must be able to be assumed to be valid for everyone a priori" (5: 290*). The same should hold for the pleasure of taste, which consists in the satisfaction of that aim: the pleasure "will allow of being rightly expected of everyone." (5: 290*)[22]

The well-known problem with a reconstruction of the deduction along such lines is that the assumption that the "subjective conditions" are *necessary* conditions for cognition seems to be needed to ensure the (subjective) universal validity of judgments of taste, while this same assumption leads to the undesirable result that every cognized or cognizable object should be beautiful. The latter follows because every cognized object satisfies those necessary conditions, which, at the same time are supposed to be necessary *and* sufficient for judgments of taste (since nothing else can be involved in these 'pure' cases of the employment of the power of judgment).[23]

Allison has suggested that even though agreement of a representation with the subjective conditions is necessary for cognition, it is not sufficient for judgments of taste; what is required in the latter case is that the conditions be satisfied 'freely' or 'in mere reflection.'[24] In this way, the unwanted conclusion that everything is beautiful is indeed blocked. The question, however, arises on what basis the deduction can justify the modified condition that is sufficient for judgments of taste (assuming that any deduction has to establish not merely necessary but also sufficient conditions for what it aims to justify). In Allison's terms: even though the

---

[21] See also Kant's re-phrasing in the footnote attached to § 38: "In all human beings, the subjective conditions of this faculty, as far as the relation of the cognitive powers therein set into action to a cognition in general is concerned, are the same, which must be true, since otherwise human beings could not communicate their representations and even cognition itself" (5: 290n.).

[22] In these quotations, I have changed Guyer-Matthews' "can ... be expected" into "will allow of being ... expected," following Rind's observation (2002: 45).

[23] For early statements of the 'everything is beautiful' problem, cf. Brasch (1896: 215f.; 245f.) and Marc-Wogau (1938: 132). Allison (2001: 184–92) gives references to more recent statements.

[24] Allison (2001: 187).

7.4 The Deduction of Judgments of Taste

'normative status,' or the authority, of the subjective conditions is guaranteed by their involvement in cognition, it is not clear why this status should be inherited by their satisfaction in a way ('freely,' 'in mere reflection') that differs significantly from the way in cognition.[25]

I return to my earlier suggestion that the operation of the power of judgment Kant identifies in § 35 is the one it engages in in concept formation ("schematizing without a concept"). The ability to do so, under the guidance of its own principle that 'for every thing empirical concepts can be found,' is indeed a necessary condition for cognition and can be assumed to be universal – even though the harmony of the faculties in this case is free since the manifold of intuition is not yet subsumed under the concept to be formed. We know, however, that this free harmony is not identical with the one underlying the pleasure of taste, for several reasons: (i) the "original pleasure of predication"[26] does not have all the characteristics of the pleasure of taste; and (ii) in concept formation, the imagination, even though it schematizes without a concept, is still bound by what is given in empirical intuition and by the laws of association (it is only 'reproductively free'), while in taste it is supposed to be free of these laws: it is here "taken not as reproductive, as subjected to the laws of association, but as productive and self-active" (5: 240). I called this the imagination's 'productive freedom.' One could speculate that in the deduction Kant assumed the cases of concept formation and taste to be similar enough, with respect to the operation of the power of judgment, so as to treat them together, without differentiating them. A passage from § 39 seems to

---

[25] Cf. Guyer (1997: 287): If the "subjective conditions of knowledge" are understood as the "capacity to unify a manifold by the cooperation of imagination and understanding in general," then this "does not entail the capacity to unify manifolds without concepts." Allison responded (2001: 190f.): The fact that the harmony required for cognition is not "equivalent" to free harmony "does not concern the norm itself, but merely the difficulty of subsuming a particular instance under it." So, agreement, "in mere reflection," with the subjective conditions of cognition (i.e., the subjective conditions of judgment) makes aesthetic judgments into "candidates" for judgments of taste; whether they really are correct judgments is an empirical question (just like the categories establish candidate cognitive judgments but their veridicality is subject to empirical evaluation). I explain below how my view agrees with and differs from Allison's.

[26] Hogrebe (1992: 73; originally published in 1981). Another author who connects the pleasure of taste with that of predication is Bernstein (1992: 55–63). He understands the experience of beauty as a "mournful" recollection of a time when all cognition was pleasurable. Bernstein thinks that Kant is forced to adopt this view because he needed to reconcile the grounding of judgments of taste on the conditions of cognition with the fact that cognition itself is not accompanied by pleasure (anymore). Makkreel (1990: 164) holds that all harmony of the faculties, including the one required for cognition, is felt (by the *sensus communis*) but that this feeling is different in the case of taste and in cognition. See also Zinkin (2014); Merritt (2014); and Cohen (2017) who suggested similar views.

indicate this: In judgments of taste, he says, a "procedure of the power of judgment" is employed,

> which it must also exercise for the sake of the most common experience: only in the latter case it is compelled to do so for the sake of an empirical objective concept, while in the former case (in the aesthetic judging) it is merely for the sake of perceiving the suitability of the representation for the harmonious (subjectively purposive) occupation of both cognitive faculties in their freedom, i.e., to sense the representational state with pleasure. (5: 292)[27]

This passage is especially obscure if we read the first clause as concept application in cognition, which would be a case of *determining* judgment. If instead we read it in terms of concept formation, it sounds more plausible and points out that it is the same procedure – schematizing without a concept, presumably – the power of judgment engages in in concept formation and in taste. The dilemma that arises from this identification, however, is the same as before: Either there is enough similarity to justify the universality of judgments of taste from their affinity to concept formation – then the 'everything is beautiful' result threatens – or we block this result by insisting on the differences – then the question about the universality of judgments of taste seems to remain unanswered.

If we look at the deduction from the perspective of the *comparison model* (Section 7.3), we have to revise the so far unsuccessful reconstruction of the deduction. What is sufficient for judgments of taste (and for the pleasure of taste to occur) is not a registration, by the power of judgment, of reproductive free harmony but of *productive* free harmony of the faculties with respect to a given representation. The task of the deduction would then be to show that we are justified in supposing that the latter ability – subsuming representations under the relation of productive free harmony – is universal, even though it itself is not a necessary condition of cognition. This ability or capacity consists in the ability to tell, upon the occasion of a given conceptualized form, that this form could have been produced freely, that is, independently of the law of association that works with what is empirically given. Such comparison of the given form with a (counterfactual) free form allows us to say that the form of a cognized object is, despite its conceptual determination, able to exemplify

---

[27] Cf. also the First Introduction: In an aesthetic judgment of reflection, "the power of judgment ... perceives a relation of the two faculties of cognition which constitutes the *subjective, merely sensitive condition of the objective use of the power of judgment in general* (namely the agreement of those two faculties with each other)" (20: 223f.; my emphasis). It is hard to read this in a way that does not lead straight to the 'everything is beautiful' problem.

7.4 The Deduction of Judgments of Taste

productive free harmony – if there is a free form it agrees with. It furthermore allows us to understand that such free harmony is connected with 'cognition in general': what is relevant for productive free harmony is the fact *that* a manifold has been subsumed under a concept; nothing is supposed to depend on the specific concept that determines the manifold of the given object. Hence, we can consider this as an agreement with a concept 'in general,' or 'indeterminate which.' In the comparison of the given with a free form – and observing the restriction put on the deduction that only subjective conditions be considered – we do not appeal to the cognition of the object but refer to a merely subjective condition, the principle of the power of judgment alone – which informs the formation of concepts – as the constraint imposed on *any* concept whatsoever. If there is agreement of a given form with a (counterfactual) free form, the latter can then be said to stand under that principle as well, without itself having been determined by (or generated according to) a concept and without itself leading to the formation of a concept.

The comparison of forms is thus constrained in two ways: (i) the given form has to agree with a free form; this, in principle, excludes many given forms from being judged to be beautiful; (ii) the free form is constrained by the agreement with the cognized given form; this excludes 'fantastic,' idiosyncratic products of the free imagination ("original nonsense"; 5: 308; 319). Constraint (ii) implies that the free form is oriented towards cognition in general, that is, cognition of an object where the specific determinate concept is bracketed and the power of judgment's constraints on any concept are considered. In a successful comparison, the faculty of imagination, in its productive free operation, can be said to have been subsumed under the "condition that the understanding in general advance from intuitions to concepts" (5: 287). What it does "in its freedom" agrees with "the understanding in its lawfulness." Such agreement is, as far as we can tell, contingent; we can therefore say that even though the given form, subsumed under a determinate concept, itself is not purposive for the power of judgment (because the agreement of intuition and concept is not contingent), in the comparison with a (counterfactual) free form, the given form reveals itself to be subjectively purposive. This is, I suggest, the *Beziehung* of judgments of taste to the a priori principle of the reflecting power of judgments (20: 243).[28] Since this principle is the principle of concept formation, every form of an object that is subsumed under a

---

[28] To quote again: A judgment of taste "wins a claim to universality and necessity ... through the relation [*Beziehung*] of the subjective purposiveness of the given representation for the power of

concept *eo ipso* stands under the principle. In other words, the principle is 'built into' every relation of *unfree* harmony of imagination and understanding. The *aesthetically* relevant issue, however, is that *even productive free harmony* has the principle built into it because of the hybrid nature of this harmony, which depends, on the one hand and counterfactually, on the free operation of the imagination and, on the other hand, it requires conceptually subsumed forms of objects. And, as we have seen, only in this case of harmony a feeling of pleasure ensues that does not end with the application of a determinate concept. From this perspective, it is also immediately obvious that a natural object that agrees with a freely produced form and which we therefore judge to be beautiful indeed 'looks like art' (5: 306), insofar as the free form can be considered a product of art. In taste as well as in concept formation, the reflecting power of judgment "proceeds with given appearances ... not as it were merely mechanically, like an instrument under the direction of the understanding and the senses, but *artistically*" (20: 213f.).[29]

Despite my emphasis on the differences between reproductive and productive free harmony, there are also significant similarities since both types of free harmony are registered by the reflecting power of judgment as attainments of its aim. In concept formation, this is done under the presupposition of its principle that for all things concepts can be found. In taste it is done non-discursively, in feeling. In both cases, the power of judgment compares forms: in concept formation, the forms of *different* objects with the aim of finding agreement with respect to certain features, in taste, the given form of *one* object is compared with a (counterfactual) free form. And finally, in both cases, judgment's own principle plays a role as a constraint on the activity of comparing.

Within the revisionist framework I am proposing, we can now also address the question, raised in Chapter 6, about the relation of the principle of systematicity and the principle of taste. I there discussed the suggestion that both principles are versions of a 'general principle of purposiveness,' which I interpreted in the sense of a discursive and a non-discursive, or "intuitive," version. I took the latter characterization from a letter Kant wrote to Johann Friedrich Reichardt (15 October 1790) in which he summarized that "the ability to make judgments of taste ... is

---

judgment to that a priori principle of the power of judgment, of the purposiveness of nature in its empirical lawfulness in general."

[29] Even though Kant is discussing only concept formation at this place in the First Introduction, the application to taste, under the comparison model, is evident.

still founded on an a priori principle of judgment (albeit an intuitive and not a discursive one)" (11: 228). According to the *Logik*, intuitive principles "can be presented in intuition and are called axioms"; discursive principles, by contrast, "can only be expressed by concepts and can be called acroame" (9: 110).[30] The only plausible way to connect this with Kant's characterization of the principle of taste as an intuitive principle, I suggest, is to understand an intuitive principle in the aesthetic context as one that can be presented only in beautiful objects and whose satisfaction can only be registered in our response to beauty, that is, in feeling the pleasure of taste. Perhaps Kant intended to express this view in the Introduction to KU when he pointed out that "we can regard *natural beauty* as the *presentation* of the concept of formal (merely subjective) purposiveness [of nature]" (5: 193).[31]

We have seen that the "condition that the understanding in general advance from intuitions to concepts" (§ 35) turned out to be the *free* (not concept-determined) harmony of the faculties. Subsumption under this condition – the task of the reflecting power of judgment – can occur in two ways, corresponding to the two forms of free harmony: (i) subsumption under the guidance of the principle of systematicity (or the principle that for all things concepts can be found) in concept formation, which establishes reproductive free harmony, and (ii) subsumption in judgments of taste, which establishes productive free harmony. Only the latter mode of subsumption is sufficient for judgments of taste, though the former is also necessary for them. In (i), the power of judgment 'presupposes' that reproductive free harmony is possible for every thing in nature; in (ii), the occurrence of productive free harmony is merely registered in the pleasure of taste. The non-discursive capacity to do so is taste. Taste can be said to 'contain a principle' of comparison (in this respect similar to the principle of systematicity) but since the relevant comparisons here involve the productively free imagination, it is an 'intuitive,' rather than discursive, principle. Free harmony, understood merely as harmony without a given concept, before the specification of the two ways of subsumption, is indeed a 'general principle of purposiveness.'

---

[30] In KrV, he correspondingly assigns "intuitive certainty" to the first two groups of the principles of the understanding, which are constitutive for intuition, including the Axioms of Intuition, which presumably are the axioms of geometry that can be presented in pure intuition of space. The other two groups, the Analogies and the Postulates of Experience, are capable only of "discursive certainty" (A 162).

[31] See Section 8. 4 for further comments on this quotation.

The subsumption in (ii), as I argued in Chapter 5, has as its only criterion of success the feeling of pleasure, while in cases of subsumption under a discursive principle there typically are criteria other than feeling. Under the interpretation of productive free harmony, I suggested, this relation of the faculties is nevertheless *also* always subsumed under the *discursive* principle of judgment, the principle that concepts can always be found or the principle of systematicity, in virtue of the fact that the (counterfactual) free form agrees with a conceptually determined form. This agreement is a necessary, though not sufficient, condition for productive free harmony.[32]

7.5 Problems with an 'Intuitive Principle': Mistaken Judgments of Taste

In the "Remark" attached to the deduction of judgments of taste, Kant explains some of the difficulties that result from the fact that these judgments rely on an 'intuitive,' non-discursive principle. In such a judgment, he repeats, we "subsume ... the given object under" the "subjective conditions of the power of judgment." This subsumption, however, "has unavoidable difficulties that do not pertain to the logical power of judgment (because in the latter one subsumes under concepts, but in the aesthetic power of judgment one subsumes under a relation that is merely a matter of sensation, that of the imagination and the understanding reciprocally attuned to each other in the represented form of the object)" (5: 290f., where "sensation" has to be understood as "feeling"). According to the discussion of § 35, this should be understood as: we discover or identify (through comparison with a counterfactual free form) the actual relation of the faculties in the cognition of the object as a case of (productive) free harmony in which the faculties are 'attuned to each other' in the sense that the *free* imagination, without constraint, operates in harmony with the understanding. The holding of the relation of free harmony, Kant emphasizes here again, can *only* be detected in feeling.

The absence of 'logical' criteria for successful subsumption Kant takes to raise the possibility of 'incorrect' subsumptions: under the specified

---

[32] To this extent, my proposal agrees with Allison's view of the deduction: "subsumability under ... 'the subjective conditions for the possibility of cognition as such' ... is merely a necessary and not also a sufficient condition for something to be judged beautiful. In order for the latter to be warranted, an object must not simply conform to ... these conditions; it must do so in a certain way, namely in free play" (2001: 187). The difference is lies in my construal of how the 'free play' should be understood.

7.5 Problems with an 'Intuitive Principle'

conditions, "subsumption can easily be deceptive" (5: 291), that is, mistaken judgments of taste can be made, which would explain certain cases of aesthetic disagreement. How can such "deceptive" subsumptions occur? There are at least two possibilities:

(1) We mistake our experience of pleasure in an object for the pleasure of taste, while in fact we are feeling the object's agreeableness or its usefulness. That is, we erroneously claim, in our judgment, that our actual pleasure has the characteristics of the pleasure of taste (in particular, universal validity), while our feeling does not indicate the occurrence of free harmony and cannot make a valid claim to universality (for instance, it might actually be an 'aesthetic judgment of sense').

(2) Within the comparison model, a further possibility arises, even though it is perhaps not completely clear that these cases should be labelled 'mistaken' judgments of taste. Suppose a subject makes such a correct judgment about an object. Another subject disagrees by saying something like 'I cannot see the beauty of this object.' (Notice that she is not expressing a judgment of ugliness, but merely of 'non-beauty' or indifference.) There is disagreement in the sense that one party is able to experience the pleasure of taste, while the other is not. We can diagnose the second subject's indifference as a failure to detect a relation of (productive) free harmony because she is unable to identify a productive free form that would correspond to the given form of the object. Her imagination, for some reason, cannot find, among the candidates for free forms, the one that agrees with the object's form. (More on this possibility below.)

In the "Remark," Kant plausibly insists that violations of the principle (by mistaken judgments of taste, i.e., deceptive subsumptions) are not to be blamed on the principle whose authority – like normative authority in general – is independent of such incidents. They concern "only the incorrect application to a particular case of the authority that a law gives us, by which the authority in general is not suspended" (5: 290n; cf. also 5: 291). But even if we grant this as plausible, the possibility of indifference, outlined in (2), raises worries, if not about the authority of the principle of judgment, then at least about my 'revisionist' reconstruction of the deduction, which suggested the diagnosis of (2).

In this reconstruction there is no productive free harmony without cognition of an object (even though what is relevant is only cognition in general). But the satisfaction of the conditions of cognition, though necessary, is not sufficient for free harmony. What has to be added to the necessary condition is the comparison with a (counterfactual) free form, which is the task of aesthetic reflective judgment or taste. It is the pleasure of taste, with its assumed characteristics, that indicates that we indeed have this capacity. I say 'indicates' because the task of the deduction, of course, is to show that we are *justified* in presuming that everybody (every human capable of cognition) possesses what is required for experiencing the pleasure of taste and for making judgments of taste. Those reconstructions of the deduction that appeal at this point to the 'subjective conditions' necessary for cognition have no further problem to solve – except, of course, the 'everything is beautiful' embarrassment. In the revisionist picture of the deduction, however, reference to those necessary conditions is not enough; I also have to justify the claim that everybody has the ability to make comparisons of given with (counterfactual) free forms. It is plausible that all cognizers are able to compare forms of objects for the purpose of concept formation and are thus capable of detecting reproductive free harmony. But this does not obviously imply that they can also compare forms with (even only counterfactually) productively free forms. Kant perhaps assumes this, for instance, when he says that the "imagination (as a productive cognitive faculty) . . . transform[s]" experiences we have had, without being bound by the law of association, "in accordance with principles that lie higher in reason. . .; in this we feel our freedom from the law of association" (5: 314). But he makes this statement in the sections of the KU that deal with *genius*.

The notion of a productively free form indeed insinuates the notion of genius, a special talent to create forms that are free in the sense that they are not reproducing what is given (presently or in the past) but 'new' and 'original.' So it might seem that the ability to detect that a given form agrees with a free form involves the special and not universally shared talent of genius. But this is somewhat misleading. The case of taste, as Kant emphasizes, is different in that taste is not creative but 'passive'; it is judging something that is given. The subject that makes a judgment of taste does not have to create an 'original' form but has to check whether a given form is such that her productive imagination could have generated this form, independently of the law of association and what is given. This requires the employment of productively free imagination; but it is not quite the same as the talent of genius.[33]

---

[33] Cf. Dobe's interpretation of taste as the "disposition" of the imagination to agree with the understanding. The "principle of taste," according to her view, is "our shared cognitive nature

7.5 Problems with an 'Intuitive Principle'

This qualification may mitigate the problem but the fact remains that the imagination has to be able to produce 'candidate' free forms in order to check for their agreement with the given form – a procedure that has some similarity with the 'testing out' of rules of apprehension in the case of concept formation. Although the similarity confirms that in both cases the power of reflecting judgment is at work, one may still have doubts about whether this ability can be assumed in every subject. A further mitigating factor could be found in the form of the argument in § 38, which commentators have not always paid attention to.[34] The section starts out with a *conditional* statement: "If it is admitted that in a pure judgment of taste the satisfaction in the object is combined with the mere judging of its form"; under this condition, we can conclude that if a subject experiences this kind of pleasure, then she is justified in demanding everybody's concurrence in her judgment, that is, her pleasure "will allow of being rightly expected of everyone" (5: 289*). The meaning of the condition is perhaps ambiguous, but if we read it as 'if somebody experiences a pleasure that satisfies the specified characteristics' and conclude that this pleasure can make a claim to universality, then it is clear that nothing follows about the correctness of the deduction or about the principle it appeals to, if another person, under the same circumstances, does not feel this pleasure and therefore does not agree with the first person's judgment of taste. As has often been pointed out, the result of the deduction should not be understood as a prediction, a claim that everybody *will* agree with somebody's pure judgment of taste. One possible diagnosis of such a case surely can be that the subject who does not experience the relevant pleasure has not yet developed the capacity of taste, the ability to make comparisons of given and free forms. It does not follow that, under these circumstances, the other subject's judgment cannot be universally valid.

In any case, the attribution of the capacity to make comparisons of given forms with (counterfactual) free forms to every cognizer is an essential but not obviously justified ingredient of the revisionist interpretation of the deduction. In the KrV, Kant emphasizes that "productive imagination" is a capacity required for the possibility of cognition (A 123/B 152). It is distinguished from reproductive imagination in that it is not dependent on what is empirically given; it has spontaneity to the extent that it is the

---

insofar as our imaginations are *predisposed* to be attuned to our understandings' need for unity" (2018: 66). Interestingly, she initially supports this reference to our 'cognitive nature' with what Kant says about *genius* – that is, the freely productive imagination – at (5: 344).

[34] Rind emphasizes this feature of the argument (2002: 45).

effect of the understanding on inner sense (B 152) and in its a priori operation it produces the schemata of the categories. There is also an empirical employment of productive imagination, which would be the employment relevant in our context, since "the image [*Bild*] is a product of the empirical faculty of productive imagination" (A 141/B 181).[35] I leave it open whether such remarks provide sufficient support for the claim needed in the revisionist interpretation of the deduction, viz., that the capacity for taste depends only on universally shared conditions.[36]

It is perhaps not altogether surprising that in the Analytic Kant can only summarily refer to the imagination in its freedom. The topic is addressed in more detail in the sections of the KU on art and in the Dialectic. Whatever can be said about it will have to import ingredients that are, as it were, foreign to the Analytic: ideas of reason and the supersensible, for instance, the rational concept "of a general ground for the subjective purposiveness of nature for the power of judgment" (5: 340). From this changed perspective (compared to the Analytic), the relation of the principle of systematicity and the principle of taste also can be characterized in different terms, as Kant indicates in the First Introduction: the deduction of the former principle "already" gives us "a ground for ascribing to nature in its particular laws a principle of purposiveness," and it is therefore "always possible and permissible, if experience shows us purposive forms in its products, for us to ascribe this to the same ground as that on which the first may rest," even though "this ground itself may lie in the supersensible" (20: 218). Thus, the connection between the principles is that they share a supersensible ground.[37] Similarly, later in the text, Kant holds that the distinguishing feature of judgments of taste is that they "relate sensible intuitions to an idea of nature, whose lawfulness cannot be understood without their relation to a supersensible substratum" (20: 247). Given the role Kant assigns to the power of judgment as a mediator between the understanding and (practical) reason, the appeal to a connection with the supersensible is to be expected.

7.6 "Taste as a Kind of *sensus communis*"

Taste as a capacity to judge that is guided by an "intuitive principle" is also characterized by Kant as a (or a "kind of") common sense. It is a *sense*

---

[35] On this, cf. especially the *Anthropologie* (7: 167; 174–77).
[36] I shall return to the issues mentioned here and in the next paragraph in Chapter 8.
[37] The beginning of § 61 (5: 359) repeats this view about the relation of the principles but does not mention the supersensible ground.

7.6 *"Taste as a Kind of sensus communis"* 153

because it judges through *feeling* rather than through concepts, as does the "common understanding" (5: 238). The "subjective principle" that underlies judgments of taste "determines what pleases or displeases only through feeling and not through concepts, but yet with universal validity. Such a principle, however, could only be regarded as a *common sense*" (5: 238). This sense is to be distinguished from other senses ("external" senses) that allow us to receive stimuli from what is empirically given; instead, Kant says, taste as a common sense is "the effect of the free play of our cognitive powers." In light of my interpretation of the free play in terms of the comparison model, the aesthetic *sensus communis* is thus the ability to detect a relation of free harmony of the faculties, that is, to subsume a given relation (on occasion of a given object) under the aim of the reflecting power of judgment in a way that is registered as pleasure.

Long before the deduction of judgments of taste Kant discusses in § 21 the question of whether we are justified in presupposing the existence of a common sense. Since § 20 ended with the result that only under such a presupposition "can judgments of taste be made," the question of § 21 seems immediately relevant to the possibility of such judgments; and the conclusion of this section – the existence of a common sense "must be able to be assumed with good reason" (5: 239) – has therefore often been understood as a 'first,' or alternative deduction of judgments of taste. Such an interpretation is further motivated by Kant's reference to different "proportions" of the cognitive powers that depend "on the difference of the objects that are given. Nevertheless," he continues, "there must be one [proportion] in which this inner relationship [of the faculties] is optimal for the animation of both powers of the mind ... with respect to cognition (of given objects) in general" (5: 238f.). Indeed, the relation of the faculties that is "optimal" for their "animation" sounds very much like a reference to their free play.[38]

With other commentators,[39] I think that it is mistaken to understand § 21's 'deduction' of a common sense as an attempt at a justification of judgments of taste. Apart from the fact that taste is not mentioned explicitly in this section, a deduction ahead of § 38 would be an extraordinary architectonic oddity. More important, however, is that Kant himself denies that the "optimal proportion" of the faculties – which has often been taken to refer to a relation of the faculties that differs from their

---

[38] For interpretations of § 21 as a deduction (and perhaps superior to the official deduction), see, e.g., Ameriks (2003 [1982]: 285–93) and Rind (2002).
[39] Cf. especially Allison (2001: ch. 7) and the earlier discussion by Fricke (1990: 168ff.).

relation in cognition – is not specific to taste at all: "The proportion of these cognitive faculties that is required for taste is also requisite for the common and healthy understanding that one may presuppose in everyone" (5: 293). It would seem that Kant is identifying the "optimal proportion" – supposedly optimal for the free play – with the proportion required by all 'ordinary' cognition. That we have "good reason" to presuppose a common sense is therefore not a result that pertains to taste in particular; it is a more general claim.

The argument of § 21 aims to show that we are entitled to assume a common sense from the communicability of cognitions. That "cognitions and judgments" must be universally communicable is entailed, according to Kant's opening move, by the rejection of skepticism: The skeptic denies that our representations correspond to objects; if our thoughts were indeed not communicable, they could not have reference to objects.[40] Communicability of cognitions, furthermore, requires that the "mental state" of the cognizer, "the disposition [*Stimmung*[41]] of the cognitive powers for a cognition in general, and indeed that proportion [of the powers] which is suitable for making cognition out of a representation ... must be capable of being universally communicated" (5: 238). If we grant this and don't worry about what Kant means by this proportion, we might also accept that the disposition of the faculties "has a different proportion depending on the difference of the objects that are given." The decisive move is now this: among the different proportions "there must be one [that is] ... optimal for the animation of both powers of the mind (the one through the other) with respect to cognition (of given objects) in general; and this disposition cannot be determined except through the feeling (not by concepts)." From the earlier steps, it is supposed to follow that the feeling that indicates the proportion that is optimal for cognition must itself be communicable. But a universally communicable feeling presupposes the existence of a common sense.

Thus, Kant is trying to infer from the communicability of cognitions to the communicability of the feeling that is involved in cognition; and this gives us "good reason" to assume a common sense "as the necessary condition of the universal communicability of our cognition" (5: 239). This inference, it would seem, can work only if the relevant feeling is the

---

[40] Cf. (A 194): "A play of representations that would not be related to any object at all." See Guyer (1997: 256–64) and Rind (2002) for criticism of the steps in Kant's argument.
[41] This could also, perhaps more appropriately, be translated as 'tuning' or 'attunement' (see the Pluhar translation).

one that indicates the proportion of the faculties that is necessary for any cognition. If the 'optimal proportion' referred to the one associated with the 'free play,' the conclusion would follow only if we accepted the implausible view that the free play itself is a necessary condition for all cognition – in which case every object we cognize should be beautiful.

I suspect that what makes it initially tempting for commentators to identify the optimal proportion (which can only be determined through feeling) with the free play or free harmony of the faculties is that they assume – as I did – that 'ordinary' cognition is not accompanied by feeling at all. And under this assumption, it would seem that Kant's reference to a proportion of the faculties that can only be felt must indicate the pleasure of taste – in which case the argument fails to establish its conclusion.

Alternatively, Allison and Fricke[42] suggested that the argument aims to establish, in line with Kant's own conclusion, a common sense that is required for *all* cognition, not a specifically aesthetic common sense. The feeling as the only indicator of the proportion optimal for cognition is then understood as a feeling that registers the successful subsumption of an intuited manifold under a concept or rule. That there must be such a feeling, Allison claims, follows from Kant's argument in KrV that there cannot be rules for judging that something falls under a rule, on pain of infinite regress: "the subsumability of an intuition under a concept [therefore] must be immediately seen, that is, 'felt.'"[43] This interpretive strategy is able to make fairly straightforward sense of § 21 and avoids the architectonic oddity of a first deduction of judgments of taste long before § 38. But the price to be paid is that we have to accept that even cases of what I called the *unfree* harmony of imagination and understanding (that is, the subsumption of intuitions under available concepts, or concept application) are associated with feeling as the only indicator of success.

I have rejected this view because it does not seem to agree with (what I take to be) Kant's general theory of pleasure. Indeed, Kant himself seems to rule out Allison's suggestion in § 40, entitled "On taste as a kind of *sensus communis*": "*only* where the imagination in its freedom arouses the understanding ... is the representation communicated, not as thought, but as the inner feeling of a purposive state of mind" (5: 296; my emphasis). This is explicitly not the case in 'ordinary' cognition, where "the agreement of the two powers of the mind is lawful, under the

---

[42] Allison (2001: 154), following Fricke (1991: 171).
[43] Allison (2001: 154), referring to (A 132f.). Kant himself, however, does not mention feeling at this point.

constraint of determinate concepts" (5: 295). This distinction is in line with the general theory that only the contingent attainment of a faculty aim is manifested in pleasure; in other words, the communication of *thoughts* (cognitions) requires the optimal proportion of the faculties in a state of unfree harmony; the communication of *feeling*, however, requires their free harmony, where the proportion is the *same* as in the case of cognition: "the proportion of these cognitive faculties that is required for taste is also requisite for the common and healthy understanding that one may presuppose in everyone" (5: 293). This sameness of proportion, of course, is an immediate consequence of the comparison model.

But what about the feeling referred to in § 21 if we agree that what is at issue is a common sense that is tied to cognition? I suggest that this can be brought in line with the Kantian view on pleasure if we understand it not as a feeling associated with concept application (unfree harmony) but with the pleasure of concept formation. I explained this as the 'free' satisfaction of the interest of the power of judgment. It is free in the sense that the imagination schematizes without (yet) being guided by the concept-to-be-formed. What is sought in this process is "the proportion [of the faculties] which is suitable for making cognition out of a representation (whereby an object is given to us)." What is given to us is a manifold of intuition, which, together with a 'fitting' concept, establishes cognition of an object. As long as the schematization has not resulted in the sought-for concept, the attunement of imagination and understanding indeed can be said to have "a different proportion depending on the difference of the objects that are given"; the "optimal" proportion is the one that the faculties have when a concept has been formed and can be applied and this proportion is associated with pleasure as the only indicator of success – no concept can provide the criterion.

As we know from the Introduction, this feeling is not experienced anymore once we have the relevant concepts available for application:

> We no longer detect any noticeable pleasure in the comprehensibility of nature and the unity of its division into genera and species, by means of which alone empirical concepts are possible ... but it must certainly have been there in its time, and only because the most common experience would not be possible without it has it gradually become mixed up with mere cognition and is no longer specially noticed. (5: 187)

The pleasure of concept formation, we also recall, is not to be identified with the pleasure of taste, even though they both are tied to the free harmony of the faculties. But while the former is based on the imagination's freedom in the sense of freedom from conceptual constraint, the latter is associated with the imagination operating not only free from concepts but, in addition, free of the task of reproducing what is empirically given.

If this distinction is granted, it is clear that § 21 establishes "good reason" for assuming a common sense that is necessarily involved in cognition (through concept formation) but not a common sense that could be identified with taste. This 'limitation' of the argument of § 21 is reflected in Kant's remarks in the following section. He wonders here – among other hints at indecision concerning taste as a common sense – "whether taste is an original and natural faculty, or only an idea of one that is yet to be acquired" (5: 240). This indecision is incompatible with the view that the relevant (namely, aesthetic) common sense has already been established in § 21 and rather seems to indicate that with respect to *taste*, the presupposition of a common sense has yet to be justified. This is the task of the official deduction in § 38.

7.7 Conclusion

In my reconstruction of the deduction, the pleasure of taste derives its claim to universal validity from the contingent agreement of a given form, subsumed under a concept of the object, with a form that the imagination could have produced freely. The two essential ingredients in judging the object in taste thus are cognition of the object and a (counterfactual) free form for comparison. But even though a concept of the object is required for cognition, the judgment of taste is not determined by this concept and hence cannot be 'proved': it cannot be established as the conclusion of an inference from conceptual premises. The way in which cognition of the object plays a role in taste is rather as 'cognition in general'; what matters is only *that* there is such a conceptually determined cognition but the specific concept is irrelevant. This is how I understand Kant's claim that the "ground" of the judgment of taste consists "only in the subsumption of the imagination itself ... under the condition that the understanding in general advance from intuitions to concepts" (5: 287). The relevant condition is the principle of systematicity that guides the formation of concepts by presupposing that nature is purposive for concept formation. Every cognition of an object, therefore, stands under this principle insofar as the concept of the object was formed so that it fits into the overall system of concepts of genera and species. The decisive point, in my view, is that in the case where a given form agrees with a free form, the latter then also stands under the principle, even though, as a free form, it was not produced under the guidance of a concept of the understanding. A judgment of taste that expresses such agreement therefore inherits the justification of its claim to universality from 'cognition in general.' It is, in this sense, a judgment that seems "as if it were objective," like a cognitive judgment (5: 281).

The ground of the pleasure of taste in some representation, accordingly, is not the representation's satisfying the interest of the power of judgment that is expressed in the principle of systematicity, that is, the interest in reproductive free harmony (that is the 'long forgotten' pleasure of concept formation), but rather the satisfaction of the interest in productive free harmony. Nevertheless, if we register such harmony in the pleasure of taste, the universality of the pleasure is bestowed on it "through the relation [*Beziehung*] ... to that a priori principle of the power of judgment", that is, the principle of systematicity (20: 243).

According to the Introduction, the reflecting power of judgment is the mediating link between the faculties of understanding and of (practical) reason. In the aesthetic part of the KU, however, the focus is on judgment's role in mediating between the imagination and the understanding. This role, in turn, depends on and requires the presupposition of the (subjective) purposiveness of nature, the principle of systematicity, that is supposed to make concept formation possible. But this very same concept of the purposiveness of nature also functions in the completion of the system of powers of the mind, as we saw in Chapter 2: it provides the link between the understanding and reason insofar as it applies what is originally a concept of reason (of a purpose, attached to a will) to nature (without assuming a will).

8
The Imagination in Its Freedom

In my interpretation of the Analytic of the Beautiful, the notion of the free harmony of the imagination and the understanding played the key role as the aim or interest of the reflecting power of judgment. I explained the possibility of such harmony with the comparison model, according to which the given form of an object is compared to forms that the imagination could have produced freely, independently of the concept that is applied to the given object. The ability to detect agreement or disagreement of the actual and counterfactual forms is taste, which crucially involves the counterfactual free operation of the imagination. At no point in the reconstruction did the notion of a 'free play' of both faculties figure. In this chapter, I discuss why I find it desirable to focus on the 'free harmony' rather than the 'free play' and to what extent the former notion can indeed substitute for the latter. I then supplement the comparison model with a more fine-grained characterization of what the (productively) free operation of the imagination consists. This characterization has to be extracted from the sections in KU about fine art (§§ 43–54), especially the doctrines of genius and aesthetic ideas, and the 'Dialectic of the aesthetic power of judgment.' I also show that the comparison model, which so far presupposed that the form of an object is given, can be applied to artistic creation, where the object is not given but has to be produced.

8.1 Problems with the 'Free Play' of the Faculties

The free harmony of the faculties, on my suggestion, involves the free operation of the imagination, but there is apparently no sense in which there is a "mutual enlivening" of the faculties that Kant wants to characterize as their free play and that he occasionally (though not in the KU) compared to a "dance" of two partners.[1] On the interpretation developed

---
[1] See (24: 707; 710), quoted by Henrich (1992: 53) and Allison (2001: 48).

so far, there does not seem to be such an intimate interaction at all: each faculty operates on its own, the understanding subsuming the given form under a concept of the object and the imagination, besides providing the manifold for subsumtion, generates free forms, independently of the understanding and, furthermore, independently of the empirically given material. Perhaps one could say that the understanding stimulates the imagination to engage in its free production so that the reflecting power of judgment (or taste) can find agreement or disagreement of the forms. But there does not seem to be a sense in which the imagination "reciprocally" stimulates the understanding, which, as it were, has already done its business by applying a concept to the given manifold.

An interpretation that ignores the free play in favour of free harmony finds some support in the structure of the KU up to the sections dealing with art (§§ 43ff.). The free play – in contrast to free harmony – does not figure at all in the published Introduction, nor in the deduction (§ 38). It is, somewhat abruptly, introduced in § 9 and then appears a few more times before § 43.[2] In my reconstructions of the arguments so far, I have avoided using the term and to get along with 'free harmony' instead, as explicated in the comparison model. But since the notion of the free play becomes prominent in the sections on art, its comparatively low profile in the Analytic is certainly not enough reason to ignore it. In fact, these sections are precisely the ones that inform us in more detail about the free operations of the imagination.

It is generally accepted that the freedom in the play of the faculties pertains in the first place to the imagination, although Kant occasionally writes about the freedom of the understanding and the freedom of the power of judgment.[3] The term free play is also suggestive in that it evokes a pleasurable activity – especially when it is opposed to 'business,' a contrast Kant often employs (cf. Section 3.1). Pleasure, however, indicates purposiveness and a frequent question that is raised about the free play, as mutual stimulation of the faculties, concerns the sense in which it could possibly be understood as purposive for cognition in general.[4] If the free play is understood as the imagination stimulating the understanding to produce

---

[2] Wachter (2006: 25–29; 93–98) has argued that in many of these places 'free play,' in the sense of a mutual stimulation of imagination and understanding, can be replaced without loss with 'free harmony.' He points out that, within the Analytic of the Beautiful, it is mainly in the General Remark (5: 240–44) that the free play becomes important.
[3] Cf. (5: 241) and (5: 270).
[4] E.g., Sonderegger (2000: 360–62); Kern (2000: 50–57); Wachter (2006); Menke (2008: 97).

8.1 Problems with the 'Free Play' of the Faculties

many concepts,[5] perhaps there is a sense in which this is purposive for cognition – though it is not clear why this would be a pleasurable activity. After all, by assumption, none of these concepts quite 'fits' the manifold, that is, with none of them harmony is established.

A related issue arises in the "General Remark," appended to the Analytic of the Beautiful: On the one hand, Kant insists that a certain irregularity of form is required for the free play; only some degree of disorderliness can keep us from getting bored (5: 242f.). On the other hand, he also claims that regularity of form is a "*conditio sine qua non*" for concept formation and application (5: 242). These requirements are clearly at a tension with each other. It is not clear how our delight in irregularity can be understood as purposive for our cognitive interests.[6]

As I showed in Section 3.1, these tensions have predecessors in Kant's notes and lectures on taste from the 1770s. I distinguished in those texts the coexistence of two models of the origin of the pleasure of taste. According to the *facilitation* view, the forms of beautiful objects are especially conducive to the aims of our cognitive faculties and therefore pleasing: "Whatever facilitates [*erleichtert*] and expands sensory intuition, pleases us according to objective laws that hold for everybody" (25: 378 [*Anthropologie Parow*]). Regular features – symmetry, harmony, clarity, and comprehensibility – assist in our "grasp[ing] the object without effort" (24: 353 [*Logik Philippi*]). In contrast to this model, the *stimulation* view found in these texts emphasizes the origin of pleasure in a heightened 'movement' of the powers of the mind. The talent for inducing such stimulation was called 'spirit' (also 'genius'); its vehicle were 'ideas' by which the understanding and sensibility were set into a state of "harmonious [*einstimige*] animation" (15: 708; R 1486) or free play (15: 364; R 817). For the stimulation view, regular figures – like the "pepper gardens" of Sumatra (5: 243) – tend to be aesthetically inert or even displeasing since they do not provide the escape from boredom or

---

[5] Guyer labels such interpretations "multicognitive" (2005: 84–87). A paradigmatic statement is given by Allison: "the imagination in its free play stimulates the understanding by occasioning it to entertain fresh conceptual possibilities, while, conversely, the imagination, under the general direction of the understanding, strives to conceive new patterns of order" (2001: 171).

[6] The problem seems to be related to the traditional view of beauty, which, as indistinctly perceived perfection, needs both unity and variety; but it remained unclear how much of each was required. Cf., for instance, Budd's gloss that the pleasure of taste is based on an object's form in which "the manifold combined by the imagination is both rich enough to entertain the imagination in its combinatory activity and such as to facilitate the understanding's detection of regularity within it" (2001: 258).

inactivity that the mind needs in order to feel pleasure; what offers pleasant stimulation is the irregularity of English gardens (5: 242), the "beau désordre."

I suggest in the following sections that these problems with the notion of the free play can be resolved in the comparison model if we supplement it with a more fine-grained characterization of what the (productively) free operation of the imagination consists in. Such a characterization is in any case overdue and it will allow us to see in the free play a division of labour, as it were, between the facilitation aspect – the free harmony as purposive for cognition in general – and the stimulation aspect that explicates the sense in which the faculties 'enliven' each other. In my interpretation, it is the former aspect, the contingent agreement of a given form with a free one, that is responsible for the pleasure of taste, while the latter aspect describes the production of such free forms in terms of a stimulation of the understanding to generate a multitude of concepts. Contrary to the old stimulation model, however, this proliferation of 'not-quite-fitting' concepts has nothing to do with the pleasure of taste itself (see Section 8.2.1).[7]

8.2 The Freedom of the Imagination, Genius, and Taste

How can the imagination generate a form on its own, without guidance of the understanding? As far as I can see, the only place where Kant says anything detailed about this achievement of the imagination is to be found in the sections on art.[8] These remarks are prefaced by the already quoted phrase from the "General Remark" (5:240): the imagination is playing freely in inventions, "*im Dichten.*" Kant deals with poetry and other forms of artistic invention in § 49 where the doctrine of "aesthetic ideas" is presented, together with "genius" as "the faculty of aesthetic ideas"

---

[7] Guyer (2005) has analyzed the problems with interpreting the free play of the faculties in great detail and has come to the conclusion that only a "metacognitive" understanding of the play can be held consistently. This view claims that in the free play we experience something over and above of what is needed for cognition of an object, a surplus. When we experience beauty, we feel "a degree or type of harmony between the imagination and understanding ... that goes beyond whatever is necessary for ordinary cognition." In this case, the imagination produces "more unity and coherence than is required for it [an object of a certain kind] to be a member of that kind" (99). In the interpretation I suggest, there is indeed a surplus in harmony. But it is not the manifold itself that has greater harmony than is required for cognition; the surplus is rather constituted by the agreement of a given form with a free form. Such agreement is indeed not required for cognition.

[8] Compare also the sections of the *Anthropologie* that deal with "free" or "productive imagination" (7: 176–82; 240f.).

8.2 The Freedom of the Imagination, Genius, and Taste

(5: 344), a talent that "displays itself ... in the exposition or expression of aesthetic ideas" (5: 317).[9]

Kant's introduction of these doctrines in the context of the *production* of art corresponds in many ways to the theory of the free play, which characterizes the *reception* or judging of beauty in nature and art.[10] In the Analytic of the Beautiful, the judgment of taste's claim to the "necessity of the ascent of all" was described as based on the assumption that the judgment "is regarded as an example of a universal rule that one cannot produce [or state]" (5: 237). Locutions like this were meant to somehow reconcile the view that there cannot be necessity without a rule and the basic feature of such judgment, that they cannot be derived from determinate concepts or rules. Although Kant intended the Deduction to provide a "resolution of these logical peculiarities" (5: 281), he took up the task of reconciliation again, much later, in the 'Antinomy of taste' where he has recourse to a concept of reason (instead of the understanding), an idea, which is supposed to allow us to see that judgments of taste are, after all, based on a concept but since this concept is "indeterminable," it does not make them capable of proof (see below in this section).

With respect to the production of artistic beauty, the analogous problem arises in the form of a conflict between an artwork being, by definition, the product of an intentional activity – an activity guided by concepts of the product – and the rejection of concepts and rules for beauty:

> We can generally say, whether it is the beauty of nature or of art that is at issue: that is beautiful which pleases in the mere judging (neither in sensation nor through a concept). Now art always has a determinate intention of producing something. If however this [something] were a mere

---

[9] Crawford (1982) seems to understand the passages at (5:240f.) and in § 49 as describing *different* activities of the productive imagination. Admittedly, one could understand the reference to "Dichten" as merely an example for the free operations of the imagination that is not meant to give a general characterizations of such operations. But since I cannot see what one could say about other free modes of the imagination, I interpret the reference in the general sense, as *pars pro toto*.

Several commentators have suggested, however, that the appropriate general characterization of the free imagination should be phrased as follows: the imagination in its freedom generates forms that are ideal or most suitable for cognition; a beautiful given form, on this view, would be one that our faculties would have designed with the aim of ideal suitability for cognition (a version of the old facilitation view). See Prauss (1981), Vogelman (2018), and Williams (2021). I have voiced suspicion about the notion of differing degrees of suitability for cognition in my interpretation of § 21 (ch. 7.6). Furthermore, I do not quite see in what sense the imagination could be said to operate *freely* according to this view: optimality of a form for *cognition* would seem to require incorporating the needs of the understanding into the free procedure of the imagination.

[10] See, e.g., Zammito: Kant's "architectonic intention was to read the production of beauty in art as structurally homologous with the appreciation of beauty" (1992: 143). Cf. also Fricke (1990: 125f.).

sensation ... that is supposed to be accompanied with pleasure, then this product would please, in the judging, only by means of the feeling of sense. If the intention were aimed at the production of a determinate object, then, if it were achieved through art, the object would please only through concepts .... Thus the purposiveness in the product of beautiful art, although it is certainly intentional, must nevertheless not seem intentional; i.e., beautiful art must be regarded as nature, although of course one is aware of it as art. (5: 306f.)

And furthermore, although "every art presupposes rules" insofar as it is an intentional activity, "the concept of beautiful art ... does not allow the judgment concerning the beauty of its product to be derived from any sort of rule that has a concept for its determining ground, and thus has as its ground a concept of how it is possible." The artist, therefore, or, as Kant says, art, "cannot itself think up the rule in accordance with which it is to bring its product into being" (5: 307).

Even though this seems to imply that art after all *cannot* be an intentional, purpose-directed activity – which would contradict its very definition – Kant's way out of this dilemma is to claim that "nature in the subject (and by means of the disposition [*Stimmung*] of its faculties) must give the rule to art" (5: 307).[11] The rule that cannot be stated, which underlies the judgment of taste's claim to necessity, appears here, in the discussion of the productive side of art, as 'nature's' own rule that is somehow not accessible to the artist's conscious awareness. Beautiful art must be regarded as if it were nature by the spectator (5: 306f.) and it is, in the genial artist, produced by nature in a way that uses the artist's conscious intentions only as a vehicle. Such artists – geniuses – have a special "talent (of the imagination)" that allows them, in the example of poetry, to "approximate a presentation of concepts of reason (of intellectual ideas)" in intuition, "by means of an imagination that emulates the precedent of reason in attaining to a maximum" (5: 314).

If this is accepted as a characterization of what genial artists aim at, it is immediately clear that they are trying to 'approximate' something that is, in principle, impossible to attain: ideas, as indeterminable concepts, cannot have sensible presentations and we therefore cannot have cognition of their objects, as the first *Critique* had shown. Thus, understanding the artist's activity must hang on the meaning Kant gives the term 'to approximate a presentation' of those ideas that artists intend to express in their work. The

---

[11] Cf. also: "In products of genius nature (that of the subject), not a deliberate end, gives the rule to art (the production of the beautiful)" (5: 344).

8.2 The Freedom of the Imagination, Genius, and Taste

first step in clarifying the meaning is to distinguish two modes of presentation of concepts in general. In § 49, Kant labels them 'logical' and 'aesthetic' presentation; later, in § 59, he makes a corresponding distinction between 'direct,' or schematic, and 'indirect,' or symbolic, presentation of concepts (see Section 8.2.4).

Notice the correspondence between the Dialectic's resolution of the antinomy with the help of indeterminable concepts – which base the judgment of taste's claim to universality on a concept whose indeterminability secures their 'as if' subjectivity – and the resolution of the 'paradox of art' through the introduction of ideas (as the ultimate subject matter of artworks) that secure a connection with the artist's intention and a special talent for their indirect presentation that cannot be governed by rules because of the indeterminability of the concepts.[12] In analogy to the KrV, ideas should play a role in the KU only in the Dialectic, not in the Analytic. They are therefore only introduced officially in the antinomy of taste and only afterwards does Kant develop the doctrine of their symbolization in § 59. But it is clear that they are already referred to in § 49, in the investigation of the work of genius, even though the focus there is on their 'counterpart,' the aesthetic ideas, as products of the imagination, not of reason.

The questions that are of primary interest in light of my interpretation of the free harmony of the faculties are:

1. In which sense is the imagination free in the production of aesthetic ideas?
2. How does Kant's analysis of the productive talent of the imagination relate to the non-productive or receptive capacity of taste? And relatedly: If the pleasure of taste, as I suggested, consists in the *contingent* agreement of a free form with a given form, how can this contingency condition be satisfied when an artist intentionally produces a form that is designed to please?

8.2.1 Aesthetic Ideas and the Free Play of the Faculties

Kant's attempt to shed at least some light on this mysterious process in the creative subject is the doctrine of "aesthetic ideas," which are the defining products of genius. Their title of 'ideas' notwithstanding, they are

---

[12] Cf. also Allison's illuminating discussion of the analogy with the 'paradox of organisms' (2001: 276–79).

intuitions, generated by the artist's imagination "in its freedom from all guidance by rules" (5: 317). An aesthetic idea is a

> representation of the imagination, associated with a given concept, which is combined with such a manifold of partial representations *in the free use of the imagination* that no expression designating a determinate concept can be found for it. (5: 316; my emphasis)

Before analyzing the ingredients in this characterization, it is helpful to look at one of the illustrations Kant gives.[13] The artist in this case chooses a concept, the idea of "the powerful king of heaven" or of "the sublimity and majesty of creation" – both of which are what Kant calls "rational ideas of invisible beings" (5: 314). These indeterminate concepts, on the one hand, characterize, at least in some sense, the artist's intention, and on the other hand, they are such that – in virtue of their status as ideas – no direct presentation in intuition (producing an example of the concepts) is possible. Instead of a direct presentation of the ideas the artist attempts to come up with an *indirect* mode of presentation, through aesthetic ideas. Any direct presentation would have to rely on the "logical attributes [that] represent what lies in our concepts"; in the example, these might be ideas of infinite power, serenity, wisdom, etc. Since these themselves do not qualify for direct presentation, the artist conceives of "aesthetic attributes" of the object of the initial concept (the king of heaven) that "yield an aesthetic idea which serves that idea of reason instead of logical presentation." Such an aesthetic attribute of the king of heaven, Jupiter, is the "eagle, with the lightning in its claws."[14] This representation of the imagination, according to Kant, "aesthetically enlarges the concept [of the king of heaven] itself in an unbounded way" and "gives more to think about than can be grasped and made distinct in [the representation] (although it does, to be sure, belong to the concept of the object" (5: 315).

Aesthetic ideas, then, as intuitions, are *associated* with a concept, not subsumed under it. Although Kant does not always make it explicit whether he is thinking of a determinate or an indeterminate concept, the context suggests that aesthetic ideas are associated with ideas of reason.

---

[13] For discussion of further examples and for an understanding of aesthetic ideas that does not restrict them to the symbolization of ideas, see Matherne (2013).
[14] Presumably we have to imagine, say, a statue of Jupiter in the form of a human being who is accompanied by an eagle with lightning in its claws. All gods or angels in works of the visual arts, according to the *Anthropologie*, have to take on the figure of a human being because any other *Gestalt* "seems to contain parts ... that are not compatible with the structure of a rational being" (7: 178).

8.2 The Freedom of the Imagination, Genius, and Taste 167

In this case, a direct presentation is out of the question; the logical attributes of the concept of the king of heaven themselves have no intuitive counterparts. At the same time, the aesthetic attributes, although they are intuitive representations, have no role to play and would not even be produced by the imagination, were it not for their association with the rational concepts. What the imagination here does, Kant explains, is to produce "forms which do not constitute the presentation of a given [rational] concept itself, but, as supplementary representation [*Nebenvorstellungen*] of the imagination, express only the implications [*Folgen*] connected with it and its affinity with others" (5: 315).[15]

It is a defining feature of aesthetic ideas that they contain "such a manifold of partial representations ... that no expression denoting a determinate concept can be found for it" (5: 316). This 'richness' of the aesthetic representations is emphasized over and over again in § 49 and Kant, at some points, seems to encourage the reader to think that what is at issue is that aesthetic ideas contain too much imaginative material to be subsumed under a determinate concept of the understanding.[16] This characteristic has to be interpreted carefully because, for our discursive minds, *every* intuition is 'too rich' for determinate concepts; after all, concepts, or their associated rules of apprehension, select marks and ignore others from a given manifold of intuition. Every determinate concept contains a finite number of marks; but any intuition that is subsumed under a concept contains a lot more that is not taken into account in the concept. Those marks selected in the concept correspond to the logical attributes, which "represent what lies in our concepts." (In principle, of course, the concept can be further specified to include more marks, as long as their number remains finite.) Furthermore, in the example of the king of heaven, it is clear that the chosen aesthetic attribute, the eagle with its paraphernalia, is a manifold of intuition, subsumed under determinate concepts. In what sense are these concepts of the eagle etc. not "fully adequate" to this aesthetic attribute?

Aesthetic attributes, Kant suggests, "give the imagination an impetus [*Schwung*] to think more, although in an undeveloped way, than can be comprehended in a concept, and hence in a determinate linguistic expression" (5: 315). It is, of course, astonishing that the imagination is supposed to think; but perhaps the qualification 'in an undeveloped way' is intended

---

[15] See Section 8.2.4 for further discussion.
[16] For instance: "An aesthetic idea cannot become a cognition, because it is an intuition (of the imagination) for which a concept can never be found adequate" (5: 343).

to mitigate this phrase. Indeed, in his discussion of examples from poetry, Kant repeats that the free imagination provides "unsought extensive undeveloped material for the understanding" (5: 317). Hence, it would seem to be the understanding that is provided with material for "much thinking" and the characteristic effect of an aesthetic idea is achieved in an interaction of imagination and understanding. Kant describes this process quite naturally as a "stimulation" or "animation" of the understanding by the imagination (e.g., 5: 315) and as a "play" that, in principle at least, does not come to an end because the stimulation of further thoughts is not halted by the subsumption of the aesthetic idea under a determinate concept.[17]

But the interaction or play of imagination and understanding in the examples Kant gives for aesthetic ideas should *not* be identified with the free harmony of the faculties that is involved in taste.[18] To see this, we have to clarify what the intended effect of such artistic products is. The remarks on poetry are especially helpful in answering the question. Kant interprets a line in a poem, "The sun streamed forth, as tranquility streams from virtue," as expressing an aesthetic attribute of the rational idea of virtue. Thinking of virtue – in the mind of the poet in the first place – is accompanied by "a multitude of sublime and calming feelings, and a boundless prospect into a happy future, which no . . . determinate concept fully captures" (5: 316). This feeling or this *"subjective Gemüthsstimmung"* the poet tries to express by choosing aesthetic attributes (of the rational concept) that are suitable to stimulate in the reader similar feelings; that is, the (successful) poet is able "to express what is unnameable in the mental state [*Gemüthszustand*] . . . and to make it universally communicable" (5: 317). Analogous remarks apply to the feelings associated with the ideas of the majesty of creation, infinite power, or the "idea of reason of a cosmopolitan disposition even at the end of life" (5: 316). I suggest, then, that what cannot be captured in a determinate concept are these *Stimmungen* in which the mind of the poet is set by a rational idea and that can be communicated not directly – since they are 'unnameable' – but only through the vehicle of aesthetic ideas, which evoke analogous feelings in other minds. According to Kant, even the physicist Segner's use of a vignette for his textbook, showing the veiled Isis, falls under this scheme:

---

[17] This view of the free play corresponds to the notes from the 1770, quoted above (Section 8.1), that portray the play as stimulated, and given a "theme," by ideas.

[18] For such identifications cf., e.g., Allison (2001: 386 n. 44); Chignell (2007); Rogerson (2008); and some of my own earlier work, Rueger/Evren (2005).

8.2 The Freedom of the Imagination, Genius, and Taste

he chose this image, Kant claims, "to fill his pupil ... with the holy fear [*Schauer*] that should dispose the mind to solemn attentiveness." (5: 316n.)[19]

The *Gemüthsstimmung* that the artistic expression of an aesthetic idea induces in the spectator is not the pleasure of taste, even though it involves a stimulation of the understanding by the imagination. "Holy fear" is plainly not the same as the enjoyment of beauty. That these feelings should not be identified is also clear from Kant's remarks in § 50 where he distinguishes 'merely' beautiful objects from those that also have "*Geist*," that is, the products of genius in cooperation with judgment (taste).[20] Furthermore, in the reception of aesthetic ideas, the understanding, though stimulated to 'much thinking,' is obviously not attempting to find a concept under which to subsume the aesthetic attribute and continues to fail in its attempts; the intuition, after all, is already under such concepts (eagle etc.). The understanding, rather, thinks about many other subjects: about all that is contained in the feeling induced by the aesthetic idea (and, ultimately, by the rational idea).

The specific *Gemüthsstimmung* induced by aesthetic ideas is therefore not the same as the free harmony of the faculties that is experienced in the pleasure of taste. The latter implies the contingent agreement of the form of an object and a freely produced form. What we learn in the sections on art is that the production of aesthetic ideas is the – or at least, one – *mode* in which free forms in general are designed by the imagination – first in the artist's mind and then, by way of recognition, in the spectator's mind (see Section 8.2.3). And because it is not the specific 'content' of aesthetic ideas (the feelings that are communicated through them) that is responsible for free harmony, Kant can claim that all "beauty (whether it be beauty of nature or of art) can in general be called the expression of aesthetic ideas" (5: 320).

---

[19] On the engraving in Segner's *Einleitung in die Naturlehre* (1746), a *putto*, presumably representing the pupil, impudently tries to peek under the veil, even though the inscription on the "temple of Isis (Mother Nature)" announces that "my veil no mortal has removed."
  Cf. a similar suggestion of Mendelssohn's: The products of architecture can touch us [*rühren*] "at least through some *Nebenbegriff*, which our soul always associates with the *Hauptbegriff*. Thus, splendid and majestic buildings can occasion awe and *Schauern* ... and a gravestone can stimulate pain and grief." (1757: 428n.)

[20] Kant asks "whether [in works of beautiful art] imagination or the power of judgment counts for more" and concludes that "since it is in regard to the first of these [genius] that art deserves to be called *inspired* [*geistreich*], but only in regard to the second [taste] that it deserves to be called *beautiful* art, the latter, at least as an indispensable condition (*conditio sine qua non*), is thus the primary thing to which one must look in the judging of art as beautiful art" (5: 319).

8.2.2 Artistic Beauty

For the artist's creative activity, we gather the following characterization from Kant: In order to communicate the disposition of the mind she experiences as connected with a rational idea, she first has to "find" an aesthetic idea that seems suitable to do this. Second, this aesthetic idea, as an "inner intuition" (5: 314),[21] has to be "expressed" in an object of "outer intuition," that is, in a manifold of intuition that is subsumed under a determinate concept (5: 317).[22] In the king-of-heaven example: the artist has to find an aesthetic attribute, associated with the rational idea, which appears capable of inducing the feeling of infinite power etc. – the artist hits on the 'inner intuition' of an eagle with a bolt of lightning in its claws; this mental image – an *Einbildung* (7: 161) – now has to be "expressed," that is, translated into an actual object, the result of the artist's work with marble, clay, or whatever, so that the actual object is able to fulfill the aim of the artist, viz., to induce the appropriate *Stimmung* in the spectator.

Kant insists that neither finding nor expressing aesthetic ideas are activities governed by determinate rules. This, formally at least, resolves the 'paradox of art': one and the same product can be the result of intentional activity and still contain enough 'freedom' so as to appear beautiful. The latter aspect is supposed to be guaranteed by the inscrutable talent for finding and expressing aesthetic ideas, while the former pertains to the, as it were, last stage in the creative process, that is, the stage when the artist has decided on an expression and therefore forms determinate concepts for the object to be produced. Since the initial rational idea is an indeterminate concept, it seems plausible to deny that there could be rules for how to find an aesthetic idea for it. With respect to this second stage, too, Kant insists that the expression of the aesthetic idea cannot be derived

---

[21] Cf. Allison (2004: 278f.) on what Kant might mean by 'inner intuition' in the KrV. Furthermore, cf. the first *Critique* on "ideals of sensibility": "The creatures of the imagination, of which no one can give an explanation or an intelligible concept; they are, as it were, *monograms*, individual traits, though not determined through any assignable rule, constituting more a wavering sketch, as it were, which mediates between various appearances, than a determinate image, such as what painters and physiognomists say they have in their heads, and is supposed to be an incommunicable silhouette of their products or even of their critical judgments" (A 570). The implication seems to be that the artist has to express those "creatures of the imagination" in concrete works of art and thereby makes them communicable.

[22] "Thus genius really consists in the happy relation, which no science can teach and no diligence learn, of finding ideas for a given concept on the one hand and on the other hitting upon the expression for these" (5: 317). This is an instance of the ambivalent use of 'idea' and 'concept' I mentioned earlier. But I think there is no other plausible way of understanding the passage than to take "a given concept" to refer to a rational idea and to gloss "ideas" as aesthetic ideas.

8.2 The Freedom of the Imagination, Genius, and Taste 171

from rules – at least not from any *pre-established* rules, since with the successful execution of a genial work, a new rule is established: when genius creates a work, she is exercising "freedom from coercion in [her] art in such a way that the latter thereby itself acquires a new rule, by which the talent shows itself as exemplary" (5: 318).[23]

The lack of rules is therefore also intended to spell out the sense in which the (artist's) imagination is free and how it can enter in a relation of free harmony with the understanding. I explicated the productive free harmony required for beauty as (1) a contingent agreement of the faculties in which the imagination (2) is not schematizing a given concept and in which it is (3) not merely reproductive (as in concept formation) but "self-active" (5: 240). Taking these points in reverse order, it is clear that, with respect to the production of aesthetic ideas, the artist's imagination is not reproductive, that is, bound by what is empirically given in intuition. To be sure, Kant emphasizes that the productive imagination does not create *ex nihilo* but uses materials provided by nature to arrange or combine them in new ways; in this activity, however, it is not bound to the "law of association (which applies to the empirical use of the that faculty)":

> The imagination (as a productive cognitive faculty) is ... very powerful in creating, as it were, another nature, out of the material which the real one gives it .... we transform the latter [real world], no doubt always in accordance with analogous laws, but also in accordance with principles that lie higher in reason (and which are every bit as natural to us as those in accordance with which the understanding apprehends empirical nature); in this we feel our freedom from the law of association (which applies to the empirical use of that faculty), in accordance with which material can certainly be lent to us by nature, but the latter can be transformed by us into something entirely different, namely into that which surpasses nature. (5: 314*)

That the imagination is guided by "principles that lie higher in reason," instead of by the law of association, requires further discussion; but for now we may take this as a reference to the connection between aesthetic ideas and ideas of reason and as a confirmation of aspect (2) of the freedom of the imagination.

How can there be – aspect (3) – a *contingent* agreement of the produced object with a free form of the imagination in the artist's mind when the

---

[23] Cf. also (5: 309f.) and (5: 317): "a new rule, which could not have been deduced from any antecedent principles or examples."

object has been produced according to the artist's intention? The lack of rules addresses this question as well. The artist has to find a determinate concept of an object (to be produced) that successfully 'expresses' the aesthetic idea presented by the free form. And since this process of 'expression' is not guided by determinate rules, the comparison of the aesthetic idea with its expression can fail to show agreement, the expression can be inadequate, the artist can fail. The contingency of the agreement is thus secured.

8.2.3 *Genius and Taste*

Since genius is a talent for the *production* of aesthetic ideas, it is not immediately clear how Kant's pronouncements in the sections on art could be employed in the discussion of taste, which is not a productive or creative capacity but "merely a faculty for judging" (5: 313; 311). If we take, as I suggested, the free operation of the imagination as modelled after the production of aesthetic ideas, and if the pleasure of taste always involves a comparison of a free form with a given form, the subject that merely judges an object to be beautiful obviously has to be able to *recognize* the expression of aesthetic ideas in that object and thereby detect that a given form agrees (or disagrees) with a form that the spectator's imagination could have produced freely. But after what I suggested above, in principle at least, the cases of production and reception should be analogous: the artist has to detect agreement of the freely created form (the aesthetic idea) with the finished product, while the spectator evaluates this product (the given form) with respect to its agreement with a form she herself could have produced freely.

This analogous structure seems to impose a considerable burden on the recipient of art, especially in light of the examples Kant uses. To recognize the eagle with lightning in its claws as an aesthetic attribute of the king of heaven requires (in the spectator as well as in the artist) quite specialized knowledge of mythology; without such knowledge, the aesthetic idea would not be recognized as appropriately associated with the rational idea. Furthermore, some conventions regarding allegories and metaphors are involved. Similar remarks obviously apply to Kant's other examples.[24]

---

[24] It might be tempting to relate the background-dependence of artistic beauty to Kant's notion of "adherent beauty" and those cases where no such background seems required to "free beauty" (5: 229–31). I have ignored this distinction so far because it does not line up with the nature/art division. Some products of beautiful art are classified by Kant as free beauties, e.g., musical "fantasias (without a theme), indeed all music without a text" (5: 229).

8.2 The Freedom of the Imagination, Genius, and Taste

If these cases require very specific background knowledge in order to recognize the aesthetic ideas expressed, *natural* beauty – which Kant also takes to be the expression of such ideas (5: 320) – raises a different worry: even if we grant that aesthetic ideas, together with their associated rational ideas, may plausibly be involved in works of art, we seem to be at a loss to say which aesthetic idea may be expressed in, say, a rose or in the appearance of "many birds … and a host of marine crustaceans" (5: 229; 347). In light of such questions, it would be desirable to have an account of aesthetic ideas that associates them with rational ideas that are less 'specialized' than the ones in the examples, ideas that are not dependent on the kind of background knowledge illustrated in the discussed cases (see Section 8.4).

Although rules of art and the background knowledge involved in the production and reception of aesthetic ideas are not supposed to 'coerce' the imagination so as to make its free activity impossible, Kant famously insists that some constraints are necessary for art. The creative imagination of the genius, he claims, "can only provide rich material for products of art; its elaboration and form require a talent that has been academically trained, in order to make a use of it that can stand up to the power of judgment [i.e., taste]." This academic training, which accounts for the "something mechanical [in art], which can be grasped and followed according to rules", furthermore constitutes "the essential condition of the art" (5: 310).[25] The genius' "free use of his cognitive faculties" (5: 318) is not a sufficient condition for the creation of beautiful art, though it may be necessary. Also necessary is the control of the free imagination by rules that ensure 'academic correctness,' a control that cannot straightforwardly be identified with taste – an identification suggested by Kant's famous claim that "taste … is the discipline (or corrective) of genius, clipping its wings and making it well behaved or polished" (5: 319). Taste itself, as Kant has insisted, does not have any "rules that could be produced." And insofar as taste is an (aesthetic) employment of the reflecting power of judgment, it clearly is not in the business of checking conformity with (e.g., academic) rules, which would be the task of determining judgment. Overall, however, despite the dependence of the work of the artist on various background conditions and rules, Kant's view is that none of this is sufficient to "deduce" the new rule that a work of genius "discloses" (5: 317).

---

[25] In the following, I am not claiming to be able to resolve all the well-known tensions in the sections on art and genius in the KU. For surveys of these difficulties, cf., for instance, Guyer (1997: ch. 12); Allison (2001: ch. 12); Kalkar (2006: ch. 4).

He summarizes the ways in which controls on the free imagination are necessary as follows:

> To be rich and original in ideas is not as necessary for the sake of beauty as is the suitability of the imagination in its freedom to the lawfulness of the understanding. For all the richness of the former produces, in its lawless freedom, nothing but nonsense; the power of judgment, however, is the faculty for bringing it in line with the understanding. (5: 319)[26]

Thus, we are to understand that the imagination in its freedom, without controls, tends to produce "nonsense," which seems to imply that this free operation is not purposive for 'cognition in general' and that it is therefore mistaken to think that this freely producing imagination, on its own, could be in agreement with the requirements of the understanding.

8.2.4 Symbols

The specter of a lawlessness imagination – free from the law of association and from what is given – that produces nonsense indicates that the *relevant* sense of the freedom of this faculty cannot merely consist in its lawlessness. And one would not have expected anything else from Kant. As Hermann Cohen put it aptly: as always in Kant, "we have to ask not 'freedom from what?' but rather 'freedom for what?'" The freedom of the imagination "is, therefore, in the last analysis, not independence *from* the understanding but suitability *for* reason."[27]

The freedom of the imagination, which has been described so far only in terms of what it is free from and which consequently requires constraints, is also tied to the indirect presentation of ideas of reason: in producing

---

[26] Zammito (1992: 124ff.) has taken pronouncements like this as evidence for his claim that in the KU Kant was reacting against views about genius as absolutely free, views that Zammito finds presented, above all, in Herder. To be sure, Kant's relations with Herder in 1790 were not friendly. But the view Kant expresses is actually a commonplace at the time. See, for example, Gerard (1774 [1966], 70f.): "Though genius be properly a comprehensive, regular, and active imagination, yet it can never attain perfection ... except it be united with a sound and piercing judgment .... It is the union of an extensive imagination with an accurate judgment, that has accomplished the great geniuses of all ages." A similar distinction is found in Garve (1779, 77f.), who had translated Gerard's *Essay on Genius* into German in 1776. And even Herder himself wrote at around the same time that "the more powers a genius has and the faster these powers operate, the more the supervision of taste is needed so as to prevent the powers from overwhelming each other" (1775, 602).

As Schmidt (1985, xii–xiv) notes, such remarks on genius were repeated, with only minor variations, over and over again. Kant's adoption of these formulas seems perfectly conventional – which is not to deny that their adoption created tensions with his own account of taste.

[27] Cohen (1889: 258).

8.2 The Freedom of the Imagination, Genius, and Taste

aesthetic ideas the imagination "strive[s] toward something lying beyond the bounds of experience, and thus seek[s] to approximate a presentation of concepts of reason (of intellectual ideas)" (5: 314). Its lawlessness thus makes it free or "suitable for reason." It accomplishes this task, as we have seen, by producing "forms which do not constitute the presentation of a given [rational] concept itself, but, as supplementary representation [*Nebenvorstellungen*] of the imagination, express only the implications [*Folgen*] connected with it and its affinity with others" (5: 315). That is, the indirect presentation of a rational idea proceeds by *analogies*.

Kant explains the distinction of direct and indirect modes of presentation further in § 59. Only for determinate concepts, pure or empirical concepts of the understanding, can presentation be "schematic" or "direct"; and for empirical concepts, their presentation consists in producing an instance, an example, of the concept in intuition. In the case of indeterminable concepts of reason, this mode of presentation is ruled out and the presentation has to be "indirect" or

> *symbolic*, where to a concept which only reason can think, and to which no sensible intuition can be adequate, an intuition is attributed with which the power of judgment proceeds in a way merely analogous to that which it observes in schematization, i.e., it is merely the rule of this procedure, not of the intuition itself, and thus merely the form of the reflection, not the content, which corresponds to the concept. (5: 351)

However this procedure is to be understood in detail, it presupposes that we have both relata of the symbolic relation, the intuition and the concept of reason, in order to reflect on them and notice an analogy. For instance, reflection on the relations of the parts of a handmill, Kant suggests, reveals an analogy with the relations of people in a despotic monarchy: "Between a despotic state and a handmill there is, of course, no similarity, but there is one between the rule for reflecting on both and their causality" (5: 352). The handmill therefore serves as an indirect, symbolic presentation of the concept of a type of state. The reference to "their causality" is important because it emphasizes that what we reflect on and compare are causal relations between otherwise completely dissimilar objects. This ensures that the relata are not the focus of reflection and, in the case of rational ideas, that we do not illegitimately project intuitions onto what cannot, by definition, be given in intuition.[28] Even though concepts of reason allow

---

[28] This is discussed in greater detail in the *Prolegomena* (4: 357–60) for symbolic cognition of God: "The concept of relation in this case is a mere category, namely, the concept of cause, which has nothing to do with sensibility" (4: 358n.). Similarly, KU § 90: analogy "is the identity of the

only of symbolic presentation, determinate concepts can be presented either directly or indirectly. For instance, when we perceive the form of a given object that is subsumed under the determinate concept "S-shaped line," the imagination has produced the appropriate schema or picture for the concept "S-line."[29] When we reflect on this given form, however, we may find that it symbolizes the further (determinate) concept of "motion" (at least better than a straight line would) because we notice an analogy between 'what follows' from the given form – change in direction in space – and from the concept – change of position in time.

Kant points out that his treatment of symbols as intuitions rather than as a discursive mode of representation is non-traditional: to consider the "symbolic in contrast to the intuitive kind of representation," as the rationalist tradition did, "is a distorted and incorrect use of the word: for the symbolic is merely a species of the intuitive" (5: 351). It is interesting to note that he used the term in the 'corrected' way already in the pre-critical *Dreams of a Spirit Seer* (1766) and in a way that comes quite close to how I earlier described the communication of a *Stimmung*, induced by an idea of reason, through the expression of aesthetic ideas. The issue in *Dreams* is how human beings could ever become conscious of influences (thoughts) from the 'spirit world,' when, by definition, such influences could not directly enter our minds. They could still migrate in an indirect way, Kant suggests: such thoughts could in humans "stimulate those images, according to the law of associated concepts, that have affinity with them and awaken analogical representations of our senses that are not the spiritual concept itself but still its symbols" (2: 338f.).[30]

8.3 The Antinomy of Taste

In sections 55–57, which open the "Dialectic of the aesthetic power of judgment," Kant introduces officially the connection of judgments of taste with rational ideas. The Dialectic, as we know from the KrV, is the fitting place to do so because ideas, as genuine products of reason, are not directly involved in cognition but can lead into dialectical error or illusion. In the first *Critique*, Kant argued that one species of such ideas, the cosmological ideas, create a conflict of reason with itself that casts serious doubt

---

relation between grounds and consequences (causes and effects)" insofar as this obtains between dissimilar things (5: 464n.) Cf. also *Fortschritte* (20: 279f.).

[29] The example is from Esser (1997: 180f.).

[30] It is notoriously doubtful that Kant is here speaking for himself; but it is clear that in 1766 he already had the non-traditional notion of a symbol as an intuitive representation ("images").

8.3 The Antinomy of Taste

("a skeptical hopelessness," "euthanasia of pure reason" [A 407]) on its employment as a higher cognitive faculty. In its strife for completeness of cognitions and for the unconditioned underlying all conditioned cognitions delivered by the understanding, reason uses the understanding's tools but applies them beyond their legitimate domain of application. In this way, it arrives at pairs of claims that contradict each other, even though each claim is capable of being proven. The resolution of this "Antinomy of Reason" is obviously highly significant for a critique of reason and Kant argues that the only way to achieve this is by accepting the distinction of a world of appearances (the world of sense) and a world of things as they are in themselves (the supersensible world), that is, transcendental idealism.

Is the aesthetic employment of reflecting judgment capable of such a life-threatening conflict with itself? A necessary condition for antinomial conflict of a faculty is satisfied, as Kant points out, namely, that the faculty has to have a priori principles and that its claims can therefore be universally valid (5: 337). The question is whether the 'principle of taste' that characterizes the power of judgment as a member of the system of the higher faculties is able to generate contradictory claims regarding the possibility of judgments of taste, thereby raising suspicions about its reputation as a faculty, and requiring, as a remedy, recourse to ideas of the supersensible world.

The answer is: no; the aesthetic power of judgment itself is in no such danger. In order to construct an antinomy involving taste, Kant has to make the power of judgment the target of reason's drive toward the unconditioned.[31] What results is, as he notes only *after* his discussion of the antinomy, "an antinomy of reason with regard to the aesthetic use of the power of judgment *for the feeling of pleasure and displeasure.*" The so-called antinomy of taste thus is another antinomy of reason, one among three: there is the antinomy from the KrV "with regard to the theoretical use of the understanding extending to the unconditioned *for the faculty of cognition*" and the same "with regard to the practical use of reason, which is intrinsically self-legislative, *for the faculty of desire*" (5: 345). From this proper labelling of the antinomies, one should suspect that it is the interference of reason that drives the aesthetic power of judgment into conflict with itself.[32]

---

[31] I follow, by and large, Allison's much more detailed interpretation of the antinomy (2001: ch. 11).
[32] The teleological power of judgment, however, is supposed to generate its *own* antinomy, which is not one of reason but genuinely one of reflecting judgment (5: 385). This is, at first glance, surprising because Kant, at least sometimes, denies that teleological judgment has its own a priori principle (e.g., 20: 233).

The three antinomies of reason listed arise "to the extent that all these faculties [understanding, power of judgment, practical reason] have their higher principles a priori, and, in accordance with an inescapable requirement of reason, must also be able to judge and determine their object unconditionally in accordance with these principles" (5: 345). We shall trace the interference of reason's requirement in Kant's presentation of the antinomy of taste. In a somewhat reconstructed form, the conflict is between two principles about judgments of taste:

> *Thesis*: Judgments of taste are not based on concepts, because otherwise conflicts between them could be decided by proofs (it would be possible to "dispute" about matters of taste).
>
> *Antithesis*: Judgments of taste are based on concepts, because otherwise we could not "lay claim to the necessary assent of others" (we could not even "argue" about them). (5: 338f.)

If we were to take these contradictory claims as indeed arising from the aesthetic power of judgment itself, serious problems would ensue because each claim individually denies that this faculty and its principle is involved in judgments of taste. If the antithesis were accepted, these judgments would be an employment of *determining* judgment (subsumption under rules/concepts).[33] The determining power of judgment, however, has no dialectic (5: 385).[34] Thus, the antithesis could not possibly arise from the aesthetic power of judgment. Since the thesis effectively denies that this power is involved in taste at all, this claim, too, cannot be derived from the assumption that there is such a faculty with its own principle.

The problem underlying the antinomy of taste, thus, cannot lie with the aesthetic power of judgment itself. The conflict instead is generated by reason's "inescapable requirement" to "absolutize"[35] what the analysis of the judgment of taste had only stated as "logical peculiarities" of such judgments (5: 281), namely, that they are not based on concepts and that they nevertheless make a claim to universality. These were 'data' that the official deduction in sections 32 to 38 had undertaken to account for. In the antinomy, these 'data' are turned into *principles* of taste – by reason, to wit – and their conflict seems obvious, notwithstanding the achievement of the deduction.

---

[33] Put differently, the antithesis would assign a 'discursive' principle to the aesthetic power of judgment, while the principle is actually 'intuitive' (see Chapter 7).
[34] Only the reflecting power in its teleological employment has a conflict of its 'maxims.'
[35] This is Allison's term (2001: 242).

8.3 The Antinomy of Taste

Kant's resolution of the antinomy applies a strategy he had used in KrV: he disambiguates the term 'concept' in the Thesis and Antithesis so that both claims are correct and in line with the results of the KU. The Thesis, Kant suggests, is about determinate concepts and thus agrees with the view of the Analytic. The Antithesis, however, is talking about an "indeterminate" – actually indetermin*able*[36] – concept. Since all universality rests with concepts, some concept has to ground the judgment of taste's claim to universal validity and since it cannot be a determinate concept, it must be an indeterminable one, an idea of reason. Since the main purpose and result of all antinomies of reason is the introduction of a special kind of idea that alone, according to Kant, can resolve the conflict of reason with itself,[37] it is, for architectonic reasons, not surprising that he asserts that "all contradiction vanishes" if we realize that the judgment of taste is based on an indeterminable concept "of a general ground for the subjective purposiveness of nature for the power of judgment" and that this ground "may lie in the concept of that which can be regarded as the supersensible substratum of humanity" (5: 340).

This specification of the indeterminable concept as one of a supersensible substratum (ignoring for the moment the further specification "of humanity") follows from the constraints on possible resolutions that are imposed by Kant's theory of taste and the fact that we are dealing with an antinomy of *reason*.[38] What is at issue in a judgment of taste is the pleasure of taste. Like all pleasure – according to the theory I ascribed to Kant – the pleasure in beauty indicates a purposiveness in the object's form: it satisfies the interest of the reflecting power of judgment in a way that is contingent from the point of view of the understanding.[39] It was indeed the task of the power of judgment to capture such contingency in a special concept of purposiveness ("without a purpose"), which does not require us to ascribe an actual purpose in the mind of a designer or some other ground. This concept, Kant emphasizes, is *genuine* to the power of judgment: it is "a special concept of the reflecting power of judgment, not

---

[36] As Allison notes (2001: 247).
[37] All three antinomies "force reason" to regard objects of experience as appearances "and ascribe to them an intelligible substratum (something supersensible, the concept of which is only an idea and permits no genuine cognition)" (5: 344).
[38] The specification is therefore not as arbitrary as Guyer claims (1997: 302). For Allison's response to this objection, which differs slightly from mine, see (2001: 250).
[39] The subjective purposiveness of nature, Kant emphasizes again in § 58, is "without any end [purpose]"; it is "an on its own and contingently manifested purposive correspondence with the need of the power of judgment in regard to nature and the forms generated in it in accordance with particular laws" (5: 347*).

of reason" (20: 216); it "still belongs among the concepts of nature," not among reason's practical concepts (5: 197). Reason's concept of purposiveness, by contrast, always includes a reference to purposes and a ground.[40] Consequently, in the antinomy of taste, then, it is 'absolutizing' reason that requires that a ground be ascribed to the purposiveness manifested in the pleasure of taste. It seems clear (i) that nature, as an appearance, cannot contain the requisite ground[41] and (ii) that not just any indeterminable concept could satisfy reason's need: it has to be the concept of a ground that lies "beyond the sensible." And since the purposiveness at issue pertains to the free harmony of imagination and understanding, we have "to seek the unifying point of all our faculties a priori in the supersensible" (5: 341). Although this paraphrase may come close to the "supersensible substrate of humanity," Kant also mentions in this context "the mere pure rational concept of the supersensible, which grounds the object (and also the judging subject) as an object of sense, consequently as an appearance" (5: 340).[42] But in each case, it is the idea of a supersensible ground that is identified as the relevant indeterminable concept — a concept of reason, not of the power of judgment. The latter introduces the indeterminate concept of the subjective purposiveness of nature; but since it is *reason* that forced the antinomy, only the idea of a *ground* of such purposiveness can satisfy reason's interest.[43]

In the text immediately following the resolution of the antinomy, "Remark I" to § 57, Kant returns to the discussion of aesthetic ideas as the counterparts to ideas of reason. Since all beauty is the expression of aesthetic ideas, we can see a correspondence between the result of the antinomy and the (earlier) doctrine of aesthetic ideas: their "inexponible" nature (5: 342) supports the Thesis (no proofs), while their association with (or symbolization of) rational ideas can be linked with the Antithesis (based on concepts). To make the correspondence complete, however, there would have to be an idea of the supersensible ground that is

---

[40] Compare the discussion of the purposiveness of nature in the KrV Dialectic (A 815f.).

[41] In support of this, in § 58 Kant argues at length that there are no good reasons why we should assume nature, as appearance, to be purposive for us.

[42] The role that reason plays in the antinomy is also evident in a different context, in § 42, where Kant argues that we take an "intellectual interest" in natural beauty. In the pleasure of taste in such beautiful objects, we experience nature as purposive without a purpose. Reason, however, goes beyond this and seeks the purpose behind the purposiveness, a purpose "we never encounter ... externally" in nature, and which reason therefore "seek[s] within ourselves, and indeed in that which constitutes the ultimate end of our existence, namely the moral vocation" (5: 301).

[43] I do not agree, therefore, with Allison's attempt to identify the required indeterminate concept as that of 'beauty' (which is roughly equivalent with subjective purposiveness). Only an idea of reason will do. Cf. Allison (2001: 244; 249–51).

symbolized by *all* aesthetic ideas, regardless of which other ideas (like the king of heaven) they may present symbolically. In the following "Remark II," Kant effectively offers a list of candidates, even though he does not here mention aesthetic ideas again. He notes that if

> our deduction is at least on the right track, even if it has not been made clear enough in every detail, then three ideas are revealed: *first*, that of the supersensible in general, without further determination, as the substratum of nature; *second*, the very same thing, as the principle of subjective purposiveness of nature for our faculty of cognition; *third*, the very same thing, as the principle of the ends of freedom and principle of the correspondence of freedom with those ends in the moral sphere. (5: 346)

The reference to "our deduction" is, of course, irritating because it was not the deduction but the antinomy of taste that supposedly revealed those ideas of the supersensible, while the deduction did not require bringing in ideas.[44] Be that as it may, we now have three ideas that Kant perhaps even intended to identify ("the very same").[45] From this list of ideas and the resolution of the antinomy, one might expect that beautiful objects (at least in nature) symbolize the supersensible ground of the subjective purposiveness of nature. Kant, however, does not elaborate on this. Instead he focuses in § 59 on the symbolization of the third idea and famously claims that beauty is "a symbol of morality" (5: 351). I shall briefly discuss the latter doctrine and then the possibility of the former.

8.4 Symbolizations of the Ideas of a Supersensible Ground

8.4.1 Morality

In order to establish the symbolization relation between an intuition and an idea of reason, analogical ways of reflecting on each relatum of the relation have to be displayed. Kant mentions four ways in which our reflection on beautiful objects, as expressed in judgments of taste, is analogous to the way we reflect on the morally good in moral judgments ("while at the same time not leaving unnoticed its differences" [5: 353]). As required by the concept of symbolization, the comparison focuses on

---

[44] The quoted remark is found in the Dialectic, which could not possibly be part of the deduction. One could, however, try to argue, that, in the second and third *Critiques*, the respective deductions indeed move from the Analytic into the Dialectic. For such a proposal, see Brandt (1989).
[45] One is reminded of the end of the *Groundwork* where Kant says about the moral imperative that all philosophy can try to do is to "comprehend its incomprehensibility" (4: 463).

relations; the most significant for our discussion is the relation of the cognitive faculties in taste, on the one hand, and that of the faculties involved in moral judgments, on the other: "The freedom of the imagination (thus of the sensibility in our faculty) is represented in the judging of the beautiful as in accord with the lawfulness of the understanding" while "in the moral judgment the freedom of the will is conceived as the agreement of the latter with itself in accordance with universal laws of reason" (5: 354). Although at the time of the KU Kant had not yet made explicit the distinction of the will and free *Willkür* (choice), it is plausible to interpret Kant's point in these terms:[46] free *Willkür*, corresponding to the imagination, is in harmony with the will as practical reason that gives the moral law, corresponding to the understanding. *Willkür*'s choosing, in its freedom, a maxim approved by the will, is supposed to be analogous to the imagination, in its freedom, producing a form that conforms with the requirements of the understanding. When we make a moral judgment, that is, we decide to adopt a maxim because it is morally right, we experience that what we freely desire is in line with the moral law. Analogously, in a judgment of taste, we feel that a given form that satisfies the requirements of the understanding is such that we could have designed this form freely, without 'coercion' from the faculty of concepts.

The purposiveness of nature for judgment, manifested in the pleasure in the beautiful, shows that a free harmony of the faculties is possible in the subject – in which the power of judgment gives the law to itself – and it shows that nature is such that it can agree with a faculty that itself does not give laws to nature. Kant sums up these considerations in this way: in taste, the power of judgment

> sees itself, both on account of this inner possibility in the subject as well as on account of the outer possibility of a nature that corresponds to it, as related to something in the subject itself and outside of it, which is neither nature nor freedom, but which is connected to the ground of the latter, namely, the supersensible, in which the theoretical faculty is combined with the practical, in a mutual and unknown way, to form a unity. (5: 353)

Thus, even though free harmony in taste, according to the resolution of the antinomy, points itself towards a supersensible ground of such harmony, it is the analogy of the pleasure of taste with moral satisfaction, according to the symbolism section, that indicates an ultimate unification of the supersensible grounds of the purposiveness of nature and of freedom.

---

[46] See Guyer (1997: 335).

8.4 Symbolizations of the Ideas of a Supersensible Ground 183

This result of § 59 is in some ways anticipated in § 42. The latter argues for a moral interest in beautiful nature (and nature alone), an interest of reason "that nature should at least show some trace or give a sign that it contains in itself some sort of ground for assuming a lawful correspondence of its products with our satisfaction that is independent of all interest" (5: 300). The basis of this argument is, like in § 59, "the analogy between the pure judgment of taste ... and the moral judgment" in terms of the similarities of the pleasure of taste and moral feeling. (Kant even proposes this analogy as an "explanation [*Deutung*] of aesthetic judgments in terms of their affinity with moral feeling" [5: 301]). That we experience nature as if it were art, as being purposive without a purpose, is the basis for our "admiration" and for reason's further speculation about the purpose behind all this, a purpose "we never encounter ... externally," in nature, and which we therefore "seek within ourselves, and indeed in that which constitutes the ultimate end of our existence, namely the moral vocation" (5: 301).

Since Kant's notion of analogy is explicitly 'formal' because of its focus on correspondences between relations rather than between the contents of the symbolizing intuition and what it symbolizes, the doctrine of § 59, therefore, can be understood to apply to *all* beauty, whether natural or artistic. The formal affinity of the pleasure of taste and the moral feeling is supposed to suffice for making the claim applicable to all manifestations of beauty. Although some beautiful objects may symbolize particular moral or other ideas, beauty in general, as the expression of aesthetic ideas, is not dependent on such more specific rational ideas.[47]

8.4.2   Systematicity

Kant mentions once, in the Introduction, that "we can regard natural beauty as the presentation of the concept of the formal (merely subjective) purposiveness" of nature (5: 193). If 'presentation' is here to be understood as 'indirect,' symbolic presentation, this brief remark might confirm that Kant indeed had in mind that natural beauty (also) symbolizes the idea of the supersensible ground of the purposiveness of nature. This purposiveness is characterized, in the same context, as something we ascribe to nature "in accordance with the analogy of an end," namely, the purpose to assist us in the task of forming concepts "in the face of this excessive multiplicity in nature (in order to be able to be oriented in it)." Since this

---

[47] See Allison (2001: 259–62).

is the presupposition of the systematicity of nature in its particular laws, natural beauty would have to symbolically present the (idea of the ground of the) systematic organization of nature in this sense.[48] In order to fill such speculations in, one could argue that the way we reflect on the system of laws (or whatever fragment we know of this system) is analogous to the way we reflect on the parts and their relations in a beautiful object in nature. According to this suggestion, those objects are not systems in any literal sense; just their parts are arranged in analogy with a literal system of laws. But I will not here pursue this speculative extension of Kant's theory.

The First Introduction contains a section about "the purposiveness of the forms of nature as so many particular systems" (20: 217). Here Kant seems to have entertained – but later apparently abandoned the idea, since it is not mentioned in the published Introduction – that we can judge (in reflecting judgment) certain products of nature as "individual things in the form of systems" and distinguish them from other products, "aggregates," where "nature proceeds mechanically." The former class of forms contains not only organisms, as one would expect, but also *beautiful* products, "e.g., crystal formations, various shapes of flowers." The difference of 'system' and 'aggregate,' as applied to such objects, however, is not clarified beyond the intuitive level. But Kant points out, significantly, that the presupposition of the systematicity of laws, which can be transcendentally justified, by itself does not imply anything about the possibility of *individual* things and their structure, since a system of laws is perfectly possible without any object being judged as a particular system. If we encounter the latter sort of things – for example, beautiful crystals – in experience, however, we are then entitled to connect their subjective purposiveness, manifested in the pleasure of taste, to the already established purposiveness of nature in its laws. This is a legitimate move, says Kant, "because we already have a ground for ascribing to nature in its particular laws a principle of purposiveness" and therefore "it is always possible and permissible, if experience shows us purposive forms in its [nature's] products, for us to ascribe this to the same ground as that on which the first [systematicity of laws] may rest" (20: 218). This "ground," he adds, "may lie in the supersensible and beyond the sphere of the insights into nature that are possible for us."

The idea, then, presented in very cautious language, is that (i) the purposiveness of nature as captured in the principle of systematicity and the purposiveness manifested in the pleasure of taste in natural objects have a common ground in the supersensible; and (ii) the purposiveness to

---

[48] Cf., e.g., Elliot (1968), Makreel (1990: 63f.), Rueger/Evren (2005).

which taste responds is experienced when we encounter objects that have the form of a system, a certain arrangement of their parts that distinguishes them, in reflection, from mere aggregates. In the KU, Kant seems to have retained only (i) but did let go of (ii).[49] But if the previous speculation about nature's systematicity being symbolized by natural beauty were to be followed, this could be seen as a modification of the view from the First Introduction: beautiful objects are now no longer characterized as individual systems but rather as symbolic presentations of the idea of (the ground of the) systematicity of nature in its laws.

8.5   Concluding Remark

Each of the three *Critiques* introduces a specific form of the presentation of concepts in intuition. In the KrV, schemata of concepts of the understanding mediate between intuitions and the products of the understanding, two kinds of representations that Kant regards as too heterogeneous to allow for subsumption of the former under the latter without the mediating assistance of schemata (A 137f.). In the KpV, a related problem of mediation arises because in moral judgments we are supposed to subsume an action, an event in the phenomenal world, under the "morally good," which "is something, which, by its object, is supersensible; nothing corresponding to it can be found in sensible intuition" (5: 68). Kant's solution to this problem is the "type of the moral law," a construct that, on the one hand, is suitable to subsume phenomenal events, and that, on the other, shares a relevant feature with the law of the intelligible world. This type is the *form* of a law of the understanding – that is, the form of a law of nature – that shares the character of necessity with the moral law while, as a law of nature, it applies to "objects of the senses." Thus, maxims for actions are to be compared with a universal natural law and the form of the latter is "a type for the estimation of maxims according to moral principles." This comparison, of course, is what the 'natural law formulation' of the categorical imperative requires. While schemata mediate between the imagination and the understanding, the type accomplishes this task between the understanding and practical reason: the faculty of concepts "can supply to an idea of reason not a schema of sensibility but a law" (5: 69). In the third *Critique*, finally, symbols are introduced as an indirect

---

[49] In KU, crystals are still examples of beautiful objects ("beautiful formations") and their possibility is explained mechanically (5: 347–50) but there is no suggestion that they are also to be judged as 'particular systems.'

(non-schematic) way of presenting ideas of reason in intuition. Given the list of mediating roles:

SCHEMA: imagination – understanding;
TYPUS: understanding – reason/idea;
SYMBOL: imagination – reason/idea,

there is at least a loose sense in which the doctrine of symbolism synthesizes the two other modes of presentation.

The relation of the imagination to ideas of reason served in my interpretation of the free harmony to provide an account of what the imagination in its freedom does: through symbolization, it produces free forms, that is, forms that are not established through schematization of concepts; these free forms can then be compared with given forms. That reason is involved in the experience of beauty naturally raises the question of how, on this account, the beautiful and the sublime are to be distinguished. The pleasure in the sublime is analyzed by Kant as a much more complex feeling than the pleasure of taste in the beautiful: as an intricate mixture of frustration in the failure of the imagination to accomplish what the "voice of reason" commands it to do (to comprehend a vast manifold in the case of the mathematical sublime), which nevertheless is combined with a satisfaction in the fact that the imagination "feels itself unbounded precisely because of this elimination of the limits of sensibility," and finally a satisfaction in the revealed superior power of reason over sensibility (e.g., 5: 269; 271).[50] It is certainly not obvious how this complex feeling can be analyzed in the framework of the theory of pleasure and displeasure I attributed to Kant, but the attempt at such an analysis is beyond the scope of the this study.

---

[50] See Clewis (2009: 81–83) for a good overview of the complexities and Guyer (2005: ch. 9) for a proposal to explain in what different ways beauty and sublimity are symbols of the morally good.

9

The Transition from Nature to Freedom

In the Introduction to the KU, Kant famously claimed that the aim of the work is to bridge the "incalculable gulf" between nature and freedom, that is, between the domains of the higher faculties of the mind, understanding, and practical reason. He explains that the *Critique*'s contribution to the bridging effort will be to show that we can conceive "nature ... in such a way that the lawfulness of its form is at least in agreement with the possibility of the ends that are to be realized in it in accordance with the laws of freedom." The end that the moral law imposes on us is the highest good – happiness in proportion to virtue – and it should be made "real in the sensible world" (5: 175f.). The power of judgment, however, "provides the mediating concept between the concepts of nature and the concept of freedom, which makes possible the transition from the purely theoretical to the purely practical ... in the concept of a purposiveness of nature" (5: 196).

We have seen in Chapter 2 how this concept "mediates" between the two parts of philosophy in what I called the *architectonic* sense, that is, how the concept and its associated faculty of judgment are required to render the division of the higher cognitive faculties complete. Furthermore, we have seen how the initially introduced concept of a subjective purposiveness of nature in the arrangement of its particular *laws* is supposed to 'prepare' us for the application of purposiveness to *individual* objects or forms: to beautiful objects and to organisms, in which case Kant speaks of *objective* purposiveness since what is involved here are not the interests of our faculties. The latter application provides the starting point of the lengthy argument in the teleological part of the KU that takes us from organisms as "natural purposes" to the notion of the world as a system of purposes that is oriented towards a final end, our moral vocation.

Since Kant divides the KU (in the First Introduction) into an "aesthetic of the reflecting power of judgment" and the "logic of the same faculty,"

I shall label the argument in the Teleology the *logical transition*.[1] There also is an *aesthetic transition* in which the feeling of the pleasure of taste supposedly plays a preparatory or promoting role with respect to moral feeling: in taste "a transition from sensory enjoyment to moral feeling" is revealed and with this "a mediating link in the chain of human faculties a priori ... would thereby be exhibited as such" (5: 297f.). With respect to both, the logical and the aesthetic transition, it is important to keep in mind that the "incalculable gulf" between nature and freedom, strictly speaking, cannot be bridged or mediated in the sense of a 'smooth' transition. That would, of course, be impossible, given the basic tenets of Kant's philosophy, as he emphasizes himself in the Introduction.[2] All one can expect under the title of a 'transition' is a kind of preparatory work in the domain of nature that makes the switch to the point of view of freedom less of a "violent leap"[3] – but a leap it has to be in any case.

It is perhaps useful to compare the transition in the KU with the different transition project Kant pursued in the *Opus postumum*, the earliest parts of which apparently date from before 1796. There he is concerned about a transition from the metaphysics of nature to physics, that is, from an a priori discipline to an empirical one. Some of the characterizations of this transition are phrased in terms similar to the ones used in KU:

> These two territories (metaphysics of nature and physics) do not immediately come into contact; and, hence, one cannot cross from one to the other simply by putting one foot in front of the other. Rather, there exists a gulf between the two, over which philosophy must build a bridge in order to reach the opposite bank. For, in order for metaphysical foundations to be combined with physical [foundations] (which have heterogeneous principles) mediating concepts are required, which participate in both. (21: 475; before 1796)

Although Kant seems to have conceived of the transition in different ways at different times in the *Opus postumum*, the above passage maps nicely onto the KU transition. Here it is the concept of a purposiveness of nature

---

[1] "The *aesthetic* of the reflecting power of judgment will occupy one part of the critique of this faculty, just as the logic of the same faculty, under the name of *teleology*, will constitute its other part" (20: 249).

[2] "The concept of freedom determines nothing in regard to the theoretical cognition of nature; the concept of nature likewise determines nothing in regard to the practical laws of freedom: and it is to this extent not possible to throw a bridge from one domain to the other" (5: 195).

[3] "Taste as it were makes possible the transition from sensible charm to the habitual moral interest without too violent a leap" (5: 354).

that serves as the 'mediating concept' because it applies *reason's* concept of a purpose, stripped of its connection with an actual will, to *nature*. This leads, in the aesthetic part of KU, to the pleasure of taste and, in the teleological part, to the view of nature as a system of ends.

Both aspects of the KU transition have been discussed at length in the literature and I can be brief in laying out the main points to which I have little to add. My central concern here rather is to explore how some facets of the logical transition indicate a shift in Kant's views about human beings between the time of the KrV and the GMS (1781/85) and the later works, that is, the KpV (1788), KU (1790), *Religion* (1793), and MS (1797). This shift, I want to suggest, motivates the emphasis Kant puts on the *aesthetic* transition in KU and explains its significance. The suggestion – conjectural as it may be – sheds some light on the otherwise puzzling facts that (i) Kant saw a need to take up the issue of the realizability of the highest good in the world again in the KU, after he had already resolved the antinomy of practical reason in KpV – the demonstration of the "real possibility" of the concept of the highest good – and that (ii) he seemed to suddenly realize, after 1788, that the moral theory laid out in the second *Critique* was "too austere" for human beings that are not only intelligible but also sensible beings.[4]

9.1 Teleology: The Logical Transition

In whatever sense the notion of a subjective purposiveness of nature 'prepares' us for the application of the concept to nature in an objective mode, Kant claims that *experience* (of organisms) forces us to apply the latter concept[5] and he provides, in §§ 76 and 77, an argument for why the nature of our mind (with its discursive rather than intuitive understanding) makes it unavoidable for us to judge organisms as natural purposes.[6] In the First Introduction, this procedure of the reflecting power of judgment is described as a comparison of what is given in experience with a concept of reason, that is, in terms that are analogous to the comparison model for the

---

[4] This is how Guyer proposed to resolve the puzzle (2005: 225).
[5] "Experience leads our power of judgment to the concept of an objective and material purposiveness, i.e., to the concept of an end of nature, only if there is a relation of the cause to the effect to be judged which we can understand as lawful only insofar as we find ourselves capable of subsuming the idea of the effect under the causality of its cause as the underlying condition of the possibility of the former." That is, we "regard the effect immediately as a product of art" (5: 366f.). Cf. also *Fortschritte* (20: 293): the purposiveness of nature "can also be an object of experience, and ... is therefore an immanent, not a transcendent, concept."
[6] A clear analysis of the argument is given by Förster (2008).

experience of beauty. While in a judgment of taste the power of judgment compares a given form of an object with a (counterfactual) free form,

> if empirical concepts and empirical laws are already given in accordance with the mechanism of nature and the power of judgment compares such a concept of the understanding with reason and its principle of the possibility of a system, then, if this form is found in the object, the purposiveness is judged objectively and the thing is called a natural end. (20: 221)

A 'system,' in Kant's sense, is possible only according to an idea; the systematic organization found in living beings thus requires an idea, a purpose, as its ground, just as products of human art come into being through a purpose in the designer's mind. In both parts of the KU, nature is therefore regarded by the reflecting power of judgment as "art," "on account of an analogy which ... [nature's] causality must be represented as having with that of art" (20: 251). Reason introduces supersensible grounds for manifestations of purposiveness in nature, as we have seen at length in the aesthetic case. The First Introduction sums this up: the aesthetic power of judgment provides a "transition ... which connects the two parts" of philosophy – theoretical and practical – a transition "from the sensible substratum of the first part of philosophy to the intelligible substratum of the second," because judgments of taste about natural beauty "are of such a special sort that they relate sensible intuitions to the idea of nature, whose lawfulness cannot be understood without their relation to a supersensible substratum" (20: 247). The same move is made, with respect to *objective* purposiveness, in the teleology – with the crucial difference that here Kant ends up with an argument for "practical belief" or "rational faith" in the existence of God. That the aesthetic part does not also lead to such an argument is at first glance surprising because in the tradition of proofs of a wise creator from the purposive organization of the world – the tradition of physico-theology – natural beauty often served as a basis for such arguments, besides other manifestations of purposiveness in nature.[7] As we will see, Kant is critical of physico-theology, since it cannot

---

[7] See, for instances, Lord Kames' *Elements of Criticism*: Following Hutcheson (*Inquiry* I. v and viii; 2004: 46ff. and 76ff.), Kames traces the pleasure of taste in natural objects to a wise and benevolent designer: "In natural objects, whether we regard their internal or external structure, beauty and design are equally conspicuous" (1785: 408). "Nature has a wonderful power of connecting systems with each other, and of propagating that connection through all her works" (413). "But the most wonderful connection of all, though not the most conspicuous, is that of our internal frame with the works of nature. Man is obviously fitted for contemplating these works, because in this contemplation he has great delight. The works of nature are remarkable in their uniformity not less than in their variety; and the mind of man is fitted to receive pleasure equally from both" (415).

lead to a god with the desired features; he may have thought that the experience of beauty could at most lead to an argument analogous to the deficient physico-theological one. But there is perhaps a further reason. Even though in teleology we judge certain natural objects – organisms – in analogy with products of art, we can produce beautiful objects ourselves in fine art; organisms, however, show an "organization ... as the internal end of nature, [that] infinitely surpasses all capacity for a similar presentation by art" (5: 383).[8] Under this aspect, the teleological strategy, starting from organisms, provides a stronger basis for physico-theology than the purposiveness of beautiful objects.

In the KpV, Kant introduced the concept of the highest good as the unique "object of practical reason," together with the claim that the moral law obliges us to the realization of this object. Since the law is a purely formal law for the determination of the will and since any determination of the will by an object, distinct from the law itself, amounts to heterogeneity, that is, an infringement on the autonomy of practical reason, it is not immediately clear how such an obligation could arise from the moral law.[9] The highest good, however, consists in the proportionate combination of (maximal) virtue and happiness, with the former as the "supreme" condition of the highest good and the latter as that which, together with the supreme condition, forms the "complete object of practical reason" (5: 109f.). With this distinction, the moral law, the supreme condition, remains the only determining ground of the will; the strife for happiness, by contrast, plays no such role. But since all human actions presuppose the setting of a purpose, and the 'matter' of our purposes (as finite beings) is happiness, the realization of *any* purpose involves the desire for happiness. This has to hold for the highest purpose – the highest good – as well. In order for humans to follow their duty to realize the highest good in the world, Kant claims, they have to be able to see that nature does not systematically exclude the combination of virtue and happiness, that is, they have to have some reassurance that – all appearances in the world notwithstanding – there can be a connection between the two components, a way in which virtue indeed leads to happiness. Our initial inability to see such a connection (since it is not in our power to make nature cooperate towards our aim of happiness), together with the moral

---

"In short, nothing can be more happily accommodated to the inward constitution of man, than that mixture of uniformity with variety which the eye discovers in natural objects" (417).

[8] Also compare Kant's remarks on the shortcomings of the analogy with art (5: 374f.).

[9] See Albrecht (1978) for an extensive overview of the difficulties commentators have had with this claim.

obligation to strive for the realization of the highest good, leads to the antinomy of practical reason, a contradiction within the very concept of the highest good, which therefore would seem impossible to realize:

> To be in need of happiness and also worthy of it and yet not to partake of it could not be in accordance with the complete volition of an omnipotent rational being, if we assume such only for the sake of the argument. (5: 110)

Likewise for finite rational beings, according to KpV, "the impossibility of the highest good must prove the falsity of the moral law ... which commands that it be furthered." Unless the antinomy is resolved, this law "must be fantastic, directed to empty imaginary ends, and consequently inherently false" (5: 114). The resolution of the conflict consists in the "postulates" of practical reason, among them the proposition that a morally benevolent god exists. Although we cannot grasp the required connection of virtue and happiness in phenomenal nature, such a connection is at least possible in the supersensible realm, through god's arrangement of nature in a way (hidden to us) that ensures the possibility of the highest good.[10] "Practical belief" or "rational faith" in god is therefore justified because finite beings that have to act according to the commands of practical reason require such belief in order to consistently execute those commands. The result of the KpV, then, is that moral action, fulfillment of our duty, is possible for creatures like us only if we have faith in the postulates. Only such faith, in particular, in the existence of god, can save us from irrationality because to follow the moral law in one's conduct while being convinced that such conduct cannot have the intended effect of contributing to the realization of the highest good would be irrational.[11] Kant succinctly summarized the issue in a *Reflexion* from 1785–88: "Without morality, the hypothesis" of a necessary being would always remain ungrounded; but without the hypothesis, "morality has no prospect of ever connecting the objective principle of the (good) will with the subjective principle (of happiness)." There would be no system of nature that corresponds to the system of reason and freedom "and thus the moral concept would concern a mere *ens rationis* which dissolves into nothing" (R 6280; 18: 547*).

The claim in KpV that without rational faith in god and, consequently, in the realizability of the highest good, the moral law itself would be "fantastic" and "inherently false" is astonishing because one would not

---

[10] See Willaschek (2010) for an analysis of the postulates and their status.
[11] Beiser (2006: 616f.) called this threat of irrationality an "existential concern."

9.1 Teleology

have expected that acting out of respect for the moral law – an unconditional imperative for us – should be dependent on any beliefs we hold about the natural world. In the KU version of the moral argument for the existence of god in §§ 86–87, in fact Kant seems to tone down the strong language of the KpV. In the KU version, if I decide to act out of respect for the moral law but do not believe in the assurances provided by the postulates, I end up with the despair Kant illustrates dramatically with the figure of Spinoza, the atheist who is nevertheless virtuous. This "righteous man" has convinced himself that there is no god and, therefore, that the realization of the highest good is impossible but he nevertheless holds firm to doing his duty.

> He would merely unselfishly establish the good to which that holy law directs all his powers. But his effort is limited; and from nature he can, to be sure, expect some contingent assistance here and there, but never a lawlike agreement in accordance with constant rules (like his internal maxims are and must be) with the ends to act in behalf of which he still feels himself bound and impelled. Deceit, violence, and envy will always surround him, even though he is himself honest, peaceable, and benevolent. (5: 452)

Such righteous people, "in spite of all their worthiness to be happy," will be subjected to nature, "to all the evils of poverty, illness, and untimely death, just like all the other animals on earth ... until one wide grave engulfs them all together (whether honest or dishonest, it makes no difference here)"(5: 452).

Since, by assumption, Spinoza actually is virtuous, it must be possible for humans to do their duty without believing in God. The atheists can – in fact, must (5: 451) – still obey the moral law; they just have to pay the high price of despair – an ultimately psychological problem that is caused by what Kant deems to be irrational behaviour.[12] The virtuous atheists thus have no sufficient reason to regard the moral law as "fantastic" or as "inherently false," unless the avoidance of psychological distress or cognitive dissonance counts as such.

It is not surprising that the doctrine of the postulates became more complex and developed inner tensions after Kant had revised his doctrine of incentives of morality in the GMS in 1784.[13] As long as he thought that belief in god and an afterlife were required, not to ground the moral law (as

---

[12] See also the remark that there is "a pure moral ground of practical reason for assuming" the existence of god – "even if for nothing more than avoiding the danger of seeing that effort [of striving to be virtuous] as entirely futile in its effects and thereby flagging in it" (5: 446).
[13] Rich material for this claim is found in Schmitz (1989: ch. 2), from which I draw in the following.

principium dijudicationis but to provide it with motivating, executive force (the prospect of divine rewards and punishment),[14] there was a fairly straightforward sense in which an atheist would be caught in 'absurd' situations, as laid out, for example, in the *L1 Metaphysics* lectures: if he decided to be virtuous, he would be a *fool* because there would be no prospect of reward ("*absurdum pragmaticum*"); if he decided against a virtuous life, he would be a *scoundrel* ("*absurdum morale*") (28: 318; cf. R 5477; 18: 193, from 1776–78). Once the moral law, however, was supposed to provide its own incentive in the feeling of respect (in the GMS of 1785), that is, once practical reason became fully autonomous, those simple calculations had to be abandoned and the role of (belief in) god in moral philosophy had to be reconceived. Kant still insisted on the 'absurd' position of the atheist but the Spinoza example in KU may indicate that cracks in the doctrine are showing. By the time of the *Opus postumum*, it seems that the postulate 'god exists' has finally lost its former significance.[15]

Kant repeats the moral proof in KU under the title of "ethico-theology" and contrasts it to the physico-theological argument. The latter argument, in Kant's version and very roughly sketched, leads from the 'fact' of organisms in nature to our need to judge them as purposes of nature and from there to judging the whole of nature as a system of purposes, in which every object is 'good for' some other object. These chains of purposive relations have to terminate in some "ultimate purpose of nature," which itself is not purposive for any other object.[16] This termination point, Kant says, can lie only in an object that is able to set purposes for itself and the only thing in nature of this kind is the human being (5: 426f.).

This is how far "physical teleology" can take us. Physico-theology attempts to go further and asks for the ground of the system of purposes in nature, thereby arriving at the concept of an "artistic intelligence" that has arranged this organization of nature (5: 440f.). But – as Kant already pointed out in KrV (A 620–30) – this concept is "indeterminate" in several

---

[14] See Section 5.2. An example from the *Metaphysik Volckmann* (1783/84, just before the GMS): "If there is no governor [*Regierer*] who will at some time distribute happiness in accordance with good behavior: then morality has no incentives" (28: 385). If somebody is virtuous and sacrifices much of her happiness without the belief that her conduct will later be appropriately rewarded, she "is a *Phantast* and pursues a figment of the brain" (28: 386). Similarly, R 6110, from the same time (18: 458).

[15] Cf. Förster (2000: ch. 5).

[16] Cf., for instance, the reconstruction of the argument in Guyer (2005a: chs. 12 and 13, 2014a).

9.1 Teleology

ways: it is an intelligence, but not necessarily a creator, it does not necessarily have wisdom (moral benevolence), and it may not even be a single being but could be a collective (5: 480). Physico-theology, therefore, leads to a "demonology," not to a theology (5: 444). In particular, we can still ask further about this intelligence's purpose in arranging nature in this way. An answer to the question, which would block the regress of more questions, would have to point to a purpose that is, as it were, self-justifying, a purpose that would satisfy reason's quest for the unconditioned. Such a purpose, however, can only be given by morality – the "final purpose of creation," the highest good or the existence of "the human being (each rational being in the world) under moral laws" (5: 448). Once this final purpose is imported by practical reason and establishes what Kant calls "ethico-theology," the concept of god can be made determinate (that is, all the traditional Christian attributes can be derived) and ethico-theology thereby compensates the deficiency of physico-theology:

> In this way moral teleology makes good the defect of physical teleology, and first establishes a theology; since the latter, if it is to proceed consistently rather than borrowing, unnoticed, from the former, could by itself alone establish nothing more than a demonology, which is not capable of any determinate concept. (5: 444)

The indeterminacy in the physico-theological concept of god corresponds to an indeterminacy in the notion of the ultimate purpose of nature. Even though we know that the addressee of this purpose is the human being, Kant insists that what this purpose consists in cannot be determined within nature itself. "To discover where in the human being we are ... to posit that ultimate end of nature," we have to refer to the final purpose, that is, to practical reason. With the help of this selection criterion, Kant identifies as the ultimate purpose what "nature can accomplish with a view to the final end that lies outside of it", that is, "that which nature is capable of doing in order to prepare [the human being] for what he must himself do in order to be a final end" (5: 431). This ultimate end in nature is *culture*, in particular, the "culture of training (discipline)," which "consists in the liberation of the will from the despotism of desires" (5: 432) and which is a condition for enabling us to make the free choices that are required for pursuing the highest good. It is only in light of the final purpose that we can recognize that nature "displays [in regard of discipline] ... a purposive effort at an education to make us receptive to higher ends than nature itself can afford." Engagement with "beautiful arts and sciences" is part of this effort to "reduce the tyranny of sensible tendencies" (5: 433), which reminds us of remarks Kant made much earlier in the KU, for instance, that "the beautiful prepares us to love something, even nature, without interest" (5: 267) or that the pleasure of taste is "teaching us to find a free satisfaction in the objects of the senses even without any sensible charm" (5: 354).

It may seem as if there is indeed a transition from nature to freedom because the teleological argument from nature leads to the human being as the carrier of the ultimate purpose, while the moral argument identifies the human being as the addressee of the final purpose. The arguments from bottom up and from top down seem to meet in the same object. But, of course, the being that qualifies as the ultimate purpose of nature is the human being as part of nature ("as a link in nature [*Naturglied*]"; 5: 443) while the being that is receptive to the duty to realize the final purpose is the human being as an intelligible being, the "human being . . . considered as noumenon" (5: 435). Kant emphasizes this difference repeatedly and finally admits the inevitable consequence of the difference: the moral proof does not really complement the physico-theological argument but rather makes it superfluous, at least in a systematic sense.

> In fact . . . only the moral ground of proof carries conviction, and only in a moral respect, assent to which everyone feels most deeply; the physico-teleological argument, however, has only the merit of guiding the mind on the path of ends in the contemplation of the world, and thereby to an intelligent author of the world . . . . The moral basis for the proof of the existence of God, however, does not properly merely supplement the physico-theological proof, thereby making it into a complete proof; rather, it is a special proof that makes good the lack of conviction in the latter . . . [The physico-theological proof can] make us . . . more receptive to the moral proof. (5: 477f.)

Since the moral argument is "entirely independent" of the physico-theological one, it would have to be accepted even by beings who live in a world without any "clear trace of organization," a world that "reveals only effects of a mere mechanism of raw matter." Such beings would have no reason to develop a physical teleology and infer to an intelligent author but they still would feel the force of the moral argument (5: 478f.).

What role is then left for the physico-theology developed in the KU with respect to the 'logical transition'? In § 88, Kant asks whether the "objective reality of the concept of a final end of creation" can be established, if not apodictically, then at least "for the maxims of the theoretically reflecting power of judgment," that is, as a regulative claim. This would mean, Kant explains, that theoretical philosophy could "connect the moral end with natural ends by means of the idea of a single end" (5: 454) and the optimism of the Canon in KrV would be vindicated, namely, that the

> systematic unity of ends in ... the moral world (*regnum gratiae*), also leads inexorably to the purposive unity of all things that constitute this great whole, in accordance with universal laws of nature, just as the first does in accordance with universal and necessary moral laws, and unifies practical with speculative reason. (A 815)

But Kant denies this prospect in KU emphatically; no such unification of the two parts of philosophy can be accomplished, because the concepts of the ultimate end of nature and of the final end of creation are so radically different that there is no ground for the earlier optimism. The concept of the final end, as a concept of practical reason, "can neither be deduced from any data of experience for the theoretical judging of nature nor be derived from any cognition of it. No use of this concept is possible except solely for practical reason in accordance with moral laws" (5: 454f.).

The role of the physico-theological proof in the end seems limited to one of persuasion:[17] It provides "desired confirmation of the moral argument, insofar as nature is thus capable of displaying something analogous to the (moral) ideas of reason" (5: 479), an analogy that Kant calls in *Fortschritte* "very conducive" for the acceptance of the moral argument (20: 300). In the language of § 59, this analogy establishes the teleological structure of nature as a symbol of "(moral) ideas of reason," just as the beautiful was earlier analyzed as such a symbol of morality. The real work with respect to convincing us of the realizability of the highest good, however, has to be done by the moral argument and practical reason's concept of a final purpose. A 'logical transition' thus can be identified in the teleological part of the KU only in a very attenuated sense: the power of judgment with its concept of an objective purposiveness of nature provides *psychological* support for the moral proof; its systematic relevance remains limited to the architectonic sense of the transition, viz., justifying the application of the concept of 'purpose' or 'purposiveness' to nature.

---

[17] This persuasive role of the proof is the reason for Kant's long-standing respect for the argument as "the oldest, clearest and most appropriate to common human reason" (A 623). Mendelssohn, in 1764, agreed that the argument does not amount to a demonstration but that it has more persuasive force (*Beredungskraft*) than even a demonstration (1764: 313).

9.2 The New 'Gulf'

I return to the question of why it seemed necessary to Kant to take up the issue of the realizability of the highest good again after the KpV had already shown, in the resolution of the antinomy of practical reason, that we can lay to rest worries that the task of attaining the final purpose may be impossible because of internal contradictions within the concept of the highest good. The result of the resolution was that speculative reason cannot prove that the highest good is impossible and that the interest of practical reason entitles us to believe in its realizability with the assistance of a wise creator (e.g., 5: 145f.). What does the teleological part of the KU really add to this? I suggested above: not much, except in terms of persuasion and psychological support. It is quite plausible, then, to think that what motivated Kant to take up the question again, shortly after he had finished the KpV, was the need he saw to go beyond the "austere" presentation in the second *Critique*. This is Guyer's view: Kant "recognizes that we are sensuous as well as rational creatures, and need sensuous as well as rational presentation and confirmation of the conditions of the possibility of morality." And he quotes from the *Religion*, where Kant "asserts 'the natural need of all human beings to demand for even the highest concepts and grounds of reason something that the senses can hold on to, some confirmation from experience or the like.'"[18] Kant therefore "believes that every means for cultivating moral feeling and thus narrowing the gap between our sensible and intellectual being must be seized."[19]

This proposal, as I said, is plausible, although it brings the project of a transition and its motivation quite close to the Baroque idea that the poet's task is to provide a sugar coating to the bitter pill of morality.[20] But there is more to Kant's project, which I hope to bring out by sketching what I take to be its background. My starting point is the "gap," Guyer mentions, "between our sensible and intellectual being." This gap is decidedly *old* in Kant's thinking in the form of the contrast between our receptive and spontaneous faculties. Could the *new* project really have been motivated

---

[18] Guyer (2005: 202); the quote is from (6: 109). Cf. also Guyer's suggestion that, after 1788, "the rationalism of the *Critique of Practical Reason* was too austere even for Kant himself" (2005: 225)..
[19] Guyer (2005: 225).
[20] Cf. Gottsched in the *Critische Dichtkunst* of 1730: "The most thorough treatise on morals is much too lean and dry for most people because the rigor of inferences of reason is not suitable for the common understanding of the uneducated. The naked truth does not please them: only learned minds can enjoy it .... Poetry, by contrast, is as edifying as morals and as enjoyable as historical narratives; it instructs and entertains and is suitable for the scholars as well as for the uneducated" (1730: 167).

9.2 The New 'Gulf'

by a sudden worry about this gap? I want to suggest that it was actually the discovery, after 1785, of a different, previously unnoticed gap that drove Kant's renewed engagement with the question of the realizability of the highest good, an engagement that does not so much modify the results of the KpV than take into account that the relevant gap is not the old one between receptivity and spontaneity but a new one *within* the spontaneous faculties themselves. This, I submit, explains why Kant, after 1788, placed so much emphasis on "finding ways in which morality, based in freedom, can be made accessible to feeling as well as reason."[21]

What I call the new gulf is implicit, if not explicit, in the distinction of the ultimate purpose of nature and the final purpose. About the former, Kant explains that, although the human being is "the sole being on earth who has understanding, and thus a capacity to set voluntary ends for himself," he is

> always only a link in the chain of natural ends; [he is] a principle, to be sure, with regard to many ends which nature seems to have determined for him in its predispositions, since he himself makes those his ends; yet also a means for the preservation of the purposiveness in the mechanism of the other links. (5: 430f.*)

The ability of setting oneself purposes is here attributed to the understanding, a spontaneous faculty, to be sure, but not to be equated with practical reason. What is striking and important, however, is that beings with this equipment still belong to *nature* as a teleological system; they do not, on account of this capacity alone, also qualify as beings with practical reason and therefore as addressees of the final end.

The same contrast is taken up again later: if a world, says Kant, contained only "rational beings ... whose reason was able to place the value of the existence of things only in the relation of nature to themselves (to their well-being), and were not able themselves to create such an original value (from freedom), then there would certainly be (relative) ends in the world, but no (absolute) final end" (5: 449). Such a world of purpose-setting beings would contain nothing but nature – a nature, in which everything is conditioned by further natural grounds or ends and that therefore would not contain anything unconditioned like the final end – even though it is populated, by assumption, with *rational* creatures. All determining grounds in nature are themselves conditioned, as one would expect. But Kant now emphasizes that "this holds not merely for

---

[21] Guyer (2005: 225).

nature outside of us (material nature), but also for nature inside of us (thinking [*denkenden*] nature) – as long as it is clearly understood that I am considering only that within me which is nature" (5: 435). The expression "thinking nature" (inside of us) is certainly striking and unexpected in Kant because the activity of thinking counts as a paradigmatic manifestation of our spontaneity – the spontaneity of apperception – and stands in contrast to our merely receptive capacities (sensibility).

Similarly, the KpV considers a scenario in which the actions of a being "have their determining ground ... in the causality of a supreme being which is distinct from him." Such a being, a "marionette", says Kant, could well be equipped with self-consciousness, with the ability to think – a "thinking automaton" – but "the consciousness of his own spontaneity, if taken for freedom, would be a mere delusion" (5: 101).[22] That is, a being could have the spontaneity of apperception and still lack freedom in the transcendental sense. A few years later, the *Vigilantius* lectures on metaphysics of morals (1793/94) confirm this possibility:

> The human being is not set free [*befreit*] from the mechanism of nature when he in his actions performs an act of reason [*actum der Vernunft*]. Every act of thinking, deliberation, is itself an occurrence in nature... such an act, however, is an inner occurrence because it happens in the human being.... Thus by the fact that he determines himself through grounds of reason and understanding to action, he is not yet free from all mechanism of nature. (27: 503f.*)

The shift in Kant appears even more clearly when we compare the claims I just quoted with his views expressed earlier in the KrV and the GMS, where the focus is on the divide between receptivity and spontaneity, between sensibility and understanding, together with (theoretical) reason, and where our possession of the latter faculties – in particular, our ability to form rational ideas – indicates that we are not merely natural creatures but also possess an "intelligible character," which qualifies us as members of the noumenal realm and, therefore, as (transcendentally) free and as standing under the moral law:

> The human being is one of the appearances in the world of sense, and to that extent also one of the natural causes whose causality must stand under empirical laws .... In the case of lifeless nature and nature having merely animal life, we find no ground for thinking of any faculty which is other than sensibly conditioned. Yet the human being, who is otherwise acquainted with the whole of nature solely through sense, knows himself

---

[22] Cf. also the "*automaton spirituale*" at (5: 97).

9.2 The New 'Gulf'

also through pure apperception ... he obviously is in one part phenomenon, but in another part, namely in regard to certain faculties, he is a merely intelligible object, because the actions of this object cannot at all be ascribed to the receptivity of sensibility. We call these faculties understanding and reason; chiefly the latter is distinguished quite properly and preeminently from all empirically conditioned powers, since it considers its objects merely according to ideas and in accordance with them determines the understanding, which then makes an empirical use of its own concepts (even the pure ones). (A 546f.)

Earlier in the Dialectic, Kant had already – albeit briefly and vaguely – suggested that speculative reason's transcendental ideas can not only "serve the understanding as a canon for its extended and self-consistent use" but also "perhaps ... make possible a transition from concepts of nature to the practical, and themselves generate support for the moral ideas and connection with the speculative cognitions of reason" (A 329). Although it is not clear what Kant had in mind at this point, one way in which transcendental and moral ideas could be connected is certainly in terms of their origin in faculties that share the aspect of radical spontaneity, as (A 546f.) claims.

The view that there is a spontaneity that is shared by our theoretical and practical faculties is one that Kant had held for a long time. In many lecture transcriptions and notes from the 1770s until the early 1780s, he apparently thought that a being with understanding – with the ability for apperception – is *automatically* also a being with moral status. This is nicely illustrated in the anthropology lecture of 1781/82: "If a horse could form the thought 'I,' I would have to dismount and regard the horse as my company. The 'I' makes human beings into persons" (25: 859).[23] That the spontaneous ability for apperception is *sufficient* for moral status is also affirmed in the metaphysics lectures from the mid-1770s: "When I say: 'I think,' 'I act,' etc., then the word 'I' is either misapplied or I am free" (28: 269). In Kant's own notes from this time, we find similar claims, for example: "The understanding itself (a being that has understanding) is ... transcendentally free" (R 4758; 17: 707; from 1775–77).[24]

Kant continued to hold this view in the GMS of 1785.[25] In GMS III, he argued that it is quite possible – "as speculative philosophy can show" –

---

[23] See Ludwig (2010: 606) [24] Cf. also R 4904 (18: 24; from 1776–78).
[25] This explains, I think, what Ameriks has called Kant's "nonchalant ambivalence" in the historical-political essays of the mid-1780s. In the "Idea for a Universal History" (1784), Ameriks finds that "the distinction between theoretical and practical considerations is not yet sharply drawn" and that Kant "casually propose[s] that we think about natural history as in effect the whole 'stage' for the advancement of freedom, while bracketing libertarian metaphysics" (2012a: 215). This is remedied

to presuppose freedom of the will without creating a conflict with the principle of natural necessity (4: 461). And for every rational being that is conscious of itself as having a will it is, "without further conditions," even necessary to think of its actions as free (4: 461). In the resolution of the third antinomy, speculative philosophy presumably has shown (i) that even though transcendental freedom cannot be thought coherently in the sensible world, it can be so thought if an intelligible realm is admitted. And furthermore (ii) that it is also possible to attribute such freedom to human beings if it can be demonstrated that humans are not only sensible creatures but also participate in the intelligible world. Kant then uses the argument from KrV (A 546f.), quoted above, in the so-called deduction of the categorical imperative, after the moral law has been established as binding for every purely rational will. Since humans are not purely rational wills – they are sensibly affected by inclinations – the question is: why should the law also be binding for them? As in KrV, Kant infers from the fact that we have *theoretical* reason (the ability to form ideas) that we are not merely sensible beings but also intelligible subjects, and hence the moral law is binding for us as an unconditional imperative (4: 451f.).

Although the interpretation of Kant's argument in GMS III is endlessly controversial,[26] I believe there is sufficient evidence to support the claim that he must have changed his mind after 1785 on the 'transition' from the spontaneity of theoretical reason to that of practical reason.[27] I have noted above what I take to be some traces of this shift in the KpV and KU. The most famous of these traces, of course, is the KpV's rejection of a deduction of the categorical imperative and its replacement with the doctrine of the 'fact of reason.' Kant now takes the consciousness of the obligation that the moral law imposes on us as a "fact of reason" that cannot be further elucidated and cannot be derived from premises like our consciousness of being members of the intelligible realm (5: 31). To the contrary, it is *only*

---

in the teleological part of the KU when Kant introduced the distinction between the "ultimate end of nature" and the "final end."

[26] One interpretive issue in the controversy is whether Kant, in the quotes from (A 546f.) and (4: 451f.) meant to refer to our ability to generate theoretical ideas (and hence was trying to argue from theoretical spontaneity to practical) or whether he actually included both kinds of ideas, theoretical and practical. For the latter interpretation, see, e.g., Puls (2016).

[27] Henrich has called the process in which Kant realized that the spontaneity of the will must not be confused with the spontaneity of theoretical reason "one of the most exciting and insightful" developments in the history of the formation of philosophical thoughts (1984: 32). Kant realized, after the GMS, that the "concept of a pure practical reason must in no way be understood as implied in the spontaneity of theoretical consciousness" (1984: 33). See also Allison (1990: ch. 12) who largely follows Henrich. In Allison (2020: 317–49), he modified his interpretation somewhat; cf. especially (330 n. 22).

9.3 The Aesthetic Transition

the awareness of moral obligation that can give us access to that realm. The role of transcendental ideas of (speculative) reason in providing us such access is accordingly played down: "In the entire faculty of reason only the practical can lift us above the world of sense and furnish cognitions of a supersensible order and connection, though these connections can be extended only as far as is needed for pure practical purposes" (5: 106). This seems to rule out the claim in KrV, quoted above, that we "know" ourselves, as intelligible beings, "through pure apperception." The argument of GMS III, in which Kant justified the bindingness of the categorical imperative through a 'transition' from theoretical to practical reason via membership in the intelligible realm, is not mentioned again in KpV. The earlier argument claimed that the obligation of the moral law ultimately rests on the fact that the intelligible realm is the "ground" of the sensible world and that the former's laws thus take precedence over the latter's; what accounts for the bindingness of the imperative for us is the supremacy of the intelligible ground, in which we participate in virtue of our ability to form ideas.[28]

So it seems that by the time of KpV and KU, Kant has complemented the old contrast of receptivity and spontaneity with a new one, a split *within* the spontaneous faculties themselves: understanding and theoretical reason on one side, practical reason on the other. This, I suggest, is the 'new gulf' and the background against which the aesthetic transition project of the KU is to be understood.

9.3 The Aesthetic Transition

The 'new gulf' is made explicit, for the first time as far as I can tell, in the *Religion*, the first part of which was published in 1792, and later again in the MS of 1797. In the introduction to the latter work, Kant reminds us of a distinction that has been a constant feature of his moral philosophy from the beginning: The moral law represents some action as a duty that is "a merely theoretical cognition of the possible determination of *Willkür*"; to this has to be added an incentive, a *Triebfeder*, which turns the theoretical cognition into an actual determination of *Willkür*, something we

---

[28] "But the intelligible world contains the ground of the sensible world and therefore also of its laws; and so in respect of my will, for which (as belonging entirely to the intelligible world) it gives laws immediately, it must also be conceived as containing such a ground. Hence, in spite of regarding myself from one point of view as a being that belongs to the sensible world, I shall have to recognize that, *qua* intelligence, I am subject to the law of the intelligible world ... and therefore I must look on the laws of the intelligible world as imperatives for me" (4: 453f.).

experience as an obligation (6: 218). It is a characteristic feature of Kant's moral philosophy after the KpV that he now identifies, and puts great emphasis on, a special disposition or capacity for feeling as a condition for subjects to be receptive for the incentive of the law. In GMS III, the deduction of the bindingness of the law did not refer to such a receptivity. The KpV analyzed the incentive – the feeling of respect for the law – at length, but it is only in the *Religion* and in MS that Kant identifies this special receptivity as the 'missing link' between beings that are rational in the sense of having theoretical reason (including the ability to set themselves purposes) and moral beings that have practical reason.

In the first part of the *Religion* he presented three "predispositions" that can be assigned to human beings:

1. The predisposition to the *animality* of the human being, as a *living being*;
2. To the *humanity* in him, as a living and at the same time *rational being*;
3. To his *personality*, as a rational and at the same time *responsible being*. (6: 26)

A long footnote, added to this distinction, elaborated on the differentiation of dispositions 2 and 3. Personality is not "already included in the concept of" humanity, he explained, but must be treated as a "special predisposition." From the fact that a being has reason – theoretical reason, including the ability for prudential calculations – it does not follow that "this reason contains a faculty of determining the power of choice unconditionally by virtue of simply representing its maxims as suited to universal legislation" (6: 23n.*).[29] Such a 'merely' rational being – even a maximally rational being – would not have an inkling of the kind of unconditional command that the moral law issues. A "most rational being" [*das allervernünftigste Weltwesen*] therefore could be "morally dead,"[30] unreceptive to the obligating force of the moral law. Thus, "the predisposition to personality is the receptivity for respect of the moral law as a by itself sufficient incentive for *Willkür*" (6: 27).[31]

---

[29] That Kant would allow it as possible that humanity and personality are not necessarily coextensive has caused puzzlement. See especially Wood (1999, 364): "There is no indication anywhere in Kant's writings that there might be a class of beings which have humanity ... but lack personality." (Wood does not mention the parallel passage in MS.) The important issue, however, is that such a class of beings is possible on Kant's premises, not whether he actually believed them to exist.
[30] This is the term Kant uses in MS (6: 400).
[31] In October 1790, the *Allgemeine Litteratur-Zeitung* reported briefly about a book, published in Dutch in the same year, in which the pseudonymous author posed, among several others, the following question to Kant: "Is practical reason ... completely different from speculative reason so

9.3 The Aesthetic Transition

A few years later, Kant made the same point, in different terminology, in the MS: a human being considers herself "first as a *sensible being*, that is as a human being (a member of one of the animal species), and secondly as an *intelligible being* [*Vernunftwesen*] (not merely as a being that has reason [*vernünftiges Wesen*], since reason as a theoretical faculty could well be an attribute of a living corporeal being)" (6: 418).³² Here the distinction of a *vernünftiges Wesen* and a *Vernunftwesen* obviously corresponds to the earlier one between humanity and personality. In analogy to the predisposition to personality of the *Religion*, Kant identifies in MS several "natural predispositions of the mind ... for being affected by concepts of duty," capacities for feeling that are given by nature to "every human being" (6: 399). These capacities are, as it were, activated by consciousness of the moral law and generate what Kant now calls "moral feeling" (among other kinds of morally relevant feeling). Although he explicitly denies that any *actual* human being lacks these predispositions (6: 400), the *possibility* of 'merely' rational beings – that can set themselves purposes and do mathematics and science, without having a moral conscience – is not excluded.

This possibility, indeed, is the basis for the (counterfactual) scenario Kant discussed in § 3 of KU (see Section 4.1.3).³³ There Kant considered rational beings who are, in the terms of MS, aware of the "merely theoretical cognition of the possible determination of *Willkür*" that comes with the moral law, but they are not receptive to the law's incentive and hence cannot make it inform their valuation of things. Kant diagnosed this lack as resulting from the crucial assumption underlying the scenario: that feelings in general are sensations and, therefore, all satisfaction reduces to the agreeable. In this case, the gap between theoretical and practical reason, or between humanity and personality, could not be filled; the subjects would inevitably lack "receptivity to concepts of duty as such" (6: 399). They would be aware of the moral law, its content, but they would be

---

that there could be rational spirits that can grasp mathematical, physical and other sciences but who are otherwise completely lacking the practical principle?" (Quoted in 13: 281). The journal judged the question, without supplying grounds, to be *"abgeschmackt"* (fatuous) and as evidence of the author's lack of understanding of Kant (*Intelligenzblatt der Allgemeinen Litteratur-Zeitung*, no. 140, 27 October 1790, 1156). Less than two years later, however, in April 1792, Kant in effect answered this question (in the essay that became the first part of the *Religion* in 1793) and explained that practical reason is indeed a capacity that does not come automatically with theoretical reason.

³² The distinction is introduced in the resolution of the *"scheinbare Antinomie"* in the *Doctrine of Virtue*.

³³ One could also think of the race of "devils" in *Perpetual Peace* of 1795 (8: 366).

incapable of the feeling by which the law "immediately influences ... [us] to obedience" (5: 452).

This development, I suggest, explains why Kant after 1788 placed so much emphasis on "finding ways in which morality, based in freedom, can be made accessible to feeling as well as reason" and that "every means for cultivating moral feeling ... must be seized."[34] The increased focus on feeling is due not so much to his belated realization that the doctrine of the KpV was "too austere" for humans. In my view, it is the loss of the 'transition' from theoretical spontaneity to moral status – the new split within the spontaneous faculties – that required the more prominent role of moral feeling as the missing link between the faculties. Kant of course had not earlier ignored the role of feeling in moral beings; but what is clearly new, after 1788, is the significance such feelings take on for him because the difference between rationality and morality consists precisely in the capacity for moral feeling.

To conclude: In the aesthetic transition, the sensible manifestation of the purposiveness of nature, the pleasure of taste, is supposed to make "possible the transition from sensible charm to the habitual moral interest without too violent a leap by representing the imagination even in its freedom as purposively determinable for the understanding" (5: 354).[35] What makes the leap supposedly less violent are *analogies* or affinities, in the aesthetic as well as in the logical transition. Analogies between the teleological structure of nature and moral ideas (5: 479) give – however problematic – "confirmation" to belief in a wise creator and affinities between the pleasure of taste and moral feeling promote "the receptivity of the mind for the moral feeling" (5: 197).[36] All of these analogies and affinities are based on the mediating concept of the (subjective and objective) purposiveness of nature. As a genuine concept of the power of judgment, it "still belongs to the concepts of nature" (5: 197), it is used 'immanently,' not as a transcendent notion, and because of this it can serve as "the mediating concept between the concepts of nature and the concept of freedom, which makes possible the transition from the purely theoretical to the purely practical, from lawfulness in accordance with the former to the final end in accordance with the latter" (5: 196). The mediating concept, as it were, replaces the old idea of a shared spontaneity of

---

[34] Guyer (2005: 225).   [35] Cf. Allison's commentary on this passage (2001: 217f.).

[36] Cf. also the preparatory notes for the *Doctrine of Virtue*: "It is an apriori law in us to observe how nature also may operate in ways that are similar to the principle of freedom and our satisfaction [in such observations] then promotes morality subjectively – the way in which to bring nature in us in agreement with freedom" (23: 375).

theoretical and practical reason, which would have been not a "bridge" to the intelligible realm but an entry ticket. But with the distinction, within the spontaneous faculties, of the moral being (personality) from a rational being (humanity), the receptivity for moral feeling, which defines the former, takes on a new significance and so do other feelings that could be obstacles to that receptivity. Under these conditions, and not merely because of the old 'gulf' between our sensitive, receptive nature and the spontaneity of our higher faculties, it is systematically important to remove such obstacles by offering opportunities to learn or get "trained," in the sense of the "culture of discipline," in ways that can prevent our 'flagging' in the effort to be virtuous.

Conclusion
The Autonomy of Taste

In analogy with his first two Critiques, Kant formulated the basic question of the aesthetic part of the third as follows: How are judgments with the characteristics we attribute to judgments of taste possible? Since the content of such judgments is a report about a peculiar kind of pleasure, this initial question thus corresponds to the question: How is this pleasure, with the characteristics of universality and independence of concepts, possible in the first place? His investigation starts with the realization that there seems to be a species of judgments that cannot be assimilated or reduced to other kinds of judgment; an account of how they are possible, therefore, will have to forego such assimilation or reduction. His answer to the question is that the possibility of such judgments requires the introduction of a new, higher faculty, that is, the reflecting power of judgment. The reconstruction of the introduction of this new faculty was the main topic of my study.

To whatever extent the early reviewers of the KU were correct in noting similarities between Kant and the rationalist and empiricist traditions, they did not seem to have noticed that Kant was interested in a question that did not quite correspond to questions that had been asked before. Granted, one could derive rules of taste from those occasions in which objects appear beautiful to us, connect such rules with the doctrine of empirical psychology – that the intuitive perception of perfection gives us pleasure – and thereby determine what is required for such perfection. Yet how could this approach account for the initial occurrence of pleasure, which obviously cannot depend on knowledge of the rules? Alternatively, an account of the peculiar pleasure of taste might require the postulation of a special sense of the sort found in Hutcheson. This would ensure a certain independence of judgments of taste from other judgments, made on the basis of the deliverances of other senses. But such a postulation would seem ad hoc in just the way Mendelssohn complained about.[1] Kant's own response – the introduction of a special faculty – might similarly seem ad hoc, were it not for the fact that the reflecting power of judgment turns out to have other tasks besides its aesthetic employment. These additional tasks, in fact, are essential to securing the universality of judgments of taste.

In my reconstruction, the introduction of the new faculty requires the principle of systematicity as a necessary, but not sufficient, condition; and the pleasure of taste, together with the general theory of pleasure, constitutes a further necessary condition. These conditions taken together, however, are jointly sufficient for the task: the principle of sytematicity ensures the universality of the pleasure, while this universality in turn justifies the requirement that a higher faculty has to play a constitutive role with respect to another faculty. To argue for this claim, I adopted two main hypotheses: (1) I attributed to Kant a theory according to which pleasure consists in the satisfaction of faculty interests, and (2) I claimed that there is nothing like a 'free play of the faculties' in the sense in which this term is usually understood. I call these two claims hypotheses because, as readers may have noticed, each of the claims violates a venerable philological maxim that one occurrence of a concept or phrase in an author's work means 'never mentioned' while two occurrences mean 'always.' My hypotheses are indeed based on two passages in the KU that each occur only once. Their plausibility thus depends crucially – besides on the historical context I lay out – on how much light they can shed on the reconstructive project.

I traced the introduction of the power of judgment into the system of higher faculties by starting from the pleasure of taste on through the interest of the new faculty and further on to the justification of this pleasure's claim to universality, which completes the deduction of "this unusual [*sonderbare*] faculty" (5: 281). In this line of argument, the free operation of the imagination turned out to be crucial. For, it is the free employment of the imagination – free, that is, both from the demands of the understanding as well as from what is empirically given – that accounts for the fact that judgments of taste cannot be assimilated or reduced to other kinds of judgment. Kant calls this the autonomy of taste (5: 281f.) and, on my proposal, it should be understood as the requirement that the reflecting power of judgment, in its aesthetic employment, has its own interest, an interest that cannot be reduced to other faculty interests. This interest,

---

[1] Mendelssohn (1757: 429f.): Hutcheson's postulation of an additional sense would block "all rational investigation".

which I identified as an interest in the free harmony of the imagination and the understanding, involves in taste the productively free imagination, which is to be distinguished from the reproductively free operation of the imagination in concept formation. The activity of the productively free imagination results in the pleasure of taste only when its products find their counterparts in nature. Whatever pleasure may be experienced in the free operation of the imagination itself, by contrast, would be an idiosyncratic pleasure since it does not consist in the satisfaction of an a priori principle. "For the imagination to be free and yet lawful by itself, i.e., that it carries autonomy with it, is a contradiction" (5: 241). That is, the imagination has no law of its own (except empirical laws of association); the law has to be given by the understanding. Taste, however, can be autonomous because it involves the aim of free harmony, the contingent agreement of the free imagination with the requirement of cognition in general. The attainment of this aim is recognized only in pleasure – hence, Kant's insistence that in judging beauty one has to 'taste for oneself,' rather than rely on the testimony of others or on general rules (e.g., 5: 285).

Taste, then, is not the capacity to detect a form's suitability for concept application or formation. Were this Kant's view, his position would be very similar to claims found in many eighteenth-century philosophers, according to which we judge objects in feeling more quickly, but less distinctly, than when we judge them through reason (and that such shortcut judgments can, after the fact, be ratified by more distinct deliberation). Wolff and Baumgarten, for instance, called the lower faculty of judging, among other capacities, an *analogon rationis*, the ability to judge *vernunftähnlich*. Kant's view is different from this: for him, we recognize in taste a freely produced form to be similar (enough) to a given conceptualized form. The point is not that we feel that a given form can be conceptualized; rather, we feel that a free form is concept-adequate because it agrees with a given conceptualized form. The freedom of the imagination is obviously essential here. And it is this freedom in its – for our discursive minds contingent and therefore unforced – agreement with the understanding that symbolizes moral freedom (Chapter 8).

The autonomy of taste gives rise to the worry that taste might lack the connection to 'cognition in general' that is, in the end, required to justify the claim to universal validity our judgments about beauty make. Given this worry, one might be tempted to identify the pleasure of taste with the pleasure that arises when we succeed in forming a concept of an object, a success that is evidently a necessary condition for any cognition of objects. The pleasure of taste then becomes one of the pleasures of the understanding, instead of a pleasure that characterizes the satisfaction of the interest of a separate higher faculty. And thus the (productive) freedom of the imagination seems hard to preserve because, in these views, the imagination is always working to promote cognition, in whatever indirect ways.[2] The pleasure of taste, accordingly, is not qualitatively but only quantitatively different from the pleasure of systematization and concept formation – which does not agree with the autonomy of taste. According to Geiger, for instance, "a critique examining the feeling of pleasure and displeasure is required because reflective judgment is a faculty of cognition that plays a necessary role in the construction of experience."[3] The contribution of taste to cognition, then, is "that the feeling of harmony expressed by aesthetic judgments is to be understood as the promissory feeling that a sensible manifold can be brought under concepts" and it is "thus through pure aesthetic judgments that objects are first given to us."[4] Such a view, as Geiger notes, stands at a tension with Kant's explicit insistence at (5: 190) that in a judgment of taste we have do not have "any intention of acquiring a concept."[5]

In accounts that assimilate the relation of imagination and understanding in taste to their relation in concept formation, the distinction of reproductively and productively free operation of the imagination is ignored or downplayed. In my view, by contrast, the requirement of productively free harmony functions as a selection mechanism that does not constrain the free operation of the imagination itself but admits as pleasurable only those free forms that actually agree with conceptualized forms.

A similar problem with the freedom of the imagination arises in attempts to transform Kant's theory into an 'objective' account. Consider Schiller, for example. It is no accident that in Schiller's *Kallias* project the free imagination does not appear to play much of a role at all. Practical reason is surprised to find among objects that are not determined by it (i.e., natural objects) some that look as if they had freely chosen their appearance; the arrangement of their parts seems free or autonomous in the sense that it seems as if it were "not from outside but through itself determined, autonomously determined."[6] Such objects appear as "imitations of free actions" or "analoga of reason."[7] Finding objects of this sort

---

[2] Accounts of this kind have been suggested, e.g., by Wieland (2001: 362–81); Zinkin (2012); Cohen (2017); and most recently by Geiger (2022).
[3] Geiger (2022: 17). [4] Geiger (2022: 189f.). [5] Geiger (2022: 197).
[6] Schiller (1992: 181): letter of 25 January 1793. [7] Schiller (1992: 179)

among objects that are not free but parts of the mechanism of nature is surprising and therefore pleasing; the pleasure of taste is therefore a pleasure of practical reason. Schiller attempts to formulate an 'objective' account of the conditions that must be satisfied if an object is to appear as self-determined. In the example of a beautifully shaped vase, "the mass [of the object] is completely dominated by the form," that is, the vase does not appear to be shaped by the external influence of gravity; and in a beautiful horse, the body is "completely dominated by ... the forces of life," rather than by external purposes as in a work horse.[8] For Schiller, then, what appears in the beautiful object – what is symbolized by it – is *immediately* the freedom of practical reason, not mediated by the freedom of the imagination. This proposal to identify features of the object that seem analogous to the idea of freedom is quite different from Kant's understanding of how beauty symbolizes morality. The freedom of the imagination, which was central to Kant's construction of the analogy, is thereby cancelled.

On my interpretation, the (subjective) purposiveness of nature for judgment that we experience in beauty has two aspects, which together are unique to this experience. (i) The understanding imposes its laws on nature but only the most fundamental laws. The production of things with specific forms in nature, however, is governed by particular, or empirical, laws that do not stand in a relation to the fundamental ones that we can grasp; to our minds, the former are contingent. Thus, we are temporarily surprised and pleased that the forms of things that result from the operation of particular laws can be conceptualized by us. Nature seems purposive for us with respect to concept formation, which we require for cognition. (ii) In the experience of beautiful things in nature we feel a similar surprise because, on these occasions, the free operation of the imagination is in harmony with what cognition delivers to us. We cannot expect or predict such occasions, nor can we understand why they occur, and the harmony is contingent for us. But they are occasions on which nature seems to have produced forms of things that agree with forms that the imagination (could have) produced freely, that is, not in the service of the understanding. It is the combination of the two aspects in the pleasure of taste that explains, from the viewpoint of the KU, the meaning of Kant's often quoted note from the 1770s: "The beautiful things indicate that the human being fits into the world" (R 1820a; 16: 127*).

---

[8] Schiller (1992: 205), letter of 23 February 1793.

Bibliography

Kant's Works

Kant, Immanuel (1900–): *Gesammelte Schriften* (Akademie Ausgabe). Berlin: Reimer, later deGruyter.

Translations Consulted

The Cambridge Edition of the Works of Immanuel Kant. P. Guyer/A. Wood (general editors). Cambridge: Cambridge University Press 1992–.
Lectures on Logic. J. M. Young (ed., transl.). Cambridge: Cambridge University Press 1992.
Opus Postumum. E. Foerster/M. Rosen (eds., transl.). Cambridge: Cambridge University Press 1993.
Practical Philosophy. M. Gregor (ed., transl.). Cambridge: Cambridge University Press 1996.
Religion and Rational Theology. A. Wood/G. diGiovanni (eds., transl.). Cambridge: Cambridge University Press 1996.
Lectures on Ethics. P. Heath/J. Schneewind (eds., transl.). Cambridge: Cambridge University Press 1997.
Lectures on Metaphysics. K. Ameriks/S. Naragon (eds., transl.). Cambridge: Cambridge University Press 1997.
Critique of Pure Reason. P. Guyer/A. Wood (eds., transl.). Cambridge: Cambridge University Press 1998.
Correspondence. A. Zweig (ed., transl.). Cambridge: Cambridge University Press 1999.
Critique of the Power of Judgment. P. Guyer/E. Matthews (eds., transl.). Cambridge: Cambridge University Press 2000.
Notes and Fragments. P. Guyer (ed.), C. Bowman et al. (transl.). Cambridge: Cambridge University Press 2005.

Primary Sources

Anonymous (1792): "Vergleichung des Baumgartenschen und Kantischen Begriffs der Schönheit." *Neue Bibliothek der schönen Wissenschaften und der freyen Künste* 46, 163–91.

Baumgarten, Alexander (1735 [1954]): *Reflections on Poetry*. K. Aschenbrenner/ W. Holther (eds., transl.). Berkeley: University of California Press.

— (1783): *Metaphysik*. Transl. G. F. Meier. 2nd ed. Halle: Hemmerde.

Boileau-Despréaux, Nicolas (1674 [1970]): *L'art poetique*. A. Buck (ed.). Munich: Fink.

Breitinger, Johann Joachim (1740): *Critische Dichtkunst*. Zurich: Orell.

Crusius, Christian August (1767): *Anweisung vernünftig zu leben*. 3rd ed. Leipzig: Gleditsch.

De Pouilly, Louis Jean Lévesque (1751): *Theorie der angenehmen Empfindungen* .... F. J. Biel (transl.). Leipzig: Wendler.

Descartes, René (1985): *The Passions of the Soul*. In: Descartes, *Philosophical Writings*. Vol. 1. J. Cottingham et al. (transl.). Cambridge: Cambridge University Press, 326–404.

— (1991): *Philosophical Writings*. Vol. 3. J. Cottingham et al. (transl.). Cambridge: Cambridge University Press.

Dubos, Jean-Baptiste (1748): *Critical Reflections on Poetry, Painting and Music*. 5th ed. Transl. Th. Nugent. 3 vols. London: John Nourse.

Eberhard, Johann August (1786): *Theorie der schönen Wissenschaften*. 2nd ed. Halle: Buchhandlung des Waisenhauses.

— (1791): "Einige Anmerkungen über die Recension meiner Theorie der schönen Künste und Wissenschaften in der Allg. Litt. Zeit." *Philosophisches Magazin* 4, 148–70.

Fichte, Johann Gottlieb (1962): "Versuch eines erklärenden Auszugs aus Kants Kritik der Urteilskraft." In: *Nachgelassene Schriften 1780–1791 (Gesamtausgabe*, vol. II.1, R. Lauth et al. [eds.]) Stuttgart-Bad Cannstatt: Fromann-Holzboog, 319–73.

Garve, Christian (1779): "Versuch über die Prüfung der Fähigkeiten." In: *Gesammelte Werke*. Vol. I.5. K. Wölfel (ed.). Hildesheim: Olms, 8–115.

Gellert, Christian Fürchtegott (1774): "Wie weit sich der Nutzen der Regeln in der Beredsamkeit und Poesie erstrecke." In: *Gellerts Abhandlungen und Reden*. Karlsruhe: Schmieder, 154–86.

Gerard, Alexander (1774 [1966]): *An Essay on Genius*. B. Fabian (ed.). Munich: Fink.

Gottsched, Johann Christoph (1730 [1962]): *Versuch einer Critischen Dichtkunst* .... Darmstadt: WBG.

Hamann, Johann Georg (1965): *Briefwechsel*. Vol. 5. A. Henkel (ed.). Frankfurt: Insel.

Herder, Johann Gottfried (1775 [1887]): "Ursachen des gesunknen Geschmacks bei den verschiednen Völkern, da er geblühet." In: *Sämmtliche Werke*. Vol. 5. B. Suphan (ed.). Berlin: Weidmann, 599–655.

Hutcheson, Francis (2004): *An Inquiry into the Original of Our Ideas of Beauty and Virtue*. W. Leidhold (ed.). Indianapolis: Liberty Fund.

Kames, Henry Home (1785 [2005]): *Elements of Criticism*. Vol. 1., 6th ed. P. Jones (ed.). Indianapolis: Liberty Fund.

Leibniz, Gottfried Wilhelm (1860): *Briefwechsel zwischen Leibniz und Christian Wolff*. C. I. Gerhardt (ed.). Halle: H. W. Schmidt.

Bibliography

(1966): *Theodicy*. D. Allen (ed.). Indianapolis: Bobbs-Merrill.
(1981): *New Essays on Human Understanding*. P. Remnant/J. Bennet (eds., transl.). Cambridge: Cambridge University Press.
(1989): *Philosophical Essays*. R. Ariew/D. Garber (eds.). Indianapolis: Hackett.
Maupertuis, Pierre Louis Moreau de (1750): *Versuch in der moralischen Weltweisheit, übersetzt aus dem Französischen des Herrn von Maupertuis*. Halle: Gebauer.
Meier, Georg Friedrich (1744): *Theoretische Lehre von den Gemütsbewegungen überhaupt*. Halle: Hemmerde.
(1752): *Auszug aus der Vernunftlehre*. Halle: Hemmerde.
(1754): *Anfangsgründe aller schönen Wissenschaften*. 3 vols. Halle: Hemmerde.
Mendelssohn, Moses (1755 [1971]): *Über die Empfindungen*. In: *Gesammelte Schriften. Jubiläumsausgabe*. Vol. 1. F. Bamberger et al. (eds.). Stuttgart: Frommann, 41–123.
(1757 [1971]): *Über die Hauptgrundsätze der schönen Wissenschaften und Künste*. In: *Gesammelte Schriften. Jubiläumsausgabe*. Vol. 1. F. Bamberger et al. (eds.). Stuttgart: Frommann, 425–52.
(1764 [1971]): *Abhandlung über die Evidenz in Metaphysischen Wissenschaften*. In: *Gesammelte Schriften. Jubiläumsausgabe*. Vol. 2. F. Bamberger et al. (eds.). Stuttgart: Frommann, 267–330.
(1770? [1971]): "Bemerkungen zu den 'Philosophischen Schriften,' 1761." In: *Gesammelte Schriften. Jubiläumsausgabe*. Vol. 1. F. Bamberger et al. (eds.). Stuttgart: Frommann, 223–26.
(1771 [1971]): *Über die Empfindungen*. In: *Gesammelte Schriften. Jubiläumsausgabe*. Vol. 1. F. Bamberger et al. (eds.). Stuttgart: Frommann, 233–334.
(1771a [1971]): "Rhapsodie oder Zusätze zu den Briefen ...." In: *Gesammelte Schriften. Jubiläumsausgabe*. Vol. 1. F. Bamberger et al. (eds.). Stuttgart: Frommann, 381–424.
Rehberg, August Wilhelm (1788 [1975]): "Rezension der 'Kritik der praktischen Vernunft'." In: *Materialien zu Kants "Kritik der praktischen Vernunft."* R. Bittner et al. (eds). Frankfurt: Suhrkamp, 179–96.
Rüdiger, Andreas (1721): *Anweisung zu der Zufriedenheit der menschlichen Seele ...*. Leipzig: Coerner.
Schiller, Friedrich (1992): *Briefwechsel. Schillers Briefe 1. 3. 1790 – 17. 5. 1794* (= *Schillers Werke. Nationalausgabe*, Vol. 26). Weimar: Böhlau.
Schlegel, August Wilhelm (1989): "Vorlesungen über schöne Literatur und Kunst." In: *Vorlesungen über Ästhetik I*. E. Behler (ed.). Paderborn: Schöningh, 179–472.
Schlegel, Friedrich (1797): "Über das Studium der griechischen Poesie." In: *Schriften zur Literatur*. W. Rasch (ed.). München: Deutscher Taschenbuch Verlag, 84–192.
Sulzer, Johann Georg (1771): *Allgemeine Theorie der schönen Künste*. Vol. 1. Leipzig: Weidmann.
(1773): *Vermischte philosophische Schriften*. Leipzig: Weidmann.
(1774): *Allgemeine Theorie der schönen Künste*. Vol. 2. Leipzig: Weidmann.

Tetens, Johann Nicolas (1777 [1913]): *Philosophische Versuche über die menschliche Natur und ihre Entwickelung.* Vol. 1. Reprint. Berlin: Kantgesellschaft.
Walch, Johann Georg (1726): *Philosophisches Lexicon.* Leipzig: Gleditsch.
Wolff, Christian (1751): *Vernünfftige Gedanken von Gott, der Welt und der Seele des Menschen.* Halle: Renger.

Secondary Literature

Albrecht, Michael (1978): *Kants Antinomie der praktischen Vernunft.* Hildesheim: Olms.
Allison, Henry (1990): *Kant's Theory of Freedom.* Cambridge: Cambridge University Press.
  (1996): *Idealism and Freedom.* Cambridge: Cambridge University Press.
  (2001): *Kant's Theory of Taste.* Cambridge: Cambridge University Press.
  (2003): "Reply to the Comments of Longuenesse and Ginsborg." *Inquiry* 46, 182–94.
  (2004): *Kant's Transcendental Idealism.* 2nd ed. Cambridge: Cambridge University Press.
  (2020): *Kant's Conception of Freedom.* Cambridge: Cambridge University Press.
Alston, William P. (1967): "Pleasure." In: *Encyclopedia of Philosophy.* Vol. 6. London: Macmillan, 341–47.
Altmann, Alexander (1969): *Moses Mendelssohns Frühschriften zur Metaphysik.* Tübingen: Mohr.
Ameriks, Karl (2003): *Interpreting Kant's Critiques.* Oxford: Oxford University Press.
  (2012): *Kant's Elliptical Path.* Oxford: Oxford University Press.
Anderson, R. Lanier (2015): *The Poverty of Conceptual Truth.* Oxford: Oxford University Press.
[Anonymous] (1790): [Review of J. A. Eberhard, *Theorie der schönen Künste und Wissenschaften*, 3rd ed.] *Allgemeine Litteratur-Zeitung* 344, 778–84.
Aydede, Murat (2000): "An Analysis of Pleasure vis-à-vis Pain." *Philosophy and Phenomenological Research* 61, 537–61.
  (2018): "A Contemporary Account of Sensory Pleasure." In: *Pleasure. A History.* L. Shapiro (ed.), Oxford: Oxford University Press, 239–66.
Basch, Victor (1896): *Essai critique sur l'esthétique de Kant.* Paris: Alcan.
Bayerer, Wolfgang (1968): "Bemerkungen zu einer vergessenen Reflexion Kants über das Gefühl der Lust und Unlust." *Kant-Studien* 59, 266–72.
Beck, Lewis White (1960): *A Commentary on Kant's "Critique of Practical Reason."* Chicago: University of Chicago Press.
Beiser, Frederick (1987): *The Fate of Reason.* Cambridge, MA: Harvard University Press.
  (2005): *Schiller as Philosopher: A Re-Examination.* Oxford: Oxford University Press.
  (2006): "Moral Faith and the Highest Good." In: *The Cambridge Companion to Kant and Modern Philosophy.* P. Guyer (ed.), Cambridge: Cambridge University Press, 588–629.

(2009): *Diotima's Children: German Aesthetic Rationalism from Leibniz to Lessing*. Oxford: Oxford University Press.
Bernstein, Jay (1992): *The Fate of Art*. Cambridge: Polity.
Brandt, Reinhard (1989): "Analytic/Dialectic." In: *Reading Kant*. E. Schaper/W. Vossenkuhl (eds.). Oxford: Blackwell, 179–95.
    (2007): *Die Bestimmung des Menschen bei Kant*. Hamburg: Meiner.
Brandt, Richard (1979): *A Theory of the Good and the Right*. Oxford: Oxford University Press.
Buchenau, Stefanie (2013): *The Founding of Aesthetics in the German Enlightenment*. Cambridge: Cambridge University Press.
Budd, Malcolm (2001): "The Pure Judgment of Taste as an Aesthetic Reflective Judgment." *British Journal of Aesthetics* 41, 247–60.
    (2002): *The Aesthetic Appreciation of Nature*. Oxford: Oxford University Press.
Caranti, Luigi (2005): "Logical Purposiveness and the Principle of Taste." *Kant-Studien* 96, 364–74.
Chignell, Andrew (2007): "Kant on the Normativity of Taste: The Role of Aesthetic Ideas." *Australasian Journal of Philosophy* 85, 415–33.
Clewis, Robert (2009): *The Kantian Sublime and the Revelation of Freedom*. Cambridge: Cambridge University Press.
    (2023): *The Origins of Kant's Aesthetics*. Cambridge: Cambridge University Press.
Cohen, Alix (2017): "Kant on Beauty and Cognition." In: *Thinking about Science and Reflecting on Art*. O. Bueno et al. (eds.). London: Routledge, 140–54.
    (2018): "Rational Feelings." In: *Kant and the Faculty of Feeling*. K. Sorensen/D. Williamson (eds.). Cambridge: Cambridge University Press, 9–24.
Cohen, Hermann (1889): *Kants Begründung der Ästhetik*. Berlin: Dümmler.
Cohen, Ted (1993): "The Relation of Pleasure and Judgment in Kant's Aesthetics." In: *Kant and Critique. New Essays in Honor of W.H. Werkmeister*. R. M. Dancy (ed.). Dordrecht: Kluwer, 117–24.
Cramer, Konrad (1985): *Nicht-reine synthetische Urteile a priori*. Heidelberg: Winter.
Crawford, Donald W. (1982): "Kant's Theory of Creative Imagination." In: *Essays in Kant's Aesthetics*. T. Cohen/P. Guyer (eds.). Chicago: University of Chicago Press, 151–78.
Di Giovanni, George (2005): *Freedom and Religion in Kant and His Immediate Successors*. Cambridge: Cambridge University Press.
Dobe, Jennifer (2018): "Kant's A Priori Principle of Judgments of Taste." In: *Freedom and Spontaneity in Kant*. K. Moran (ed.). Cambridge: Cambridge University Press, 68–88.
Düsing, Klaus (1968): *Die Teleologie in Kants Weltbegriff*. Berlin: deGruyter.
Dumouchel, Daniel (1994): "La découverte de la faculté de juger réflechissante." *Kant-Studien* 85, 419–42.
Dyck, Corey (2016): "Spontaneity before the Critical Turn." *Journal of the History of Philosophy* 54, 625–48.

Elliot, R. K. (1968): "The Unity of Kant's 'Critique of Aesthetic Judgement'." *British Journal of Aesthetics* 8, 244–59.

Engstrom, Stephen (2007): "Kant on the Agreeable and the Good." In *Moral Psychology*. S. Tenenbaum (ed.). Amsterdam: Rodopoi, 111–60.

— (2010): "The 'Triebfeder' of Pure Practical Reason." In: *Kant's Critique of Practical Reason. A Critical Guide*. A. Reath/J. Timmermann (eds.). Cambridge: Cambridge University Press, 90–118.

Esser, Andrea (1997): *Kunst als Symbol*. München: Fink.

Fabbianelli, Faustino (2004): "Einleitung." In: K. L. Reinhold, *Beiträge zur Berichtigung bisheriger Missverständisse der Philosophen*. Vol. 2. K. L. Fabbianelli (ed.). Hamburg: Meiner, ix–ciii.

Feder, Johann Georg Heinrich (1790): [Review of KU]. *Göttingische Anzeigen von gelehrten Sachen* 114, 1137–47.

— (1791): "Kant's Critik der Urtheilskraft." *Philosophische Bibliothek* 4, 180–94.

Förster, Eckart (2000): *Kant's Final Synthesis*. Cambridge, MA: Harvard University Press.

— (2008): "Von der Eigentümlichkeit unseres Verstandes in Ansehung der Urteilskraft." In: *Kants Kritik der Urteilskraft*. O. Höffe (ed.). Berlin: Akademie, 259–74.

Fricke, Christel (1990): *Kants Theorie des reinen Geschmacksurteils*. Berlin: deGruyter.

Friedman, Michael (1992): "Causal Laws and the Foundations of Natural Science." In: *The Cambridge Companion to Kant*. P. Guyer (ed.). Cambridge: Cambridge University Press, 161–99.

— (1992a): *Kant and the Exact Sciences*. Cambridge, MA: Harvard University Press.

Frierson, Patrick (2014): *Kant's Empirical Psychology*. Cambridge: Cambridge University Press.

— (2018): "'A New Sort of A Priori Principles.' Psychological Taxonomies and the Origin of the Third Critique." In: *Kant and the Faculty of Feeling*. K. Sorensen/D. Williamson (eds.). Cambridge: Cambridge University Press, 107–29.

Geiger, Ido (2022): *Kant and the Claims of the Empirical World*. Cambridge: Cambridge University Press.

Ginsborg, Hannah (1990): *The Role of Taste in Kant's Theory of Cognition*. New York: Garland.

— (2015): *The Normativity of Nature*. Oxford: Oxford University Press.

— (2017): "In Defense of the One-Act View: Reply to Guyer." *British Journal of Aesthetics* 57, 421–35.

— (2018): "Why Must We Presuppose the Systematicity of Nature?" In: *Kant and Laws*. A. Breitenbach/M. Massimi (eds.). Cambridge: Cambridge University Press.

Giordanetti, Piero (1999): "Kants Entdeckung der Apriorität des Geschmacksurteils." In: *Aufklärung und Interpretation*. H. Klemme et al. (eds.). Würzburg: Königshausen, 171–96.

Guyer, Paul (1993): *Kant and the Experience of Freedom*. Cambridge: Cambridge University Press.
   (1997): *Kant and the Claims of Taste*. 2nd ed. Cambridge: Cambridge University Press.
   (2005): *Values of Beauty*. Cambridge: Cambridge University Press.
   (2005a): *Kant's System of Nature and Freedom*. Oxford: Oxford University Press.
   (2008): "The Psychology of Kant's Aesthetics." *Studies in History and Philosophy of Science* 39, 483–94.
   (2014): *A History of Modern Aesthetics*. Vol.1. Cambridge: Cambridge University Press.
   (2014a): "Freedom, Happiness, and Nature: Kant's Moral Teleology." In: *Kant's Theory of Biology*. I. Goy/E. Watkins (eds.). Berlin: deGruyter, 221–37.
   (2017): "One Act or Two? Hannah Ginsborg on Aesthetic Judgment." *British Journal of Aesthetics* 57, 407–19.
   (2018): "What Is It Like to Experience the Beautiful and Sublime?" In: *Kant and the Faculty of Feeling*. K. Sorensen/D. Williamson (eds.). Cambridge: Cambridge University Press, 147–65.
   (2020): *Reason and Experience in Mendelssohn and Kant*. Oxford: Oxford University Press.
Heathwood, Christopher (2007): "The Reduction of Sensory Pleasure to Desire." *Philosophical Studies* 133, 23–44.
Henrich, Dieter (1960): "Der Begriff der sittlichen Einsicht und Kants Lehre vom Faktum der Vernunft." In: *Die Gegenwart der Griechen*. Henrich et al. (eds.). Tübingen: Mohr, 77–115.
   (1963 [1984]): "Ethik der Autonomie." In: *Selbstverhältnisse*. Stuttgart: Reclam, 6–56.
   (1992): *Aesthetic Judgment and the Moral Image of the World*. Stanford: Stanford University Press.
Hogrebe, Wolfram (1992 [1981]): "Die ursprüngliche Lust der Prädikation." In: *Metaphysik und Mantik*. Frankfurt: Suhrkamp, 73–79.
Höwing, Thomas (2013): *Praktische Lust*. Berlin: deGruyter.
Horstmann, Rolf Peter (2018): *Kant's Power of Imagination*. Cambridge: Cambridge University Press.
Kalkar, Brent (2006): *The Demands of Taste in Kant's Aesthetics*. London: Continuum.
Kern, Andrea (2000): *Schöne Lust*. Frankfurt: Suhrkamp.
Kim, Jaegwon (1998): *Mind in a Physical World*. Cambridge, MA: MIT Press.
Kleingeld, Pauline (1998): "Kant on the Unity of Theoretical and Practical Reason." *Review of Metaphysics* 52, 500–28.
Klemme, Heiner (2006): "Bibliography." In: Kant, *Kritik der Urteilskraft*. H. Klemme (ed.). Hamburg: Meiner, 557–86.
   (2010): "The Origin and Aim of Kant's 'Critique of Practical Reason.'" In: *Kant's Critique of Practical Reason. A Critical Guide*. A. Reath/J. Timmermann (eds.). Cambridge: Cambridge University Press, 11–30.

Kuehn, Manfred (2004): "Einleitung." In: *Immanuel Kant Vorlesung über die Moralphilosophie*. W. Stark (ed.). Berlin: deGruyter, vii–xxxv.

Kuhlenkampff, Jens (1978): *Kants Logik des ästhetischen Urteils*. Frankfurt: Klostermann.

La Rocca, Claudio (2012): "Von den regulativen Funktionen des Urteilskraftprinzips." In: *Worauf die Vernunft hinaussieht . . . .* B. Dörflinger et al. (eds.). Hildesheim: Olms, 13–29.

Lin, Eden (2020): "Attitudinal and Phenomenological Theories of Pleasure." *Philosophy and Phenomenological Research* 100, 510–24.

Longuenesse, Beatrice (1998): *Kant and the Capacity to Judge*. Princeton: Princeton University Press.

(2003): "Kant's Theory of Judgment and Judgments of Taste." *Inquiry* 46, 143–63.

(2005): *Kant on the Human Standpoint*. Cambridge: Cambridge University Press.

Ludwig, Bernd (2010): "Die 'consequente Denkungsart der speculativen Kritik'. Kants radikale Umgestaltung seiner Freiheitlehre im Jahre 1786. . . ." *Deutsche Zeitschrift für Philosophie* 58, 595–628.

Makkreel, Rudolf (1990): *Imagination and Interpretation in Kant*. Chicago: University of Chicago Press.

Marc-Wogau, Konrad (1938): *Vier Studien zu Kants Kritik der Urteilskraft*. Uppsala: Lundequistka.

Matherne, Samantha (2013): "The Inclusive Interpretation of Kant's Aesthetic Ideas." *British Journal of Aesthetics* 53, 21–39.

(2015): "Images and Kant's Theory of Perception." *Ergo* 2, no. 29.

McAndrew, Matthew (2021): "Three Kantian Accounts of Concept Formation." *Kant-Studien* 112, 159–94.

Mellin, G. S. A. (1798): "Dunkelheit." In: *Encyclopädisches Wörterbuch der kritischen Philosophie*. Vol. 2. Züllichau/Leipzig: Frommann, 156–75.

Menke, Christoph (2008): *Kraft. Ein Grundbegriff ästhetischer Anthropologie*. Frankfurt: Suhrkamp.

Menzer, Paul (1952): *Kants Ästhetik in ihrer Entwicklung*. Berlin: Akademie.

Merritt, Melissa M. (2014): "Kant on the Pleasures of Understanding." In: *Kant on Emotion and Value*. A. Cohen (ed.). Cambridge: Cambridge University Press, 126–45.

Morrisson, Iain (2008): *Kant and the Role of Pleasure in Moral Action*. Athens: Ohio University Press.

Pollok, Anne (2018): "Beautiful Perception and Its Object. Mendelssohn's Theory of Mixed Sentiments Reconsidered." *Kant-Studien* 109, 207–85.

Pollok, Konstantin (2006): "Von der Transzendentalphilosophie zum Vergnügen." In: *Die Vollendung der Transzendentalphilosophie in Kants "Kritik der Urteilskraft."* R. Hiltscher et al. (eds.). Berlin: Duncker&Humblot.

(2017): *Kant's Theory of Normativity*. Cambridge: Cambridge University Press.

Prauss, Gerold (1981): "Kants Theorie der ästhetischen Einstellung." *Dialectica* 35, 266–81.

Puls, Heiko (2016): *Sittliches Bewusstsein und Kategorischer Imperativ in Kants "Grundlegung."* Berlin: deGruyter.
Reath, Andrews (2006): *Agency and Autonomy in Kant's Moral Theory.* Oxford: Oxford University Press.
Reicke, Rudolph (1889): *Lose Blätter aus Kants Nachlass. Erstes Heft.* Königsberg: Beyer.
Rind, Miles (2002): "Can Kant's Deduction of Judgments of Taste Be Saved?" *Archiv für Geschichte der Philosophie* 84, 20–45.
Rogerson, Kenneth (2008): *The Problem of Free Play in Kant's Aesthetics.* City University of New York Press.
Rueger, Alexander (2008): "The Free Play of the Faculties and the Status of Natural Beauty in Kant's Theory of Taste." *Archiv für Geschichte der Philosophie* 90, 298–322.
– (2008a): "Beautiful Surfaces: Kant on Free and Adherent Beauty in Nature and Art." *British Journal of the History of Philosophy* 16, 335–57.
– (2009): "Enjoying the Unbeautiful: From Mendelssohn's Theory of 'Mixed Sentiments' to Kant's Aesthetic Judgments of Reflection." *Journal of Aesthetics and Art Criticism* 67, 181–89.
– (2011): "Aesthetics." In: *Oxford Handbook of Philosophy in Early Modern Europe.* D. Clarke/C. Wilson (eds.). Oxford: Oxford University Press, 201–23.
– (2018): "Pleasure and Purpose in Kant's Theory of Taste." *Kant-Studien* 109, 101–23.
– (2018a): "Kant on Beauty and Morality c. 1784." In: *Proceedings of the XII. International Kant Congress* (ed. V. Waibel et al.). Vol. 4. Berlin: deGruyter, 3063–70.
– (2020): "Kant on Feelings and Sensations and the Gap between Rationality and Morality." *Kantian Review* 25, 125–48.
Rueger, Alexander/Şahan Evren (2005): "The Role of Symbolic Presentation in Kant's Theory of Taste." *British Journal of Aesthetics* 45, 228–47.
Ryle, Gilbert (1949): *The Concept of Mind.* London: Hutchinson.
Schlösser, Ulrich (2013): "Concept Formation, Synthesis, and Judgment." In: *Self, World, and Art.* D. Emundts (ed.). Berlin: de Gruyter, 177–205.
Schmidt, Jochen (1985): *Die Geschichte des Genie-Gedankens in der deutschen Literatur, Philosophie und Politik 1750–1945.* Vol.1. Darmstadt: WBG.
Schmitz, Hermann (1989): *Was wollte Kant?* Bonn: Bouvier.
Schulze, Gottlieb Ernst (1793): [Review of KU] *Allgemeine deutsche Bibliothek* 115, 398–426.
Schwaiger, Clemens (1995): *Das Problem des Glücks im Denken Christian Wolffs.* Stuttgart/Bad Cannstatt: Frommann-Holzboog.
Shell, Susan Meld (2003): "Kant's 'True Economy of Human Nature.'" In: *Essays on Kant's Anthroplogy.* B. Jacobs et al. (eds.). Cambridge: Cambridge University Press, 194–229.
Sonderegger, Ruth (2000): *Für eine Ästhetik des Spiels.* Frankfurt: Suhrkamp.
Teufel, Thomas (2011): "Kant's Non-teleological Conception of Purposiveness." *Kant-Studien* 102, 232–52.

Tonelli, Giorgio (1966): "Kant's Early Theory of Genius." *Journal of the History of Philosophy* 4, 109–31, 209–24.
Tuna, Emine Hande (2016): "A Kantian Hybrid Theory of Art Criticism: A Particularist Appeal to the Generalists." *Journal of Aesthetics and Art Criticism* 74, 397–411.
Vogelmann, Rafael G. (2018): "Can We Make Sense of Free Harmony?" *Studia Kantiana* 16, 53–74.
Wachter, Alexander (2006): *Das Spiel in der Ästhetik*. Berlin: deGruyter.
Warner, Richard (1980): "Enjoyment." *Philosophical Review* 89, 507–26.
Wieland, Wolfgang (2001): *Urteil und Gefühl. Kants Theorie der Urteilskraft*. Göttingen: Vandenhoeck&Ruprecht.
Willaschek, Marcus (2010): "The Primacy of Practical Reason and the Idea of a Practical Postulate." In: *Kant's Critique of Practical Reason. A Critical Guide*. A. Reath/J. Timmermann (eds.). Cambridge: Cambridge University Press, 168–96.
    (2018): *Kant on the Sources of Metaphysics*. Cambridge: Cambridge University Press.
Williams, Jessica (2022): "Attention and the Free Play of the Faculties." *Kantian Review* 27, 43–59.
Windelband, Wilhelm (1880): *Die Blüthezeit der deutschen Philosophie*. (*Geschichte der neueren Philosophie*, vol. 2.) Leipzig: Breitkopf&Härtel.
Wolff, Michael (1995): *Die Vollständigkeit der kantischen Urteilstafel*. Frankfurt: Klostermann.
Wolfsdorf, David (2013): *Pleasure in Ancient Greek Philosophy*. Cambridge: Cambridge University Press.
Wood, Allen (1999): *Kant's Ethical Thought*. Cambridge: Cambridge University Press.
Wuerth, Julian (2014): *Kant on Mind, Action, and Ethics*. Oxford University Press.
Zammito, John H. (1992): *The Genesis of Kant's Critique of Judgment*. Chicago: University of Chicago Press.
Zelle, Carsten (1987): *"Angenehmes Grauen." Literaturhistorische Beiträge zur Ästhetik des Schreckens im 18. Jahrhundert*. Hamburg: Meiner.
    (1995): *Die doppelte Ästhetik der Moderne*. Stuttgart: Metzler.
Zinkin, Melissa (2014): "Kant and the Pleasure of 'Mere Reflection.'" *Inquiry* 55, 433–53.
Zuckert, Rachel (2007): *Kant on Beauty and Biology*. Cambridge: Cambridge University Press.
    (2007a): "Kant's Rationalist Aesthetics." *Kant Studien* 98, 443–63.

Index

achievement principle, 50, 58–59
aesthetic ideas, 166–70
Allison, H., 103, 142, 148, 155
Alston, W.P., 74, 76
Ameriks, K., 153, 201
Anthropology from a Pragmatic Point of View, 28, 56, 162, 166
antinomy
 of practical reason, 192, 198
 of taste, 163–65, 176–81
apprehension, 121–23
art, 5–6, 168–72
autonomy
 of morality, 100–4
 of taste, 209–11
Aydede, M., 74–75

Baumgarten, A.G., 8–11, 14, 28, 31, 36, 38, 118, 210
Beck, L.W., 64–65
Beiser, F., 9–11, 13, 36, 41, 192
Boileau, N., 40
Breitinger, J.J., 12
Buchenau, S., 29, 35–36, 38
Budd, M., 136, 161
Burke, E., 11

Clewis, R., 186
Cognition in general, 132–35, 157–58
Cohen, A., 131
Cohen, H., 174
concept formation, 116–23
Cramer, K., 95, 133
Critique of Practical Reason, 52, 57, 59, 65–69, 86, 90, 185, 191–92, 200
Critique of Pure Reason, 8, 16–19, 24, 52, 68, 94, 99, 102, 108, 111–12, 116–17, 126, 133, 151, 197, 200–1
Crusius, C.A., 37–38

de Pouilly, L., 34, 39, 41, 43
deduction
 of categorical imperative, 202
 of judgments of taste, 138–46, 157–58
 of principle of systematicity, 111–12
Descartes, R., 34, 39, 47
desire, faculty of, 21, 26, 57, 77–78, 80, 87–88, 98
Dobe, J., 150
Dreams of a Spirit Seer, 176
Dubos, J.B., 34, 39–41
Düsing, K., 107

Eberhard, J.A., 9–12
Engstrom, S., 56, 92, 135

faculties
 interests of, 59–61, 125–28
 system of, 16, 26–29
Feder, J.G., 10
feeling of pleasure and displeasure
 attitudinal theories of, 74–75
 as desire satisfaction, 76–81
 distinct from sensation, 63–65, 71–72
 facilitation view, 42–45, 161–62
 nominal definition, 47–48
 relation to judgment, 29–32, 86–91
 stimulation view, 39–40, 43–45, 161–62
 transcendental definition, 51–53, 55
Fichte, J.G., 60, 119
Förster, E., 18, 24, 189, 194
free play of the faculties, 6, 159–62, 168–69
Fricke, C., 98, 121, 153, 155, 163
Friedman, M., 24
Frierson, P., 15, 29–30, 54

Garve, C., 10, 174
Geiger, I., 5, 119, 211
Gellert, C.F., 12

genius, 12, 43, 150, 162–65, 171–74
Gerard, A., 174
Ginsborg, H., 88
Gottsched, J.C., 198
Groundwork of the Metaphysics of Morals, 68, 92, 100, 102, 104, 201–2
Guyer, P., 2, 50, 58, 64–65, 72, 76, 88, 198

Hamann, J.G., 100
harmony of the faculties
 productively free, 130–41, 166–69
 reproductively free, 130
 unfree, 129
Heathwood, C., 76, 80–81
Henrich, D., 103, 136, 159, 202
Herder, J.G., 174
Hogrebe, W., 5, 143
Horstmann, R.P., 6
Hutcheson, F., 64, 190, 208

imagination. *See* harmony of the faculties

judgment, power of
 determining, 4, 120, 124
 reflecting, 4, 121–24
judgments of taste
 deduction. *See* deduction
 determining ground, 89–91
 mistaken, 148–49

Kames, H.H., 190
Kuhlenkampff, J., 127

laws of nature
 general, 112
 particular, 112–14
Lectures on Anthropology (Collins), 42
Lectures on Anthropology (Mrongovius), 77
Lectures on Anthropology (Parow), 42, 161
Lectures on Ethics (Vigilantius), 200
Lectures on Logic (Blomberg), 42, 46
Lectures on Logic (Philippi), 42, 45, 161
Lectures on Metaphysics (L1), 26–31, 45, 49, 194
Lectures on Metaphysics (Mrongovius), 49, 54, 101
Lectures on Metaphysics (Volckmann), 194
Leibniz, G.W., 9, 14, 34–35, 38–39, 47
Locke, J., 64
Longuenesse, B., 56, 88, 90–91, 121–24, 130

Maupertuis, P.L.M., 47–48
Meier, G.F., 35–36, 45–46
Mellin, G.S.A., 110
Mendelssohn, M., 10–12, 34–35, 38–41, 44–45, 47–50, 169, 197, 209

Metaphysics of Morals, 54, 73, 80, 203–6
moral feeling (Kant), 68–73, 102–4, 204–7

Opus postumum, 188

perfection
 in Kant, 45–47
 in Mendelssohn, 38–39
 in Wolff, 34–38
physico-theology, 38, 46, 190–91, 194–97
Pistorius, H.A., 86
pleasure. *See* feeling of pleasure and displeasure
Pollok, K., 23, 26
principle of systematicity. *See* deduction
 for concepts, 120–23, 140–41, 145–46
 for laws, 114–20
principle of the power of judgment
 discursive and intuitive versions, 107–10, 146–48
Prolegomena to Any Future Metaphysics, 133, 175
purpose
 etiological notion, 55–58
 final, 23–24, 187, 195–99, 202
 teleological notion, 55–58
 ultimate, 194–96, 199, 202
purposiveness
 defined, 54
 of nature as a mediating concept, 23–24, 188, 212

reason, maxims of, 114, 120
Reath, A., 67, 80
Rehberg, A.W., 65, 69
Reichardt, J.F., 12, 107, 146
Reicke, R., 100
Reinhold, K.L., 14–15, 31, 99
Religion within the Boundaries of Mere Reason, 203–4
Rind, M., 140, 142, 151, 153–54
Rüdiger, A., 37
Ryle, G., 75–76, 81

schematism, 121–22, 124, 185–86
Schiller, F., 13, 211–12
Schlegel, A.W., 10
Schlegel, F., 8, 13
Schulze, G.E., 9–11
Schwaiger, C., 34–35
Segner, J.A., 168
sensus communis, 153–57
Spinoza, B., 193–94
sublime, 186
Sulzer, J.G., 10, 12, 34, 38, 41, 43, 45, 49–50
symbols, 174–76, 181–85
 of morality, 181–83
 of systematicity, 184–85

Tetens, J.N., 49–50, 65, 67
Teufel, T., 55
transcendental
  meaning, 107, 114–16
transcendental definitions, 51–61

unity
  of experience, 111–13
  of reason, 17–18

Wachter, A., 55, 160
Walch, J.G., 34, 37

What Real Progress Has Metaphysics Made in Germany..., 133, 189, 197
Willaschek, M., 114–16, 125, 192
Windelband, W., 4
Wolff, C., 8–9, 14, 28–29, 31, 34–39, 42, 45, 47, 66, 118, 210
Wolfsdorf, D., 74–75
Wood, A., 17, 204

Zammito, J.H., 15, 163, 174
Zelle, C., 40, 42
Zuckert, R., 26, 31, 55–56, 62, 65, 72–73, 83, 121

For EU product safety concerns, contact us at Calle de José Abascal, 56–1°,
28003 Madrid, Spain or eugpsr@cambridge.org.

www.ingramcontent.com/pod-product-compliance
Lightning Source LLC
LaVergne TN
LVHW011816060526
838200LV00053B/3803